EXCHANGE RATE CHAOS

EXCHANGE RATE CHAOS

Twenty-five years of finance and consumer democracy

Charles R. Geisst

London and New York

First published in 1995
by Routledge
11 New Fetter Lane, London EC4P 4EE

Simultaneously published in the USA and Canada
by Routledge
29 West 35th Street, New York, NY 10001

© 1995 Charles R. Geisst

Typeset in Garamond by Florencetype Ltd,
Stoodleigh, Devon
Printed in Great Britain by
T J Press (Padstow) Ltd, Padstow, Cornwall

British Library Cataloguing in Publication Data
A catalogue record for this book is available from the
British Library

Library of Congress Cataloguing in Publication Data
A catalogue record for this book has been applied for

ISBN 0-415-10981-7

For Meggie, whose first book is yet to come

CONTENTS

FIGURES AND TABLES

FIGURES

TABLES

INTRODUCTION

Over the last seventy years, the financial markets and financial institutions of the major industrialised countries have had a significant impact upon politics as well as upon the fortunes of the individual. Unlike in other periods of recent history, however, the markets and institutions have managed to remain in the news for a sustained period of time, more so than at any other period since the Great Depression. Scandals and financial maelstroms have certainly helped. The junk bond scandal, the Hammersmith swaps debacle, the American thrift institutions crisis and sterling's problems in the European Monetary System are only a few examples that have pushed finance to the forefront of the news. Finance, and somewhat surprisingly international finance, has come out of the closet and has begun to occupy centre stage.

Despite its new-found notoriety, the reasons that events have turned increasingly financial are not particularly clear. Perhaps that is because the major financial event of the last thirty years occurred at a time when money matters took second place to political dissent and social change. After being announced along with other economic measures, it was quickly forgotten except among those who make their living at foreign exchange dealing and international trade. Nevertheless, in the twenty-odd years since that particular announcement, the world has begun to take notice that many contemporary events have economic and financial determinants that tended to go unnoticed previously.

Part of this new interest in things financial is a direct legacy of the 1980s. The merger and acquisitions trend, bank crises, the market collapse of 1987, the property boom and bust, widely fluctuating currencies and structural problems within the European Monetary System occupied centre stage for a good deal of the decade after the 1980–82 recession. When combined with many other fast-moving developments in telecommunications and computer science, they helped characterise the decade as one of fast movers with large bank-rolls. Many of the financiers became household names, as well known as sports figures or politicians.

Two countries that have had many shared experiences in this past once

1

again found themselves united more than at any time in recent memory. Always close in the twentieth century since the time that two of their central bankers – Montague Norman and Benjamin Strong – struck a close relationship in the 1920s, the British and Americans in the 1970s found themselves united again in a close relationship between their central banks that also spilled over into the financial markets and the commercial banking sector. On the surface, this may seem at odds with other trends of the last twenty years. Britain joined the European Community and the European Monetary System while the Americans have been forging even stronger links with Canada, Mexico and the Pacific Rim countries. Superficially, the relationship appears to have grown more distant rather than integrated.

In the 1920s, when both countries were on the gold exchange standard the close relationship was easy to understand. Both relied on the gold standard to maintain stable exchange rates so that trade could be facilitated. Deals between the Bank of England and the Federal Reserve were also common, with the bargain struck between Norman, then Governor of the Bank of England, and Strong, head of the Federal Reserve Bank of New York, perhaps the most famous. Even the general outline of the deal illustrated how close the two central banks were when adjustments needed to be made in one country or the other.

The deal struck between the two allowed the British to insulate their markets against capital outflows by protecting sterling. At the same time, many international borrowers were lured to New York by low interest rates and the American market began to develop its modern international reputation. During the First World War, most international borrowing and financing was still done through London. By 1926 the tide had slowly begun to turn.

The honeymoon did not last long, however. During the Depression, Herbert Hoover was severely criticised for being 'soft' on the British by forgiving war debts in 1932. In fact, he froze all international payments for one year, not just those owed by the UK. But while the public outcry remained loud, the reliance of the two countries on each other still could be found in institutional developments that were certainly less shrill. The Americans closely examined the British Companies Act in effect at the time to determine whether elements of it could be applied to the new regulatory environment that was developing in the US after the market crash of 1929. While some were accusing the Republicans of being too close to the British, reformers in Congress were actively studying British legislation in order to construct a more rigorous regulatory system than the patchwork system that had allowed such widespread fraud to be committed by companies selling new securities issues prior to the Depression.

Despite the similarities between British and American finance, many disparities also exist because of the structural differences between the two political and economic systems. The traditional political independence of the Federal Reserve has not been matched at the Bank of England. The money markets operate differently in the two and the conspicuous absence of a UK corporate bond market since the late 1960s–early 1970s has led many companies to rely more upon roll-over financing from banks than has been the case in the United States. But, as will be seen, the similarities that do exist stem from a common experience that extends beyond clubbiness or historical ties. Both the British and American financial systems depend to a large extent upon the consumer to generate spending. Consumers' behaviour since the Second World War has made both countries consumer democracies, a term that will be discussed below.

Throughout the four decades following the war, the institutional reliance was kept firmly in place as the dollar supplanted sterling as the major international reserve and trading currency. But it was after 1971–72 that the old alliances and reliances again surfaced noticeably. When the Bretton Woods system of fixed parity exchange rates that had been framed by John Maynard Keynes and others after the Second World War finally collapsed in August 1971, the financial systems of both countries came under pressures that were remarkably similar. While there were obviously vast discrepancies between the economies of the two, financial developments in them still displayed a similarity that cannot be attributed to circumstance. And neither were the similarities all American-inspired, as many critics of contemporary Britain might believe. In the cross-currents spanning the Atlantic, many originated on the eastern side and found their way west as well as the other way round.

However, as notable as the collapse of the Bretton Woods system has become, its effect on sterling and other currencies has usually been minimised in Britain. Many of the economic events that followed hard on its heels have been attributed to purely British causes or failures in domestic economic policies. Perhaps this oversight can be attributed to the fact that sterling was still protected by exchange controls in 1971–72 and was not liberalised until 1979. Whatever the reason for the oversight, many significant financial events in Britain in the early 1970s were directly affected by the collapse of the agreement because the dollar was affected and sterling's role as a major dollar alternative was also similarly affected.

The financial world changed substantially after 1971 when the currencies of the major industrialised countries began to float against each other. The *de facto* collapse of the Bretton Woods system, discussed in Chapter 1, may well prove to be the most important post-war financial event of the twentieth century because of the changes in international finance that followed. Hard on its heels came the first OPEC price rise, Britain's emergence as a major oil producer, rising worldwide inflation, the collapse of sterling and major financial reforms on both sides of the Atlantic. In the next decade – the 1980s – change would continue at a frenzied pace, only to be temporarily subdued by the 1990s recession.

3

Britain's international economic ties have changed substantially over the last twenty years. Membership in the European Community, now European Union, and joining the exchange rate mechanism (ERM) of the European Monetary System has brought the pound into closer contact with the Europeans than was previously the case. The pound/dollar rate was once the most carefully monitored of all exchange rates. But when Britain forged closer ties with the Continent, the Deutschmark/pound rate became more important while the Americans began to shift their attention to the rates of the Deutschmark and the yen against the dollar. Britain's foray into the European Community paralleled the decline of sterling as a premier reserve currency. This will be examined more carefully in Chapter 4.

Comparing the two financial systems is made considerably more difficult by the differences in legal attitudes in the two countries. The Bank of England is responsible to the UK Treasury while its American counterpart, the Federal Reserve, is an independent institution, not responsible to any political body. The legislative comparison is easier: both Parliament and Congress have ultimate power in framing financial legislation. Neither body can affect the day-to-day workings of their central banks nor do they have any direct control over their long-range policies. Traditionally, governors of the Bank of England are chosen from the mandarin class of civil servants and almost never come from the financial services sector. Chairmen of the Federal Reserve Board, on the other hand, have often come from the private sector. While these disparities may affect differences in the way the two systems function, they are not strong enough to hinder the close alliances forged between the central banks in the last fifty years.

As Chapter 1 will illustrate, severing the dollar's convertibility into gold in 1971 produced strains in the financial system that have yet to be remedied. But perhaps more importantly, the trouble that those strains have caused has not been confined to the financial services sector. Volatile currency fluctuations have caused periodic bursts of anti-foreign feeling in both the United States and Britain, in varying degrees. These outbursts have fallen short of outright xenophobia and usually are conveniently attributed to other factors more vague in origin. But they are the indirect products of currency fluctuations nevertheless.

The currency problem has also embedded itself deeply in the domestic social fabric of each country. In both cases, it has led to deep social divisions that have been characterised in the popular press as the increasingly wealthy versus the increasingly poor in a growing class conflict, pitting the 'haves' against the 'have nots' of society: the prosperous of the Reagan and Thatcher years against those who have fallen off the edge. The poor in both societies are poorer today than they were ten years ago. While it does not take an acute sense of finance to realise that money has something to do with this, Chapter 7 will show that the merger and acquisition trend of the 1980s, more distinct in the US than in Britain, is responsible for many of the business excesses of the Reagan/Thatcher era. Clearly, the trend owes its origin to the demise of Bretton Woods and the inflation that followed. Simply, it became cheaper to mount a raid to acquire assets than to build them from the ground up. The social consequences of the merger trend are still being debated.

Much of the political turmoil of the two decades can also trace its origins to the events of 1971–72. In the United States, Jimmy Carter clearly was a victim in the 1980 election. In Britain, Harold Wilson and Edward Heath also felt the effects of currency turmoil and inflation. Richard Nixon, too, was a candidate but for the Watergate events that overtook his presidency. The beneficiaries were also obvious. Ronald Reagan and Margaret Thatcher cleverly capitalised on their predecessors' misfortunes by attributing the social and economic turmoil of the 1970s to the profligate spending habits of their opposition when they were in power.

True to many recent revolutions, the events leading to and following the demise of the Bretton Woods system went largely unnoticed by most of the public. The twentieth anniversary of the events were actually mentioned in the press but the details of the original event are still largely overlooked. When Richard Nixon suspended the convertibility of the dollar into gold in his anti-inflation package of August 1971, the assumption was that the suspension was nothing more than a temporary palliative that was conveniently packaged along with temporary wage and price controls. But once the dollar was set free it never returned to a fixed parity system. The floating dollar ushered in the new financial environment that witnessed more changes in the next twenty years than it had in the previous thirty.

Part of the reason for the public apathy for the new financial environment was that the new exchange rate system appeared to have little direct effect upon the average consumer. Only when the decline of the dollar led to higher petrol prices and general inflation did the American public realise that times had changed. The reaction swiftly followed: unions demanded higher wage settlements and companies found it more expensive to raise capital. Politicians eventually experienced the fallout. But not all were losers in the process. Wall Street and the City of London responded to the volatile times by creating several new generations of financial instruments that actually thrived on the volatility in the financial markets. Those products, discussed throughout Chapters 6 and 7, stretched the boundaries of the financial imagination and in many cases provided the capital and jobs that were missing in the wake of the old system. But the real effect of the currency turmoil has had a profound impact upon the consumer that is not easily apparent because it is intertwined with the politics of every country it has affected.

CONSUMER DEMOCRACY

The vast and sudden changes that have affected currencies in the last twenty-odd years have led to profound changes in the 'consumer democracies'. A consumer democracy is an economy driven, to a large extent, by individual consumption expenditures. Politically, governments realise that in such advanced industrial societies consumers must constantly be given as wide a range of choices as possible. The wider the choice, the more 'freedom' the consumer thinks he or she experiences on an everyday level. Consumer choices become equated with political choices, but are more plentiful and easier to make.

Consumer democracies are characterised by the high percentage of their GNPs that are dominated by consumer spending. The United States remains the best example. About two-thirds of GNP is driven by personal consumption and has been since the Second World War. In Britain, well over 70 per cent of GDP is normally attributed to consumer spending, using traditional measures. Consumers in both countries, and especially the United States, have been courted by an increasingly large number of foreign manufacturers eager to sell their goods in the world's single largest market. When the dollar began to decline after 1971, many foreign companies actively began their expansion plans into the United States to tap this vast market, either by selling directly to it or by opening American manufacturing operations.

The political side of this phenomenon has always been recognised. But with the increase in international capital flows and investment, the process has been speeded up considerably. Governments failing to recognise that their consumer constituents are unhappy with a decline in purchasing power or with the choice of goods available will be quickly under pressure. Consumers have only begun to feel these international pressures since the uncoupling of the Bretton Woods system from the American-dominated quarter-century that preceded it. Given the differences in political cultures between the United States and Britain, it was no coincidence that the governments of both James Callaghan and Jimmy Carter fell out of favour within the same general time period. As inflation rose and both currencies came under pressure, consumers finally revolted against the administrations that were associated with an ostensible decline in their standards of living. Those governments failed to recognise what their successors learned well: increased consumer confidence, availability of credit, and a general feeling that the economy was expanding were more important than how that expansion was financed or how many of their fellow citizens actually benefited.

There are many examples in banking and finance of consumer democracy at work since the 1970s. Many of the examples are American although the British joined in this phenomenon in the late 1970s. As will be seen in Chapters 2 and 3 when constrained by interest rate ceilings at banks in the 1970s, American savers turned their attention to the new money market funds paying higher rates of interest. As a result, interest rate ceilings were removed from the banking system within five years, effectively ending a forty-year tradition. Temporary credit restraints aimed at consumers during Jimmy Carter's administration proved so unpopular that they helped to elect Ronald Reagan in the 1980 election. The list of instances of consumer power being exercised in this way is quite long and George Bush was its latest victim in the contemporary period. As will be seen in the conclusion, the exchange rate and interest rate regimes require that the new rules of the game be understood and recognised if political adminstrations are to survive.

One of the foundations of consumer democracy is access to consumer credit. The period since 1971–72 has been one of relatively easy consumer credit, first in the United States and later in Britain. In order to provide that credit, banks and finance companies needed access to relatively cheap sources of funds. That has been provided by the money markets, domestic and international, that have grown in the same period. Almost simultaneously, the use of credit cards, the development of the commercial paper market and the switch to floating exchange rates have changed the face of consumerism to the point where withdrawal of that credit would have serious consequences if it were politically motivated.

The political marketing side of this phenomenon is also becoming understood as the selling of candidates via the media becomes more sophisticated. The successful political parties recognise that the candidate offering more consumer choices to constituents is more likely to be elected than those preaching something else. Equally, candidates themselves packaged as consumer goods have become more prevalent, with the British following the Americans into this chapter of television advertising. While politics has usually been considered the master science since Aristotle, a strong case can be made in the contemporary United States for marketing having overtaken it. In the short history since the collapse of Bretton Woods, candidates have been elected on alternate platforms but only after a boom period characterised by excess. While 'chicken in every pot' politics is hardly new, a dozen consumer varieties of that bird was never thought to be a part of everyday freedoms until the modern financial era began.

Foreign exchange values affect consumer democracies in two ways. The first is the traditional trade method whereby strong currencies encourage imports while weak currencies encourage exports. Consumers clearly benefit more when their native currency is strong because the increasing number of imports that it can buy adds to the menu of available products or services. A weak currency supports domestic industries that see less foreign competition because the price of imports rises. But neither position is clearly achievable politically unless supported by economic fundamentals. But if conditions are correct, either position can be easily exploited.

The historical record of the last twenty-odd years supports this. Sterling was quietly allowed to depreciate during the 1970s after several post-war devaluations, using International Monetary Fund, (IMF) standby facilities for support. But after the 1976 depreciation fiasco when the IMF facility extended to Britain became very well publicised, sentiment turned against the Labour government that presided over the IMF negotiations. When the Labour government was voted out of office in 1979, Britain joined the United States as a modern consumer democracy. The fear of Labour returning, eroding some of these principles of consumer democracy, did more to keep Labour out of office for over a decade than it did to keep the Conservatives in power.

Theoretically, consumer democracy appears superficial. It is a term that has little application in defining contemporary political activity. But politicians may find it useful to foster consumer choices while actually limiting the electorate's political choices, all in the name of democracy. Such cynical policies may not be the intent but when faced with what voters value the most, many politicians realise that the standard of living is the top priority. The pendulum only swings away from the standard of living when it is not a pressing issue.

Equally, fostering a weak exchange rate against the economic competition is not an issue when a country's political strength is not an issue. Most Americans or Britons only view a weak dollar or pound as a sign of national weakness when other factors are also pointing in the same direction. That is not to imply that a strong dollar at the time of the Iran hostage crisis would have mitigated the Americans' frustration with the Democratic administration but it certainly helped underline the failures of American foreign policy for those who voted for Ronald Reagan in the following election. But fifteen years later, a weak dollar was actively pursued against the Japanese yen at a time when the United States was in a stronger position than most of its economic competition, because the strong yen made Japanese exports to the US expensive, allowing a window of opportunity for American manufacturers.

The contemporary consumer is not unlike Thorstein Veblen's conspicuous consumer of the last century but now has a more prominent political role. The consumer has moved far beyond the voter who was guaranteed a chicken in every pot to one who wants a full range of chicken and chicken parts to choose from, willing to voice discontent against any politician who interferes with that choice, whether the source of the product be domestic or foreign. If the foreign product is deemed superior to the domestic, then the wise government recognises the necessity of a continuous flow of imports to satisfy demand. If that means a strong local currency at the expense of some unemployment then a balance must be struck between the two. That balance is easier to achieve under floating exchange rates than it was under the Bretton Woods system of fixed parities.

Contemporary finance has had a great deal to do with the shaping of modern consumer democracy. In order to supply credit to consumers, American banks and credit companies began to make ample use of the commercial paper market in the late 1960s and early 1970s, insuring themselves of a cheap source of funds free of reserve requirements. Much of the money raised by bank holding companies was able to finance consumer credit expansion despite the continued presence of credit ceilings in the 1970s. As credit card use became widespread and foreign banks, including the British, took up the concept as their own, the modern period of personal finance began, at about the same time as the Bretton Woods system was crumbling.

DEREGULATION AS A RESPONSE

Despite all of the innovation in the 1970s and 1980s, the new deregulatory environment could not be said to provide the panacea for economies that were undergoing radical restructuring and social upheaval. In this respect, the American example is more striking than the British. The new deregulatory legislation of the 1980s was intended to liberalise the rules by which banks competed in the financial system and lift, at least partially, some of the old legislation passed in the 1930s. After the legislation had several years to become effective, many banks and thrift institutions still failed, as they had during the Depression. The period of banking crisis that followed, and sporadically continues today, witnessed a great consolidation in the banking industry that was a corollary of the legislation. By lifting the protections that had insulated banks and thrifts for over fifty years, the deregulators lifted the only protection that some of them had against competition. Publicly, the failures were lamented while privately they could only have been expected.

What legislation was not able to accomplish was remedied in some cases by financial innovation. Currency and interest rate volatility spawned an entire new generation of financial derivatives that became the fastest growing segment of the financial markets ever devised. Originally designed as hedging instruments, they also became speculators' instruments in a short time but still served a basic hedging purpose for companies and investors. As will be seen, the development of these instruments was a response to the collapse of Bretton Woods. Their success may be part of the reason that a new foreign exchange regime was never organised; through these instruments the markets were able to impose some stability where the major industrialised countries were never able to agree.

What the breakdown of Bretton Woods created was a crude series of causes and effects that continues into the contemporary era. Exchange rate volatility caused OPEC to raise oil prices which in turn caused higher infla-tion, high real interest rates, high unemployment, shifts in the structure and performance of major economies and a general 'grab it while you can' attitude. But crude etiologies can themselves turn corollaries into nonsense. As will be seen in later chapters, a declining dollar after Bretton Woods helped prompt massive Japanese investment in the United States and else-where. A weak pound and Britain's entry into the European Community attracted foreign investment to the UK despite a generally decried poor management culture. Foreigners were willing to tolerate British industrial and management eccentricities as long as their tolerance gave them a foothold in the world's largest market, the EC.

While many events within the last twenty years owe their origins to the breakdown of Bretton Woods, developments in Britain and the United States are not without their light side. Although it is difficult to think of financial legislation and regulations as having a humorous aspect, the British have constantly shown a far better penchant for seeing irony in the changes in the regulatory climate than the Americans. When the major piece of financial legislation of the post-war era (until that time) was passed in the United States in 1980, it was cumbersomely known as the Depository Institutions Deregulation and Monetary Control Act (see Chapter 5). In short, it was known affectionately as the DIDMCA or the Monetary Control Act. Its major achievement was to begin dismantling interest rate ceilings over a six-year period although economic realities begged for a much shorter period of time.

In 1986, the UK experienced an equally jarring piece of legislation that affected the stock market more than the commercial banking system. The Financial Services Act of 1986 became universally known as 'Big Bang', suggesting the stock market version of astrophysics: the legislation and all of the changes it introduced occurred in one fell swoop. No six-year plans or gradualist approaches usually favoured by the Americans. But perhaps more importantly, no antiseptic acronyms for this particular piece of legislation. As will be seen later, Big Bang did not prove successful for all parts of the financial services industry despite its sudden impact, but it will certainly always be remembered for its name.

Equally important are the implications of the timing of financial reforms. Suddenness did not necessarily mean that the British reforms were more timely than those in the United States or elsewhere; in fact, it may be argued that the market reforms embodied in the Financial Services Act were long overdue and could not wait any longer if the UK market was to remain internationally competitive. But, unlike the American examples in the past, the 1986 reforms in Britain were accomplished with a certain fanfare that the acronyms across the Atlantic were not able to match.

Despite the furious pace of financial reform in the 1970s and 1980s, not all of which had the intended results nor could have been said to successfully remedy weaknesses in the financial system. When Ronald Reagan hailed the Depository Institutions Act of 1982 (Garn–St Germain Act) as the greatest piece of financial deregulation of the century, no one could have foreseen the devastating effect it would have eventually on the thrift industry. Loosening regulations on thrifts allowed them to buy corporate bonds as assets, something that had not been permitted since the Depression. Logically, that lessened their reliance on mortgages and allowed them to diversify their assets in order to become less dependent upon residential home loans. But who would have imagined that so many of them would have turned to the junk bond market, helping to fuel demand for the new, low-quality corporate security? Within five years, the pigeons would come home to roost on those particular 'innovative' investments, destroying a substantial part of the savings industry in the process.

The controversies surrounding the reforming legislation of the 1980s were the obvious products of years of regulation and then rapid deregulation. Equally important but less obvious were the changes in trade patterns and international investment brought on by rapidly changing currency values. The breakdown of Bretton Woods was not immediately thought of as responsible for a redirection in foreign direct investment but it started a trend that is still continuing today. The trend has become more pronounced in the United States than in Britain. After the dollar's devaluation in 1971 and the rise in the price of gold, the currency began to decline over the rest of the decade before beginning its remarkable rise in 1981. The intervening period produced a dramatic change in the international productivity and wealth creation that have become the visible signs of the financial revolution.

Immediately after the currency crisis in 1971, Japanese direct investment in the United States was minimal, totalling only several billion dollars. By 1980, the amount had exploded to almost $50 billion and by 1989 was second only to Britain's longstanding investment in the United States. Rather than simply export to the US, fearful of the potential trade barriers and tariffs that could be erected, the Japanese began a conscious programme of building operations on American soil. Any products made would therefore carry the appellation 'Made in America' although the parentage was obvious. But equally important, the investment in American assets provided a currency hedge against a volatile yen at the same time.

Much of the capital used to fund those operations was imported from home, meaning that the funds were relatively cheap, being generated in yen rather than in dollars. At a time when US interest rates were rising along with inflation and American manufacturing beginning to decline in quality and productivity, Japanese goods began to fill the vacuum and establish a reputation for quality. Social tensions naturally began to mount as a result.

These problems also were familiar to the British, whose cost of capital was more closely controlled by the banks than by the markets during the 1970s and early to mid-1980s. Poor productivity, labour unrest and high costs of financing eventually took their toll on British manufacturing and massive redundancies occurred in industries that were once the mainstays of the British economy. While many companies were not willing, or able, to make capital investments for the long term, the service industries got an unexpected shot in the arm from the poor financial climate and continued to thrive. They did not require the same large amounts of capital. As a result, hamburger chains, financial services and computer software companies began to dot both the British and American business landscapes.

Generally, it is fashionable to think of the products of service industries as simply outcomes of a good idea that did not cost much money to develop. While that may not be entirely true, what those products do reflect is a cost of capital that may be too high for manufacturers and others that make 'real' products. High real rates of interest, especially after 1980–81, shortened many businesses' time horizons. Companies producing goods or services with short life spans were more adequately placed to adjust to changes in the marketplace than were manufacturers producing consumer durables or capital equipment. For about a ten-year period, Britain and America shared this common problem although in varying degrees. The shared problem would lead to continued sharing of ideas in the financial services sector.

All of this currency-inspired change produced some strange side-effects, bordering on the comical. British fondness for the swaps market as a way of turning a trading profit led to a relatively small London borough causing the first major scandal in that market's relatively short history by acting as a trading front for other borough councils with less savoury political reputations. As will be seen later, the Hammersmith swaps debacle grew out of a trader's predilection for creating profit while taking enormous risks along the way. The idea of a 'politically correct' council (Tory) acting as a front for others (Labour, etc.) that were not in favour with banks is almost laughable if it were not for the billions in losses it created for the banks that did business with them.

The vast Japanese investment in American portfolio investments, accumulated during the 1980s in addition to the slightly older direct investments, led to an increased Japanese presence on Wall Street and in heartland America as well. Besides trying to crack the clubby barriers of Wall Street and gain admittance to the underwriters' club, many Japanese investment and commercial banks also sought business in the interior of the country, trying to win business from groups as diverse as local mid-American manufacturers and Indian reservation enterprises. By 1990, Japanese banks would be a major force in commercial lending in certain parts of the country, only to slow down their efforts after the Japanese banking crisis developed at home after 1991.

Although the Japanese presence outside Japan usually draws notice because of manufacturing prowess or the trade surpluses it creates, the surge in Japanese overseas investment and business was also due to the decline of the Bretton Woods system. After the Japanese authorities allowed the yen to move more freely after 1980, Japanese investment multiplied quickly, almost as if it were seeking to quickly gain all of the lost ground of previous years when its movements were restricted. As the Dutch, British and Americans in generations before them, the Japanese sought markets for their goods that were not available at home: exports were prompted in part by efficiency and capacity utilisation that required more markets than the mother country alone could provide.

In short, currency movements favouring Japanese direct investment overseas helped create the most recent example of an emerging, and then quickly mature, industrial giant flexing its muscles in international trade and investment. Public reaction in its target markets was not always friendly, as would be expected. When the British expanded a century earlier, the operative term was imperialism. When the Americans began to expand overseas investments between the two wars and then again immediately after the Second World War, the older Latin American cries of 'Yankee go home' were replaced with charges of 'Coca-Cola imperialism' and talk of pop culture dominance through American consumer goods. When the Japanese made their presence felt, it was natural to hear of Western fears of the dreaded keiretsu arrangements that had made Japanese industry and markets so effective on the one hand while being so closed to foreigners on the other.

It is tempting to think that once the Bretton Woods system had disappeared from view that it had been forgotten in favour of free market theories of foreign exchange, at least for the major hard currencies. There is no point in determining a level for the sterling/dollar relationship because the market will decide ultimately what the rate should be. And adopting such a position would also be politically opportune. Rather than face potential devaluations or unpopular revaluations, finance ministers and their superiors could simply claim that the rate had to be adjusted by the market, not because of any specific government actions. When devaluing sterling in 1968, Harold Wilson blamed his actions on speculators who had attacked sterling's value and necessitated an official adjustment by the British government. Again in 1992, when sterling dropped out of the ERM, speculators were blamed for the pound's embarrassment. In 1971, when Richard Nixon cut the dollar free from the Bretton Woods Agreement, he too blamed speculators who had forced him into unpalatable but necessary adjustments. No need for such embarrassments under floating exchange rates.

Unofficial depreciations are still more favourable for political life in consumer democracies than official devaluations would ever be, but over time the market makes its wishes known, regardless of the intent of finance ministers and others. Indeed much of the political history of the last twenty years has been affected to a great extent by currency alignments and realignments. Third World countries seem to realise this best because so much of their standard of living is based upon currency fluctuations. When their own rates fall, the standard of living falls with them. This is especially true when the IMF was asked for assistance and meted out a prescription that the host found difficult to swallow. But while 'IMF Go Home' has been a familiar piece of graffiti in many developing countries in the 1980s, it has not become a familiar body in most developed countries, Britain being the brief example during the sterling crisis in 1976. But even then the IMF would have been hard to blame for political meddling because so few people actually knew what it was to begin with. Floating exchange rates and the ubiquitous 'speculator' serve the purpose much better.

While even a brief discussion of the topic in general terms reveals that much of the history of the last twenty years is integrally related to the dismantling of Bretton Woods, its successor regime has introduced elements of risk and uncertainty that have come to characterise the contemporary era of finance and politics. The floating exchange rate system that succeeded Bretton Woods has caused serious distortions in international finance and the movement of capital. Now more than ever, the markets are ruled by speculators and 'hot money' flows seeking a temporary home. The impact that these factors have on the politics and economies of contemporary life is enormous but still little understood. This can be seen nowhere better than in August 1971 when the contemporary era of finance emerged, almost unnoticed at the time.

Throughout this book, two distinct themes dominate the post-1971 era. The first has to do with the cause of many of the economic events of the last twenty-odd years. As will be seen in Chapter 1, the major events of 1973 were the OPEC price rise and the fringe (or secondary) banking crisis in Britain. Most commentators have seen these two events as separate, only coincidentally having occurred almost contemporaneously in December 1973. Upon closer examination, the events appear to be more closely related. The secondary banking crisis was caused by a shift in funds by those anticipating a petrol price rise and the smaller UK banks were caught in the squeeze. The UK bank crisis, and the ensuing 'Lifeboat' rescue operation mounted by the Bank of England, was therefore the first casualty of hot money flows in the contemporary period of monetary instability.

The second theme that emerges here is the reaction of the two financial systems to the wrenching changes of floating exchange rates and rising inflation. On the basis of the evidence to date, the British financial system certainly has weathered the storm better than the American. Both systems have seen their share of economic setbacks. The British banks have experienced the secondary banking crisis, the Third World debt problems at the clearing banks, several property market collapses and the Hammersmith swaps debacle. The Americans have also experienced the Third World debt crisis and a fall in real estate values, but the junk bond scandal, the thrift crisis and the record number of bank closings and mergers have shown that the American system, for all of its intrinsic strengths and self-promotions, was much more vulnerable than its less regulated cousin during the same time period.

Financial changes in Britain and the United States over this tumultuous period move in similar directions despite the obvious differences in the two financial systems and cultures. While it may be argued that the move toward financial liberalisation and then re-regulation has occurred internationally in most developed countries, the tandem movements are still very disting-uishable. One generalisation that holds up for the entire period will be seen many times in the following pages: changes in the British banking system are followed by similar changes in the American banking system while changes in the American financial markets are followed by changes in the UK markets.

Throughout this essay, a strong case will be made for changing interest rates and foreign exchange rates as being the prime determinants in con-temporary British and American history since 1971. Certainly, a similar case could be made for the entire post-war period but 1971 still remains a watershed in contemporary affairs. Such a strong point appears obvious at first glance and then equally obscure at the same time. Both the Thatcher and Reagan 'revolutions' succeeded because interest rates were brought down from previous levels that characterised previous governments. As we shall see, both administrations were quick to recognise and adapt to the demands of consumers who, in some cases, voted more with their currencies than with their actual ballot papers. The economic booms they triggered were equally prompted by a lowering of interest rates, especially during the second Reagan administration in the US. Even the debate over the Maastricht Treaty and sterling's withdrawal from the ERM and all of the political furore caused as a result were at heart matters of interest rate and exchange rate considerations. If Britain had not suffered high real rates of interest during its short-lived membership of the ERM, causing sterling to rise to almost the $2.00 level, then its membership of the exchange rate regime would not have been in doubt and the Major government would have saved itself the serious embarrassment that followed.

The history of the last twenty-five years has shown that all sorts of dis-parate social developments have been affected by interest rates. But what of exchange rates? Since exchange rates are driven by interest rates, it is not possible to discuss the two separately. But as recent economic developments have shown, when exchange rates weaken considerably foreign companies often step into the breach created by lack of domestic invest-ment and create employment through direct foreign investment. As markets, companies and manufactured products become more international, more foreign influence will be felt in those countries that allow it. How well these investments are and will be received by the locals is quite a different matter.

This is not to imply that these two determinants can be applied to all sorts of events over the last twenty-odd years. But as will be seen, the events that have been triggered by the startling yet little-understood announcement in August 1971 concerning exchange rates have made that single event one of the most important, and overlooked, of the post-war period. In 1991, on the twentieth anniversary of the demise of the Bretton Woods system, *Forbes* magazine proclaimed it a 'baleful anniversary; [of] a misbegotten decision that is still costing us, and the world, dearly'. Not since the Great Depression have financial events had such a long and far-reaching impact upon everyday life. In the past, only economists and international traders realised and felt the impact of exchange rates upon their immediate surroundings. At best, exchange rates were said to have an impact upon domestic prices. In the new financial environment, exchange rates were to have a direct impact on all aspects of social life felt by all, not just specialists.

Despite the volatility and disruption caused by the exchange rate and interest rate regimes, the history of the last two decades nevertheless has left a lasting imprint from which to draw some useful policy conclusions about the potential future course of the international monetary system. Many of the conclusions and suggestions are based upon political leadership: without a strong commitment to designing a new exchange rate regime, currencies will continue to float. Politically, this sort of chaos can be managed if it is properly anticipated. Whether this is desirable or only leads to short-term policy making is a separate issue. These matters will be discussed in the Conclusion.

1

THE SYSTEM DISSOLVES

The summer of 1971 ushered in a period of economic crisis for the United States that had its origins in the Vietnam War and the free spending habits of the 1960s. After several decades of unparalleled growth, the American economy had developed both a growing inflation rate and growing unemployment at the same time. The reaction in the international financial markets caused strains that would rapidly contribute to a new emerging world financial order. In this new order, sterling was rapidly declining in importance while the yen and the Deutschmark were rising. The dollar remained the premier reserve currency but was under attack by traders who assumed that its value was bloated in comparison with other hard currencies.

The new emerging order would also place the United States in an embarrassing position. In the twenty-five years since it had signed the Bretton Woods Agreement in New Hampshire in 1947, the country had experienced unequalled prosperity. The standard of living had increased, the population had grown, higher education had become more accessible to greater numbers of people and the dollar had become the undisputed international reserve currency. How much the Bretton Woods Agreement itself had to do with America's success was not as much an issue as the fact that it would soon unravel, leaving the international financial markets in turmoil and changing the role of the United States in the world economy. The disintegration unleashed forces to which the country was unaccustomed after decades of economic success.

Since 1945, the dollar had been the pre-eminent currency in the world and had no challenges from any other currency. During that time, world trade patterns had evolved into currency blocs, with many countries tying their currency, and their fortunes, to the currency of their major trading partner. The Deutschmark had come to dominate Europe, excluding Britain, while the yen dominated parts of Asia and sterling remained central to many Commonwealth currencies. But the dollar maintained the dominant position among them, accounting for about 70–75 per cent of the world's foreign exchange reserves. Within the parity system constructed at Bretton Woods, the dollar was the sovereign currency.

In Britain, the unravelling of the agreement would lead to several international embarrassments centring around the pound and finally would lead to the acknowledgement that Britain was no longer a world power. In both cases, there was more than a subtle irony at work. Post-1971 economic forces had brought the two economic powers to heel although certainly in varying degrees. The irony was that forty years before, the unilateral actions of each had contributed to economic mayhem during the Depression. It was those unilateral actions that had caused the original Bretton Woods system to be constructed in the first place. Four decades later similar forces were again at work.

Before 1947, the last time that the major trading nations had had an orderly market for foreign exchange was in the 1920s. The dollar and sterling adhered to what was known as the gold exchange standard. Under that system, each currency was given a specific value in gold, which in turn was used to settle official claims among nations. The system worked well during the 1920s but after the stock market crash of 1929 and the Depression that followed, the lack of a central authority to administer it became obvious. No one central international institution was established possessing mediatorial power to settle international financial disputes. While many would be instituted during the Depression, they would not be fully appreciated until after the war had ended.

As unemployment grew in the industrialised countries and exports began to fall for lack of demand, both Britain and the United States devalued their currencies in order to make exports cheaper. The problem was that the actions were essentially unilateral and almost totally nationalistic; the best way to invigorate trade was to devalue, usually angering other trading partners in the process. The devaluations were a contributing cause of the Depression itself, hindering trade rather than fostering it. The international trade problem led to the establishment of the General Agreement on Tariffs and Trade, or GATT, in 1934. The currency problem was addressed later, first in 1940, but the Second World War intervened and it was not until 1944 that meaningful progress was made toward constructing a system that would help prevent problems in the future.

Arguments for and against the Bretton Woods system had always existed but one point remains undisputed: the foreign exchange system has been significantly more volatile without its fixed parity system to guide it. For better or worse, freely floating currencies have contributed immeasurably to the financial chaos that has reigned since 1972, especially during the period 1981–85. Yet at that time, the demise of the system built by the Allies immediately after the war suggested nothing but darkness and uncertainty. The last vestige of gold, once the centrepiece of foreign exchange values, was gone forever. With one stroke of the pen, Richard Nixon helped sink a system that had pulled the Western economies up by the bootstraps after the war and given them a semblance of order after almost fifteen years of unmitigated chaos in the 1930s and 1940s.

The original idea behind the Bretton Woods Agreement was simple yet devilishly political at the same time. The two major architects of the new monetary order – John Maynard Keynes of Britain and Harry Dexter White of the United States – realised that the new system would have political ramifications as well as economic ones. Yet if the two could be linked tolerably, the political temptations against acting unilaterally would be discouraged. Unlike the Depression years, the major economies would now have to recognise the shortcomings of acting purely in their own interests.

All currencies were given a parity value in terms of US dollars, itself given a distinct value against gold. Currencies were then allowed to fluctuate plus or minus 1 per cent against the parity value. If the market forces pressured a currency above or below its allowed band, the country itself would have to intervene by buying or selling its currency in the markets to return it within the allowed limits. The values were well understood and the system worked tolerably well until market forces dictated that new values be imposed.

The newly constructed system did not emerge immediately. Until 1959, the hard currencies were all protected by controls and convertibility was still impractical. The foreign exchange market was ruled by monetary authorities which dictated fixed prices for their currencies, making the notion of fixed parities within trading bands seem somewhat distant. Britain made an attempt to float the pound in the 1950s only to find itself short of foreign exchange reserves within a very short period of time. The market in the 1950s would only cast a vote of confidence in currencies backed by substantial reserves and a solid international trading position – a position that most countries would take time to achieve after the war.

When parity values became unrealistic, monetary authorities would consult with the IMF to determine new values. The IMF itself was a progeny of the Bretton Woods Agreement along with its sister institution, the World Bank. Its major purpose was (and still is) to make loans to members who experience balance of payments problems. When such problems became intolerable, putting a country's exchange rate under pressure and affecting its import/export position, the IMF would help arrange a devaluation or revaluation of the currency's parity value. Devaluation meant that the value would fall while revaluation meant a rise. In either case, the political consequences at home could be quick and unpleasant.

Devaluations mean that a country's exports become cheaper while imports become more expensive. Revaluations cause the opposite effect. Politically, devaluations are something of an embarrassment to authorities because they are usually interpreted as signs of weakness in an economy. Revaluations, on the other hand, suggest strength in the domestic economy but can lead to adjustments in the future unless the economy continues to move ahead strongly, shaking off the effects of stronger currency and more expensive exports.

When a country required a change in its parity value, the other members of the IMF would have to be consulted in order to avoid disagreement and any potential retaliation by other trading partners. In the early 1930s, both Britain and the United States acted alone at different times in declaring a devaluation of their currencies in vain attempts to stimulate exports and stem imports. Their actions were fruitless but the political ramifications were felt long after the Depression ended. Unilateral devaluations were one of the major problems the Bretton Woods Agreement sought to prevent in the future.

But whether done in consultation or alone, devaluations were embarrassing. Since the Agreement was signed, Britain underwent several devaluations of sterling. In 1947, the pound traded at $4.80. By 1971, its value had eroded to $2.40, the sort of fall that ordinary market drift could not account for over the years. The most recent devaluation prior to 1971 was in 1967 when Prime Minister Harold Wilson had announced a 15 per cent adjustment. Equally important was the effect that the various devaluations had on Britain's reputation as a world power. By 1968, after the devaluations, the Suez Crisis of the previous decade and the spate of independence ceremonies following the break-up of the old colonial empire, it became apparent that Britain's hold over world affairs, both economic and political, had faded.

The 1967 devaluation came in a time of deteriorating economic conditions. Upon taking office in 1964, the Labour government had presided over a strong economy that had seen strong industrial production, a surge in the GNP, and relatively low inflation and wage demands. But over the next three years, conditions deteriorated markedly. By 1967, wage demands had shot up, inflation had risen, and President de Gaulle of France had effectively sabotaged Britain's potential entry into the European Community. The thought of devaluation was not a pleasant one for Wilson's government but, then again, it was not an alien idea either. Britain had undergone devaluations before and the new pressures developing in the markets made it clear that the pound needed to undergo an adjustment.

In the months preceding the actual devaluation announcement of November 1967 Britain had unsuccessfully used many of its standby facilities that normally are used to shore up a currency. The swap arrangements with the Federal Reserve and other major central banks were employed but sterling still floundered in the markets. Much attention was paid to the 'international speculators' cited by many politicians and Treasury officials as the cause of sterling's weakness. This has always been a method used to blame anonymous elements in the markets for a currency's troubles and it was amply used in the months preceding November. The British avidly used the term coined by a Treasury official several years before, referring to the traders and speculators as the 'gnomes of Zurich'. Somewhere in the money houses of Switzerland were little money grabbers bent on forcing down the value of the pound.

The devaluation announced in November did not end Britain's problems in the foreign exchange markets but it did provide a temporary palliative. Although the actual decision to devalue was Britain's alone, consultations had been taken with its major trading partners and the IMF prior to Prime Minister Wilson's announcement. Yet despite the measures, within a decade the pound would again be under serious pressure due to the effect of a miner's strike in 1974 and other work stoppages that did little to enhance Britain's reputation internationally. Under the Labour government of Harold Wilson and, later, James Callaghan, Britain developed a cranky reputation as a place where little was done but at a high cost nevertheless. This would again cause a flight from sterling that would require IMF assistance in the near future.

The next currency to suffer serious problems would be the dollar, the central *numéraire* of the IMF fixed parity system. As will be seen, the official reaction of the United States was not dissimilar to that of Britain. Politically, someone else would have to be blamed for the plight of the dollar. The money inflation created by financing the Vietnam War and the failure of Lyndon Johnson to balance the budget in 1968 made the dollar less appealing to traders and others who had the option of seeking other currencies in which to direct their 'hot money' flows. Their activities would provide a convenient excuse for the actions of August 1971 that so drastically changed the structure of the international financial system.

THE CAMP DAVID DECISION

The Bretton Woods Agreement concerning the fixed parity system came to an abrupt end on the evening of 15 August 1971. In a televised news conference, President Richard Nixon announced measures designed to curtail the inflation rate and aid the balance of payments, which was showing a deficit. Although the decision to end the convertibility of the dollar into gold for official purposes was without doubt the most momentous part of the economic package, it certainly was not announced first in the address. In fact, it was the last part of the anti-inflation package to be mentioned.

The Nixon administration was compelled to act against inflation for several reasons. Wage demands had grown substantially in the late 1960s. After a seventy-day strike, car workers at General Motors had negotiated a 20 per cent wage increase. Large increases were also found in the construction industry, just beginning to feel the benefits of the new housing policies of the late 1960s and early 1970s. Yet, at the same time, unemployment stood at 6 per cent and showed no signs of receding. Although the United States was the largest foreign investor in the world (direct foreign investment), American tastes for foreign produced goods had steadily increased since the Second World War and was now contributing to the trade imbalance and balance of payments deficit.

Other economic indicators also were showing signs of nervousness and inflation. Treasury bond yields were near 8 per cent and the Dow Jones index was hovering in the 700 range after Nixon took office. Despite his optimism that 'now was a good time to buy' stocks, investors tended not to believe. This was disappointing because conventional wisdom held that Republicans were good for the stock market while Democrats tended to depress it with their free spending policies. Moreover, the first Nixon administration did show signs of traditional Republican thinking by being preoccupied with international rather than domestic affairs. The Vietnam War consumed much of the administration's time but re-election year was not far away and the domestic economy required attention.

The details of the 15 August announcement were finalised at the Camp David retreat immediately before the televised address. A devaluation of the dollar had been rumoured for some time. Finance Minister Valéry Giscard d'Estaing of France had suggested it earlier in the year although the Americans steadfastly had maintained that devaluation was not an option for the administration. Governor John Connally of Texas, Nixon's Secretary of the Treasury, had stated emphatically as late as May that devaluation would be resisted and that the price of gold would remain stable. Equally, Connally maintained that wage and price controls would not be implemented although Arthur Burns, Chairman of the Federal Reserve, had suggested just such a course of action. Clearly there were divergent views on the best method to combat inflation.

The divergent views finally came together on the weekend of 12–15 August as the administration announced measures designed to reduce unemployment and inflation. As Nixon laid out his plan in the televised address, domestic considerations came first. All of the measures announced were implemented under the Economic Stabilisation Act of 1970. He announced a 10 per cent 'job development' credit, or tax credit for capital investment by industry. He also repealed the 7 per cent excise on motor cars then in effect while insisting that the car industry pass on the savings to car buyers. He also ordered a $4.7 billion cut in federal spending and a 5 per cent pay cut for government employees. Finally, on the domestic side, he ordered a ninety-day freeze on all wages and prices in the country.

On the international side, the measures were equally stringent. US foreign aid was ordered to be cut by 10 per cent. But the measures designed to protect the dollar were saved for last. Acknowledging that the dollar was under intense pressure in the foreign exchange markets, there was little doubt who would be blamed for the problem:

> In the past seven years, there's been an average of one international monetary crisis every year. Now who gains from these crises? Not the

working man, not the investor, not the real producers of wealth. The gainers are the international money speculators: because they thrive on crisis, they help to create them.[1]

Following this statement, Nixon announced that he had ordered the United States to halt the convertibility of the dollar into gold for official purposes.

The final measure announced was a temporary 10 per cent tax on all imported goods, designed to dilute American enthusiasm for imports. Taken in its entirety, the package *was* designed to be only temporary. But the dollar part was purposely left more vague. 'In full cooperation with the International Monetary Fund and those who trade with us, we will press for the necessary reforms to set up an urgently needed new international monetary system,' Nixon concluded. 'I am determined that the American dollar must never again be a hostage in the hands of international speculators.'[2] As it turned out, all of the other measures either would be repealed or expire. The dollar convertibility issue never would be resolved.

At the time, the dollar devaluation was seen in context with the other measures rather than taken on its own. *The Economist* noted that the incomes policy was of paramount importance: 'The devaluation of the dollar was welcome and overdue, but it will have been dearly bought if one of the prices turns out to be another devaluation of the idea that a sensible incomes policy really can be made to work.'[3] Apparently, no one thought that the devaluation would lead to a total dismemberment of the fixed parity system within a year.

From the moment of the announcement, the currency markets plunged into turmoil. When other currencies were revalued or devalued, adjustments were certainly made in the markets but when the central currency of the entire system was devalued, momentary chaos certainly could be expected.

The effects of the dollar devaluation were felt almost immediately. Most commentators were immediately concerned with the trade and balance of payments effects of the measures on the international side and the price and employment effects at home. Overlooked in Nixon's statement and in many of the immediate commentaries thereafter was the effect of the dollar devaluation on the financial markets. A cheaper dollar dissuaded many foreign investors from American portfolio investments and many took action to shift their funds away from the dollar into other hard currency financial markets. In the early 1970s, the choice was still relatively limited. The United States and Britain possessed the two largest stock markets at the time as well as the two largest government bond markets.

The decline of the dollar was shadowed by a rise in sterling. The pound moved up immediately after the 15 August announcement by about 2.5 per cent and remained in a higher range for the balance of the year. The Bank of England took preventive measures to protect the pound from even further rises and to protect it from flight capital coming out of dollars but the currency still remained strong. Being protected by exchange controls at the time, sterling was relatively easy to protect while the dollar continued its slide. The behaviour of the pound compared to the dollar and the Deutschmark can be found in Figure 1.1. It should be noted that the pound was able to maintain itself against the dollar before and after 1971 but was less successful against the Deutschmark.

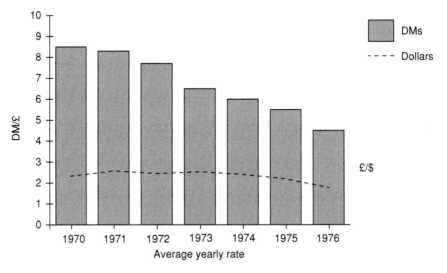

Figure 1.1 Sterling v. dollar and Deutschmark, 1970–76

Source: Central Statistical Office, *Financial Statistics*, various issues

One indication of fears for the dollar surfaced as early as 1969 when the IMF sanctioned the use of special drawing rights, or SDRs, to be used by its member states in official transactions. The SDR was (and is) a basket currency based upon a weighted average of other currencies. Originally, it included over a dozen of the major trading currencies although currently it contains only five.[4] Using the weighted concept, the IMF was able to construct a currency that was less subject to swings in the dollar. If the dollar declined then the other currencies would appreciate, mitigating the movement of the major reserve currency. In short, the SDR was less volatile than any one of its individual components and helped many countries offset wide dollar swings when valuing their reserve assets.

While investor confidence was eroded by the actions of the United States, many foreign officials also expressed shock at the measures that were imposed unilaterally. The accepted path for the dollar devaluation should have been more official, i.e., certain trading partners agreeing to revalue their currencies while the dollar was officially devalued. The foreign exchange markets were closed for the balance of the week after the announcement while finance officials from the major trading countries began to schedule meetings to determine further courses of action. The matter of the price of gold still had to be settled as did the consequences for the fixed parity system.

Immediately after the announcement, interest rates began to decline in the United States, apparently in response to the anti-inflation measures. Long-term corporate bond rates fell one-half of 1 per cent and municipal rates fell almost three-quarters of 1 per cent. Short-term rates also fell a bit later in September. While these developments were a bullish sign domestically, the drop in interest rates would only further dissuade foreign investors from purchasing American bonds and money market instruments. But the longer-term effects would not be as salubrious. The seeds of interest rate volatility and exchange rate volatility were sown that would cause serious disturbances for decades to come.

The next major attempt to patch the system together was held in Washington, DC, at the Smithsonian Institution in December 1971. This meeting was a direct outcome of a meeting between Richard Nixon and President Pompidou of France the previous month in the Azores, where they had attempted to work out a meaningful solution to the currency crisis. The European view, best expressed by the French president, was that the dollar could be allowed to decline while the European currencies were revalued, but that a general float was out of the question. Negotiations since September had not decided the role of gold after the link to con-vertibility had been broken. The currency markets remained nonplussed and the dollar declined against the other major currencies, but was not yet floating. Only in December was an agreement finally reached that addressed the matters of currency values as well as the price of gold. At the meeting, gold was officially revalued from $35 to $38 per ounce and a new parity system was established. Instead of the old band of plus or minus 1 per cent, a new band of plus or minus 2.25 per cent was established. Currencies would now be allowed to fluctuate within this wider band in a new attempt at monetary stability.

Although the Smithsonian Agreement would prove to be short-lived, the devaluation of the dollar was almost complete. Being the central numéraire of the system, it was difficult to determine exactly how the devaluation could be calculated across the board. In most cases, it depended upon the currency being quoted against the dollar, with some registering higher revaluations than others. Generally, about 10 per cent on average was a close approximation, with the Japanese yen and the Deutschmark registering some of the highest gains. The pound increased in value by about 8 per cent.[5]

The devaluation caused funds to be shifted out of dollars into the other major currencies, including sterling. Several financial and economic realities began to emerge that were not lost on the financial markets. The dollar was now cheaper than it had been previously and the depreciation was official. This would make American assets cheaper than before and would begin to change the marketing and investment strategies of many non-American international companies that had desired a toehold in the United States. International investment patterns would begin to change as a result.

Foreign investment patterns in the United States prior to 1970 provide an example. While foreigners had always found the United States an attractive place in which to invest, foreign portfolio investments in the US always outstripped direct foreign investments by a fairly sizeable margin. Foreign investors usually had preferred stock and bond investment to direct investments since the First World War although direct investments had steadily grown in popularity. But now a change was about to take place. The new environment, characterised by a weaker dollar, would help spur new direct investments. More precise motives for this phenomenon will be seen in later chapters.

The Smithsonian Agreement was short-lived. Although the new divergence band was certainly more flexible than the original Bretton Woods 1 per cent band, it did not satisfy the market. Market forces had now begun to assert themselves over the managed bands that the industrialised countries maintained must govern foreign exchange trading. Both the Canadian dollar and Dutch guilder had floated in the time leading up to August so the idea of freely floating exchange rates was certainly not novel. But more specifically, the new currency favourites – the Deutschmark and Japanese yen – represented countries that were on the rise economically. Having rebounded after the war, both countries would begin to challenge the United States, and to a lesser extent Britain, for a premier role as what would become known as the 'locomotives' of international economic growth. Naturally, those currencies would become viable substitutes for the holders of dollars who wanted to diversify their holdings.

Most of the major trading nations would not agree to a larger devaluation. The market took up the cause instead. The dollar continued to weaken after the agreement. Sterling was allowed to float in June 1972. Consequently, the dollar was devalued again in February 1973 and gold was revalued at $42 per ounce, amounting to another 10 per cent devaluation. Clearly, the fixed parity system was not working and the market continued putting pressure on the dollar. Finally, in March 1973, the horse bolted from the barn and the major industrial countries agreed to let their currencies float against each other. The process that had begun in August 1971 had finally reached its conclusion a year and a half later with a bow to ineluctable market forces.

CHANGING MARKETS

Although the Bretton Woods system finally ended with the demise of the Smithsonian accord, how much of a system *per se* actually existed after the Second World War is not entirely clear. The par value system never placed the International Monetary Fund in a commanding position to dictate to member countries, especially the industrialised ones. Its ability to dictate to any member depended upon the goodwill of individual countries to accept its positions. Too much emphasis on a 'system' tends to mask the years of monetary crisis that characterised much of the 1960s and 1970s. However, the original spirit of the Bretton Woods Agreement – that countries consult each other on exchange rate matters rather than act in a purely unilateral fashion – was a substantive improvement over the Depression years when unilateral devaluations were common. In this respect, the original system is analogous to much of the banking and securities legislation passed in the United States during the 1930s. A framework to prevent the abuses of the past was constructed to prevent groups with special interests gaining hegemony over a particular part of the market, ultimately putting the entire system at risk. Market forces had by 1971 destroyed the exchange rate system; ten years later institutions and domestic markets in Britain and the United States would feel the same sorts of pressure.

As part of the Smithsonian Agreement, the United States agreed to abolish capital controls that had been in force since 1963. Specifically, the controls attempted to stem the flow of both short- and long-term capital out of the United States. Of the two sides, the control of long-term capital through the Interest Equalisation Tax (IET) was the more contentious because it affected foreigners' ability to raise money in the American capital markets, especially the bond markets. Since the United States had been an exporter of long-term capital to the rest of the world since the 1920s, removing the barrier standing in the way of foreign companies and governments was essential to preserving international monetary peace.

The IET had been enacted in 1963 by the Kennedy administration as a means of preventing American investors from purchasing foreign securities denominated in dollars. Any investor purchasing a foreign security would be taxed at a rate that made the security equal to a comparable American stock or bond. Without the risk premium normally attached to the dividend or coupon yield, investors would be loath to purchase a security that yielded no more than a domestic one. This measure effectively slowed the issuance of new foreign securities in the American market to a trickle.

What could not be foreseen by this measure was the almost immediate birth of a new capital market – the Eurobond market. Realising that the American market was soon to be effectively closed to most foreign entities save the best known, British authorities and bankers immediately took up the gauntlet by paving the way for a new capital market, located in the City, to take up the slack in raising capital. But in this case, it was not the reintroduction of sterling into the international marketplace that was at issue. The new market initially was conducted almost exclusively in US dollars.

The second round of controls following the IET sought to stem the outflow of short-term dollars into the offshore market, better known as the Euromarket. Banks in London and other money centres had been accepting dollar deposits since the early 1960s and American companies had become accustomed to depositing money offshore as well as at home. American banks had also begun to use the market as a way of circumventing domestic regulations, and the credit controls imposed by the Johnson administration sought to interrupt the flow of dollars and companies to offshore depositories. In many cases, the dollars went back to the United States for the same purposes that domestic banks used them for − lending. By using the offshore route, many depositors helped foreign banks especially by providing them with funds and also aiding a balance of payments disequilibrium in the process.

Neither type of capital control proved terribly successful and both were eventually lifted. The United States' loss and Britain's gain, especially in the long-term sector, was the Eurobond market. Within twenty years, the Eurobond market would actually surpass the New York corporate bond market as the world's largest corporate market. Adding insult to injury was another event that was integrally tied to the capital markets, giving the American financial markets a bloody nose, at least in the opinion of foreign investors.

Since the 1930s, the American stock and bond markets had prided themselves on investor protections built into the market mechanisms. These protections, actually built up over the years, led many American regulators to claim that the United States had the best regulated (and safest) markets that investors could hope for internationally. While no market could be entirely free of manipulation and unforeseen risk, the US stock and bond markets were considered the most 'efficient' in the world. Being efficient meant the relative lack of friction (or difficulty) in obtaining a good price on a security and selling or buying even large amounts without materially affecting the price under normal market conditions. Two events occurring in the late 1960s and early 1970s helped to negatively alter that perception.

While the IET was in force, many American investors eschewed investing in foreign securities because of the penal tax. Existing stocks or bonds could only be sold to foreign investors who would not incur the supplemental rates of the IET. Foreign investors thus became the prime targets of US investors seeking to divest themselves of their foreign holdings. It was not long thereafter that a major scandal developed whereby foreign investors were sold bogus securities at knock-down prices only to find that the serial numbers on the shares and bonds were false. The implications of the bogus securities swindle were far-reaching although the amounts involved could only be estimated at between $100 million and $1 billion. But the damage done to the domestic markets in the eyes of foreign investors was inestimable.

By the time the Bretton Woods Agreement had unravelled, sentiment was clearly on the side of flight from the dollar rather than on that of increased confidence. This was one of the major reasons that the Bank of England sought to protect sterling by dissuading international investors from purchasing sterling denominated financial assets, particularly short-term ones. But as will be seen in further chapters, other currencies did not offer the full range of alternatives to the American capital markets because of the sheer size of the American stock and bond markets. As a result, the Eurobond market would benefit although many instruments traded within it were denominated in dollars (Eurodollar bonds for instance). Since the market could not sell as many dollars as might be required, it diversified internally, relying upon market segmentation – mainly tax differences and yield discrepancies – to allow investors to shift out of lower yielding US domestic investments into higher yielding Eurobonds.

When the currency volatility began in the early 1970s, the American stock and bond markets were the world's largest in terms of total capitalisation. Markets in the United Kingdom ranked second followed by Japan, West Germany, Switzerland and the Netherlands. But not all were as easily accessible. The flow of funds into the UK and Japan were controlled by the monetary authorities in varying degrees while the German market was indirectly controlled by the Bundesbank, which had the final say concerning the potential use of the Deutschmark as an international currency. Despite the fact that the dollar had fallen out of favour, the investment alternatives were limited. Pressure on the currency notwithstanding, there were no viable alternatives to the dollar in the international monetary system.

During the early 1970s, the American and British financial markets were the two undisputed leaders of the international marketplace. Both stock markets attracted sizeable international investments. The American bond market, both for corporate and Treasury issues, had a decided advantage over the UK since the British bond market was confined to Treasury issues, or gilts. The corporate market had been moribund because of exchange controls. Local authority (municipal) issues in the UK remained of interest only for local residents, as did municipals in the United States. But the seeds of change were apparent nevertheless. The American markets would be the first to be reformed in response to domestic and international pressures. The UK markets would remain protected for another decade before succumbing to similar pressures.

Since the dollar suffered more than the pound after the events of 1971–72,

29

the movement for reform in the American markets was certainly logical. Equally, the rapid development of new hedging markets, using options on common shares and interest rate futures, was another indication that the markets were in a state of transition, attempting to devise new products designed to help investors mitigate against loss in the capital markets. The UK financial markets enjoyed built-in protections and would be slower in responding to international developments. Because the London Stock Exchange traded so many foreign and Commonwealth shares as well as domestic shares, it served a vital function for territories outside the UK. While its capitalisation was smaller than that of the American stock exchanges, it traded more listed shares than the New York Stock Exchange and was a centre of trading because of London's central position in the Commonwealth. At the same time, gilt-edged securities were probably better known internationally than American Treasury bonds, for the same reason.

Although the two exchanges ranked first and second in terms of market capitalisation and turnover, the New York Stock Exchange, representative of the American market as a whole, was thought to be more efficient and economical to deal upon than the London Stock Exchange. The commission structure for dealing was fixed in both markets although the UK market charged proportionately more for commissions. In addition, investors incurred other charges such as the stamp (turnover tax) which was not a factor in New York.

In addition to the higher costs, the method of dealing was different on the London exchange from that of New York. The British method of floor trading in an auction market used floor brokers that traded for their own accounts only. When a broker representing a client approached the exchange floor, that broker's counterparty would be a broker who acted for his or her own account, in a single capacity system. New York, on the other hand, employed floor brokers, or specialists, who traded in a dual capacity, both with customers and with other brokers as well. As a result, New York stock pricing was considered more efficient because the specialist could always lay off the risk of buying or selling to a client by trading with other floor brokers. The UK method suggested that brokers would act in their own best interests first, sometimes at a cost to the customer.

Within three years of the general currency float, the American stock exchanges would abolish their fixed commission schedules in favour of negotiated commissions. The financial markets would be quick to realise that some of their business and much of their influence was tied to international events more than at any time in the past. When investors became disgruntled and sold securities they also sold the currency in which those securities were denominated. Thus, pressure on securities became pressure on currency spot rates, a phenomenon that was always recognised but not fully appreciated until after currencies began to float freely against each other.

CHANGING FINANCIAL INSTITUTIONS

Not only the financial markets were caught off guard by the new floating exchange rate regime. Banks and banking-type institutions in both Britain and the United States would also feel the effects of rapidly changing exchange rates and increased hot money flows. Again, the direct effects would be felt at different times due to the structural and functional differences in the two banking systems. The more protected banking system of the two – that in the United States – would experience a somewhat delayed reaction not dissimilar to the protected financial markets in Britain. As is usually the case, protectionist regulations insulated the American banks for a short time before international and market pressures made reform in the banking system inevitable.

At the time of the August announcement, the banking systems of the two countries were quite dissimilar in terms of regulations and supervision. In the United States, exactly what activities constituted commercial banking (as opposed to investment banking) could be found in the Banking Act of 1933, also known as the Glass–Steagall Act. That definition of banking applied not only to national banks that were members of the Federal Reserve bank in their respective districts but also to all banks in the country. Simply, commercial banks were separated from thrift institutions (building societies) as well as investment banks that underwrote and traded corporate securities.

In Britain, the actual definition of banking activities was not clearly written down until the Banking Act of 1979. Banking had a distinctly common law element to it in that it was regulated and (partially) defined by a series of prior Acts of Parliament, but still lacked a contemporary definition. As a result, a number of banking-type institutions had opened performing some, but not all, commercial banking functions, mostly on a wholesale level. These institutions performed these functions in a different manner than the clearing banks that dominated British retail and wholesale banking. By not dealing directly with the public, they were able to avoid many of the Bank of England's winks and nods that governed bank supervision. This group is referred to as the 'fringe banks', or secondary banks.

The other two institutions performing banking functions were quite similar to their American counterparts. Building societies were retail institutions that dominated the residential mortgage market while merchant banks and brokers contented themselves with securities issues and trading. Clear legalistic lines of demarcation between them did not exist as they did in America. However, the similarities persisted. Building societies, as their American counterparts, the thrifts or savings and loan associations (S&Ls), accounted for the majority of residential mortgages created. The investment banks and merchant banks maintained a monopoly on securities issues with the assistance of brokers.

Aside from the structural differences between the two financial systems, the other clear difference between them was their different attitudes toward regulation and supervision. The American financial industry, comprising both commercial and investment banks, was probably the most regulated in the country, subject to a panoply of both federal and (to a lesser extent) state rules. The British system of supervision was somewhat looser, with the Bank of England the nominal regulator of the major commercial (clearing) banks. This would allow the Bank of England some flexibility on the one hand while inviting trouble on the other.

On a higher level of comparison, the British system was clearly more reliant upon commercial banks than was the United States. Since commercial and investment banking had been forcibly divorced since the early 1930s, American corporations had come to rely upon the capital markets for long-term financing while using banks for short-term loan facilities. Smaller companies relied more upon the banks because they did not have access to the markets and commercial banks were their only external source of funds in many cases. That arrangement limited the influence of the commercial banks and, equally, brought the bond and stock markets to centre stage.

Britain, on the one hand, relied much more heavily upon the commercial banks and less on the capital markets. Banks therefore controlled the cost of funds to companies in Britain, both for short-term and long-term money. Companies needing medium-term loans negotiated term facilities with the banks because there was no corporate bond market to speak of. As a result, companies were subject to whatever sort of interest rates the banks charged and in Britain that simply meant floating rates of interest.

The Americans, on the other hand, relied upon fixed-rate financing because of the influence of the bond markets. In the short term, American banks also were protected by Federal Reserve regulations that set a limit upon the amount of interest they paid depositors. Regulation Q, established in the 1930s, allowed the Federal Reserve to dictate the maximum amount of interest banks could pay on deposits.[6] That regulation became the bane of the banks in the latter 1970s after having protected their cost of funds for over forty years. A comparison of short-term interest rates in the US and Britain can be found in Figure 1.2.

During the 1960s, the British clearing banks had operated under a system akin to Regulation Q called the interest rate cartel. Under this arrangement, the clearing (major) banks agreed among themselves to limit the interest paid on deposit accounts to 2 per cent below the rate in the money market that was affected directly by the Bank of England. The deposit rate, like the American deposit rates, was below the money market rates and also had the net effect of keeping lending rates somewhat lower than the market might have allowed. This arrangement protected UK banks well

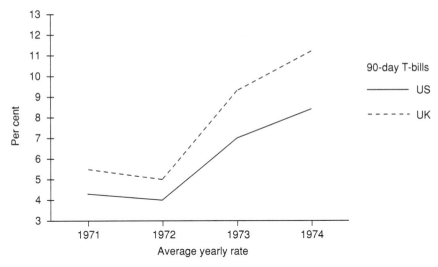

Figure 1.2 Short-term interest rates in the US and UK, 1970–76

Source: Federal Reserve System *Bulletin*, various issues

enough until competition for funds began to develop in the 1960s. Newer, and smaller, banks emerged that began to compete directly with the clearers for funds and, as a result, the clearers' share of the deposit market began to decline.

The cartel was abolished in September 1971 under a plan proposed by the Bank of England. Originally known as the Competition and Credit Control (CC&C) plan, it abolished the cartel and lowered liquidity requirements for the clearers. As a result, UK banks were on a more equal footing from that time and interest rate controlled ceilings were effectively abolished. The timing of the implementation was extremely fortuitous since sterling did not decline in the wake of the August 1971 announcement and the British banking system was able to maintain its central role in the world markeplace. For the second time in a decade, UK authorities had anticipated a contemporary event correctly and had been able to make economic gain from it. Allowing the opening of the Euromarket in London at the time of the Interest Equalization Tax in the US had been the first.

Because of the differences in market structure, the Americans had come to rely upon fixed rate financing while the British relied on floating rate financing. That difference was crucial to the way that both national markets developed quickly in the 1980s and consequently began to converge by the early 1990s. The interest rate spiral of the 1970s and 1980s would be more detrimental to the United States and would help destroy the old banking structure by creating ineluctable forces that would sweep through the bond and money markets, forcing banks to adjust themselves to a new era when interest rate ceilings would no longer be applicable. The British would feel the new environment more in the financial markets because UK banks already had years to adjust to floating interest rates.

Despite their differences in banking, both British and American commercial banks shared other common factors. Both were deposit driven to a great extent rather than driven by the money market. This means that they both relied upon their depositors to provide the funds used for lending.[7] In this respect, the American banks had a decided advantage since Regulation Q limited rates of interest paid. Savers desiring higher yields would be forced to find investments with substantially higher risk. In Britain, the deposit rate varied with the minimum lending rate (MLR), the base rate by which bank rates were set at the time. Also protecting the American banks' deposit bases was deposit insurance provided by Federal Deposit Insurance Corporation (FDIC) insurance. In the early 1970s, the maximum amount insured in any one account at an insured bank was $40,000.

In the mid-1970s, inflation and market rates of interest would create great pressures on both banking systems but especially the American. The banks would have to be quick in responding in order to maintain their depositors' business. When foreign exchange rates began to float, risks to international business increased considerably. From 1972 until the present, businesses have constantly had to cope with exchange rates capable of rapid change. The reasons that rates change so quickly is a combination of interest rates, exchange rates themselves, and foreign investment patterns, all of which combine to create exchange rate volatility unheard of in the Bretton Woods era. The driving force usually has been interest rates that in turn have affected exchange rates, which in turn have prompted foreign investment by international companies and investors. While the sequence of events in that cycle sometimes was changed, interest rates lay at the heart of the matter. Investors now had a convenient way of responding to interest rate changes in one country against another. They simply bought or sold currency depending upon the level of interest rates. High rates (especially high real rates) made a currency attractive. When interest rates fell, the currency became less attractive, depending upon the levels found in alternative countries' currencies.

Even retail depositors, or savers, could not be expected to be captive customers when interest rates began to rise. New investment products would be devised that would seriously compete with the depository institutions for funds, only adding to the banks' general woes. As will be seen in the following chapters, British banks would be more insulated from this trend in the 1970s because the trend toward developing new products was slower in Britain than in the US.

The combination of interest rate and exchange rate pressures put the markets and the banks under new strains not witnessed since the

Depression. Since American banks were protected by Regulation Q, they were slower in feeling the strains than were British banks, which were already accustomed to changeable interest rates. The British markets were slower to react because they were more protected than the American stock and bond markets. Any institution that was not subject to close regulation or protected by custom or outdated regulation would be subject to rapid change both from inside and outside the domestic financial system. The demise of the fixed exchange rate system was about to unleash forces that could not have been foreseen in 1972.

CHANGING FOREIGN INVESTMENT PATTERNS

One of the significant forces that would be unleashed by the currency realignment was foreign investment. Both the United States and Britain had been significant foreign investors in their own right and had also benefited significantly from foreign investment themselves, both portfolio and direct.[8] During the course of the twentieth century, Britain traditionally had been the largest foreign investor in the United States while the US returned the favour by becoming the largest foreign investor in the UK. This two-sided relationship was perhaps the strongest single tie that the two countries had established over the years.

This fact, not particularly well known outside financial circles, became a crucial factor as the two countries attempted to co-ordinate their financial policies in the 1980s. The British traditionally split their American investments between portfolio investments and direct investments while the Americans tended to favour direct investments in Britain rather than portfolio investments. On the direct investment side, the policies worked extremely well. Americans had come to accept such companies and brand names as Lever, Lipton and Shell as household names while Britons embraced such names as Ford, Hoover and Woolworth as their own. Using their common language to best advantage, companies from both countries were able to market and manufacture in the other without the stigma of being 'foreign'.

In the financial markets, the attraction was equally as strong. Britons had been the most avid investors in US securities since the nineteenth century. Without British investors, many municipalities and (later) railways would have found a much more difficult time raising funds. After the First World War, portfolio investments turned toward common stocks rather than bonds and remained heavily invested in them until the 1990s. Many British unit trusts (mutual funds) invested heavily in US shares, mainly as a hedge against the value of the pound. These strong relationships helped make the dollar/pound relationship one of the key foreign exchange rates over the years and proved to be the prime motivating factor in cross-border investing after 1972.

In the twentieth century, British investments began to gravitate toward North America, and particularly the United States, as British influence in the world began to wane. While it was natural that money should follow common language and cultural ties, the simple fact was that the pound was declining in importance and many British investors used the dollar to hedge its diminished stature. As noted earlier, the pound's dollar rate at the beginning of the Bretton Woods agreement was about $4.80. After several devaluations, it stood at $2.40 in 1972, a 50 per cent depreciation that technically could not have occurred under the normal fixed parity system without adjustments. For UK investors, the dollar was the natural place to diversify, although rates of return in dollar investments would not always compensate for the risks involved, as will be seen later.

American investments in Britain were equally substantial, as they were for Europe as a whole. Contrary to popular opinion, the majority of American direct foreign investment after the war was found (on a total value basis) in Europe rather than in Latin America or other parts of the Third World.[9] Although the total amount invested overseas was substantial, Western Europe and Britain remained the favourite of American companies. Therefore, when critics of American influence voiced their concern about the spread of that influence, they most often complained about it from a domestic perspective rather than worrying about the potential effects upon the developing countries. In Britain, there were relatively fewer complaints about American influence than in France or other countries with a vociferous left-wing anti-American intelligentsia.

While it might appear natural that the two countries would have been each other's favourite place to invest because of common language and shared traditions, there were many other significant economic differences between the United States and Britain in 1971–72. Many of Britain's industries and public services were nationalised, the pound was protected by exchange controls and the Conservative government of Edward Heath was beset with domestic labour problems that finally culminated in the miners' strike of 1974. But the economic ties between the two predated contemporary politics and dictated that the two countries would nevertheless have to maintain close ties despite their post-war economic differences. The business and economic relationship between the two countries gives one of the best examples of private enterprise developing relationships that eventually cause governments to take heed and acknowledge. As the two financial systems came under stress twenty years later, previous divergences would begin to disappear in favour of policies that came to look remarkably similar.

Despite the investment patterns of the past, the post-Bretton Woods era would nevertheless change trends in both the UK and US. Perhaps the greatest beneficiary of the changing currency values was Japan, itself still protected by currency controls in 1971–72. In 1972, Japanese direct investment in the US was minimal, amounting to less than $1 billion. Virtually all Japanese motor cars sold in the US were imported from Japan, as were most other manufactured products of Japanese origin. And the aura of quality that developed in later years had not yet been totally established. Manufactured goods were not yet entirely free of their shoddy image, derived from the days when imported electronic equipment and some clothing from Japan were noted for poor quality.

While the devalued dollar made Japanese imports more expensive, the stronger yen also made dollar denominated investments more favourable. As a result, the Japanese began to look at American investments in the same light as the British had done for years, realising that strong trade patterns engendered stronger direct investment, which in turn would generate even stronger trade in the future. As the dollar lost strength against the yen, the stage was set for an influx of Japanese direct investment throughout the 1970s.

The growing foreign presence put the United States in an unfamiliar and somewhat uncomfortable position. Since the Second World War, the United States had been the world's largest exporter of long-term capital. Its foreign investments exceeded foreign direct investment in the country by a ratio of five or six to one. The period 1945–72 witnessed the expansion of American industry overseas and all of the criticisms that accompanied it, from cultural (mostly pop culture) imperialism to meddling in developing countries' economic affairs in order to exploit them. For roughly twenty-five years, the Americans had dominated foreign trade and investment, based chiefly upon a strong dollar and freedom of capital movement, something the Europeans and the Japanese could not yet entirely afford. But now the stage was set to be changed. Within twenty years, the discontent that had surrounded the growing American influence abroad would shift to the Japanese, who, like the Americans, took continued advantage of their strong currency in order to expand. The Americans would pass the mantle of being *nouveaux riche* and all of the accompanying criticisms to the production-oriented Japanese.

In 1972, none of this would be predicted with any reliability. The Vietnam War was still being waged but America's problems were still mostly domestic, with the national character and the quality and veracity of its political leadership being hotly debated. In Britain, the outlook was a bit brighter, fuelled mainly by a consumption boom during the Heath government. It would be two years before similar forces were at work, manifest in the miners' strike and the shortened working week in early 1974. While the dollar was declining, the pound did not fare well despite the natural inclination of many investors to view it as an alternative to the dollar. Britain's spotty economic performance and labour troubles helped push the Deutschmark to the forefront as the second major reserve currency, faster than the Bundesbank had hoped.

Much of the gloom and uncertainty of the 1970s could therefore be attributed to the August 1971 announcement. The dollar devaluation had shown that investors and traders would have liked alternatives to the dollar but that the Germans and Japanese were less than accommodating for fear of inflation and the other problems that currency internationalisation could bring. When political problems began to appear, with the Watergate scandal and the fall of the Heath government, the problems became compounded because the political will necessary to patch up the international currency regime did not exist. As a result, the float continued until it became a *fait accompli* and currency volatility became the norm rather than the exception.

Although the demise of Bretton Woods was difficult if not impossible to predict, many in the financial community had anticipated some sort of change based upon exchange rate and interest rate volatility. As will be seen in Chapter 3, new products and exchanges were being planned in the United States designed to help investors hedge the increasing risks in the marketplace. But in many cases, as useful as that forward planning eventually proved to be, the immediate effects upon financial institutions was not foreseen, nor was the reaction of the oil-producing nations. The international financial system was set for further shocks that would permanently change the course of future events.

2

EMERGING CRISES

After the smoke had cleared from the confusion of 1972, several significant developments occurred in 1973 that have been considered the prime causes of the inflation of the 1970s and early 1980s. While these events were direct consequences of the collapse of the Bretton Woods system, at the time they were more narrowly considered as the products of poor banking regulation and a shift in the hegemony of world economic power. No one had yet assumed that exchange rates would not again be put under some sort of peg system. As a result, the fast-moving events following August 1971 left little time to make a logical connection between a British banking crisis and the worldwide spiral in the price of oil that would occur a year-and-a-half later.

Both of these events produced an increase in flight capital from traditional currency havens and also increased the volatility of hot money flows. The increase in money flows only exacerbated the crises even more. Policymakers on both sides of the Atlantic eventually would realise that the financial system in each country was not adequately equipped to deal with this new phenomenon. The American practice of adhering to fixed interest rates would provide some insulation against these shocks, while the British reliance on floating rates would leave UK institutions vulnerable. Capital flight was not new; what was new was the quick reaction in the financial markets that would leave financial institutions out of step and gasping for breath.

Despite the quick reactions of currency traders, the situation in 1973 was not as pronounced as it would become in the 1980s nor was it attributed to the same set of circumstances. The dollar was still under the protective net of short- and long-term capital controls (of a sort) and the Deutschmark and the yen were similarly protected. Sterling was still technically protected by exchange controls and the other major currencies were of limited use for purposes of diversification. Almost all finance ministers and heads of central banks agreed that a new monetary system would be devised to replace Bretton Woods, even after the demise of the short-lived Smithsonian Agreement. No one was yet able to contemplate a new order in which the hard currencies would float against each other without regard for any sort of central parity. Not that floating currencies were unheard of; they were just never contemplated.

THE OPEC PRICE RISE

At the same time as a banking crisis burst upon the scene in Britain, a shattering event of international magnitude occurred in Tehran when the Organisation of Petroleum Exporting Countries (OPEC) voted to raise the price of its exported oil. The largest OPEC oil price rise to date came in December 1973 as the price of petrol was officially doubled from $5.50 to slightly over $11.00 per barrel. Smaller previous increases had caused it to rise from about $2.50 to $5.00, so the net increases effectively quadrupled the price within the year. In addition to increasing import costs in the industrialised world, the move thrust some of the obscure oil producing nations on to the world stage.

The increase occurred for a variety of economic and political reasons. The demand for oil had surged in the mid-1960s, especially in the United States, where as in other countries there was a shift from energy produced by coal to that produced by oil for environmental reasons. American oil demands began to increase rapidly while domestic production actually fell due to import quotas that were avidly defended by domestic producers. As a result, the domestic price remained high while imports were restricted under the quota system, although the gross amount of imports increased nevertheless.

At the same time, the United States was not producing enough oil to meet its expanding energy needs. The mid- and late 1960s were a time of energy shortages. Electrical supply was not always able to keep up with demand. Periods of 'brownouts' were becoming common in some cities, especially in summer when supply was not adequate to meet the demand for air conditioning, which was becoming more widespread. An energy crisis was actually developing several years before OPEC began to raise prices.

In Britain, North Sea oil reserves were discovered in the late 1960s and fully fledged production began shortly thereafter, making the UK a major producer in its own right by the mid-1970s. However, Britain's bill for imported oil would also increase after the first price rise although the country remained more dependent upon coal than did the United States. The bill for energy imports rose before any tangible benefits from exporting oil became evident. Despite the fact that both Britain and the US were major oil producers in varying degrees, they still suffered from what became known as oil price 'shocks' beginning in the early 1970s and lasting for almost a decade.

Politically, the oil price rise was in retaliation for the Arab defeat at the hands of the Israelis in the October 1973 Yom Kippur War and for the United States' continuing support of Israel's security. The posturing by Arabs and Israelis prior to the outbreak of hostilities was intense, especially in light of the deepening energy crisis and the support of Israel by the United States. As Daniel Yergin noted, the months prior to the actual Egyptian–Syrian attack on Israel had so intensified international tensions that King Faisal of Saudi Arabia, usually publicly passive to political developments, became actively engaged in helping finance the Arab cause and using oil as a weapon against Israel's supporters.[1] The 'oil weapon' became one of the key strategic concepts of the 1970s as otherwise small, developing countries exercised what seemed to the advanced capitalist economies disproportionate power in world affairs.

But the balance of power in the Middle East was not the only motive for raising the price precipitously. The other side of the argument was equally political but less visible. A rise in the oil price eventually would lead to weakness of the dollar on the foreign exchange markets. That meant that OPEC's major financial asset would purchase less in the future.[2] This was the less obvious side of the petrodollar equation. As oil prices rose, the balance of payments of the United States would slip into deficit to cover the increased costs and that would put pressure on the currency. At the same time, however, the increasing demand for dollars to pay the higher costs should have increased its value on the foreign exchange market. When the two opposite forces collided, the only way for major producers to compensate would be to radically increase the price of their oil.

A rise in the price of oil benefited many members of OPEC for different reasons and those reasons, when combined, provided the consensus needed to raise the price. For instance, the increased price would help Venezuela develop its domestic infrastructure and reduce its balance of payments problems while at the same time potentially helping fund the Shah of Iran's ambitious plans for developing his country into a substantial regional power. Aside from oil politics on an international scale, the currency factor was the one that all members shared in common. The dollar already was under pressure and that helped depreciate the reserves of dollar-based OPEC members. The only way to adjust for the depreciation would be to raise the price of petrol to offset the currency loss.

Seen realistically, the price rise was unjustified, at least in the early winter of 1973. The dollar had depreciated by about 24 per cent against the Deutschmark and by about 20 per cent against the yen in early 1973, but the price of oil had been increased by more than 100 per cent.[3] While the OPEC countries could argue for a price increase in the face of increasing demand, the rise to over $11.00 per barrel appeared excessive. But the cartel members could counter by saying that they had been hurt for years by the US quota system which, while certainly providing them with revenues, had nevertheless discriminated against them because they were foreign producers.

Currency factors are usually overlooked in most discussions of the OPEC cartel, at least in the early years. Subsequent price rises in the later 1970s would continue pressure on the dollar and lead to the more explosive inflation of 1980–81. One of the major reasons currency is overlooked is because of the limited alternatives to the dollar. Diversifying from the dollar was not that easily accomplished in the early 1970s because both the West German and Japanese authorities frowned upon their currencies being used as reserve currencies. The other hard currencies (Dutch guilder, sterling, Canadian dollar and Swiss franc) were not all viable either, because the Canadian dollar and the pound were closely related to movements in the dollar, while the guilder and the Swiss franc paralleled movements in the Deutschmark. Thus, the price rise can be viewed as an attempt to adjust for the dollar's devalued purchasing power given that alternatives were not easily found in the same quantities.

When diversification was attempted, the pound was not a primary beneficiary, at least not according to market values. As Table 2.1 shows, the pound's appreciation in the first six months of 1973, prior to the price rise, was less than that of the Deutschmark, yen or French franc. And when the dollar made a comeback in the second half of the year, sterling's depreciation was also less than other hard currencies. Until sterling was officially freed from exchange controls in 1979, the dollar/pound relationship was close enough to consider sterling in the dollar's orbit rather than in the European camp, although Britain was now a fully fledged member of the European Community (EC). The pound was not considered an alternative to the dollar because it was viewed as being too closely related to it. Given Britain's recent entry into the EC, this was a fragile position at best since some original EC members, notably the French, remained sceptical about Britain's commitment to the ideals of European integration.

The strength of the dollar in the second half of 1973, continuing well into 1974, can be suspected to be as much a result of OPEC producers realigning their currency portfolios as a reflection of fundamental economic factors. For instance, the pound declined in the second half of the year despite a rise in interest rates begrudgingly administered by the Heath government, which saw rises in bank and money market rates as inimical to its growth policies. At the same time, the London Stock Market and (especially) the property market were assuming bubble-like proportions. Before assessing the impact that a price increase would have on the balance of payments, it was natural to assume that an increase in petrol prices would indeed prop up the dollar since more dollars would now be needed to purchase supplies. But the weakness of the pound during this period did little to help the British banking system, which was on the brink of crisis. This crisis was to prove that Britain's place in international finance was well deserved but that the lack of regulation in the London banking market left much to be desired.

Table 2.1 Dollar v. major hard currencies, 1973–74 (cents per currency unit)

Month	Pound	Deutschmark	Yen	French franc	Swiss franc
1973 Jan	235.62	31.288	0.33136	19.671	26.820
Feb	242.75	33.273	0.36041	20.987	29.326
March	247.24	35.548	0.38190	22.191	31.084
April	248.37	35.352	0.37666	21.959	30.821
May	253.05	35.841	0.37786	22.341	31.494
June	257.62	38.786	0.37808	23.472	32.757
July	253.75	42.821	0.37801	24.655	35.428
Aug	247.57	41.219	0.37704	23.527	33.656
Sept	241.83	41.246	0.37668	23.466	33.146
Oct	242.92	41.428	0.37547	23.718	33.019
Nov	238.70	38.764	0.35941	22.687	31.604
Dec	231.74	37.629	0.35692	21.757	31.252
1974 Jan	222.40	35.529	0.33559	19.905	29.727
Feb	227.49	36.844	0.34367	20.187	31.494
March	234.06	38.211	0.35454	20.742	32.490
April	238.86	39.594	0.36001	20.541	33.044
May	241.37	40.635	0.35847	20.540	34.288
June	239.02	39.603	0.35340	20.408	33.449

Source: Federal Reserve *Bulletin*, various issues

THE FRINGE BANKING CRISIS

At first glance, the breakdown of the Bretton Woods system appeared to have little effect in Britain. The Heath government had implemented a small boom by allowing the money supply to increase and relaxing many of the previous Labour government's restraints against competition. Sterling had held up well against the dollar although it did not appreciate substantially in the months immediately following the devaluation. Even after the full dollar float in June 1972, conditions changed little although sterling did slip against the other major currencies.

During the 1960s, a group of secondary banks had sprung up in Britain, challenging the clearing banks in a number of fringe or marginal areas that the big banks eschewed, mostly for regulatory reasons. These institutions became known as 'fringe' or secondary banks because they did not fill the comprehensive definition of 'bank' in the strict sense of the word. Most confined themselves to specialised areas of banking such as securities, real estate and foreign exchange dealing and funded themselves in a manner somewhat different from the large English, Scottish and Northern Irish clearers.

Unlike the larger banks, the fringe group relied on wholesale funding in order to obtain funds for making loans or purchasing other assets. They either would receive large deposits from corporate customers or sell negotiable certificates of deposit (CDs) in the London money market. In the late 1960s and early 1970s, this part of the money market became known as the parallel market.[4] This would require the fringe banks to pay more for those funds than the high street banks would pay because they were not subject to the interest rate cartel. On the other side of the coin, however, neither did they incur the same overheads that the larger banks faced since most of their loans were larger business loans.

Even when the CC&C programme was introduced, the fringe banks did not experience that much competition from the larger banks because they were already well established in their limited businesses. But one vulnerable spot remained: the mainly short-term sources of funds were loaned for the longer term. While a natural mis-matching exists at most banks, this sort of mis-match was potentially dangerous for the fringe banks because the liabilities were incurred in the money market whose customers could not be expected to be as slow in reacting to interest rate changes as did retail customers at the high street banks. Thus, conceivably it was possible that money market depositors could request their money back at short notice and the smaller banks would have little choice but to comply.

In addition to the money market fundings, many of the fringe banks were also heavily involved in real estate lending. Traditionally, real estate lending to home owners was dominated by the building societies while the clearing banks had little interest because of regulations limiting their exposure to the market. A path was clear to the market, especially for commercial real estate lending, and the fringe banks quickly exploited their advantage. When the CC&C was introduced in 1971, the clearing banks also rushed to gain additional exposure to the fast-growing real estate market with results that would prove disastrous within a short period of time.

The real estate boom was aided by the Heath government's expansionist monetary policies after it took office in June 1970. The money supply grew at a very strong rate, creating a speculative boom both in real estate and the stock market. In their rush to make more and more property loans, many of the fringe banks continued to borrow short and lend long in amounts that would not be sustainable when depositors refused to roll over their funds and demanded cash instead. The troubles began when the pound officially began to float against the dollar and the other major currencies after June 1972.

By the winter of 1973, the fringe banks were in serious financial straits. In December, the Bank of England organised a rescue operation for a relatively small bank called Cedar Holdings. The clearing banks were co-opted into the rescue effort and put up the majority of the funds necessary at the central bank's behest. The effort was unprecedented. Cedar Holdings was on the verge of failure and the central bank was worried about the consequences of an outright failure in both the stock market and the money market, where Cedar obtained much of its funding by issuing CDs. The small bank, as many of its counterparts later in the crisis, hit the rocks because of a non-performing portfolio of real estate loans.

By winter, many of the developers and speculators found themselves unable to pay back loans to the fringe banks as well as to the clearers, and the crisis began. Shortly after the Bank of England arranged for the support of Cedar, it became apparent that many other secondary banks were in dire straits. As a result, the Bank of England arranged a more general facility for all of the secondary banks that was quickly dubbed the 'Lifeboat'. Within five days of propping up one bank, it became readily apparent that the Lifeboat would be full very quickly.

The Lifeboat facility was unusual in that the Bank of England was effectively acting as lender of last resort for institutions that did not actually merit the support in a strictly legal sense. But much more was at stake than simply the loans of a fringe group of banks. London's reputation as an international financial centre was in jeopardy since the City was also home to the foreign exchange markets and the newly emergent Euromarket as well. If the Bank of England could not maintain order in the secondary banking sector then its reputation would have been seriously tarnished.[5]

The speed with which the Lifeboat was launched was unusual. The terms and conditions were also quite generous. Aid was offered to any institution that required it without exception. The speed with which the Bank of England acted and the quick acceptance by the clearing banks to aid in the rescue often has been pointed to as an intrinsic strength of the British system of relatively loose regulation and informal controls. With less legal or bureaucratic encumbrances than many other central banks, the Bank of England was able to get down to business very quickly. Its authority among the major banks was never questioned and the support deal was struck very quickly. Since the Bank of England is not independent of the UK Treasury, naturally it was assumed that the Lifeboat had government support as well.

On the other hand, if the fringe banks had been regulated in some meaningful way then the crisis may not have occurred in the first place. Although their individual influences were not great in banking terms, the fringe banks presented a serious threat to the British banking system when considered as a group. One of the lesser known but nevertheless important points about the Lifeboat also has to do with the clearers, fringe banks and the Euromarket. Many of the clearers and fringe banks also had interests in consortium banks that operated in the Euromarkets.[6] If a failure were allowed at the fringe banks, a possible knock-on effect might have been felt in the Euromarkets. That would have put the central bank in the unenviable position of having an adverse effect upon a market that had little to do with sterling and everything to do with US dollars. By stemming the tide early, the Bank of England was able to maintain order in what otherwise could have proved to have been a nasty loss of confidence in more than one marketplace, all located in the same city.

Ten years earlier, the Bank of England had openly encouraged the new Euromarket to use London as its centre in an attempt to win back business for the City despite the declining popularity of sterling as a reserve currency. The Euromarket for both currency deposits and Eurobonds had succeeded beyond most expectations and brought with it important business in foreign exchange and trade finance. This growth also provided a great irony. The largest international financial centre had obtained its position in largely unregulated waters. The Euromarkets were unregulated as were the fringe banks. Any financial crisis that could not be resolved quickly would certainly have disastrous consequences for London's stature as a banking centre. Yet, oddly, it was only two years before that Britain had adopted the decimal system for its currency, replacing the quaint but outdated shilling and old penny with 100 pence per pound.

Although the Lifeboat was launched in December 1973, its life span was longer than the Bank of England or the stock market would have hoped for. Numerous fringe banks had to be rescued throughout 1973 and 1974. The amount of the rescue attempt continued to increase beyond original estimates and the operation became more political, especially since the heads of some of the failing institutions had close political ties with the Heath government, especially Jim Walker of Slater Walker Securities, another bank that failed in 1975. While the fringe banking crisis had a beneficial effect by shaking out the weaker institutions in the banking system, it put a severe strain upon the Bank of England and the clearing banks, not to mention the Conservative government.

THE FINANCIAL MARKETS AFTER OPEC

While these events were occurring, the industrialised nations were still looking for a solution to the currency crisis. Within the IMF, a working group called the Committee of Twenty began assembling in 1973, seeking a viable framework for a new international monetary system. Since the general hard currency float had begun *de facto* in the spring of 1972, almost all finance officials believed that floating currencies were only a temporary state of affairs that would be doomed to oblivion as soon as a new framework could be worked out among the major industrialised nations with necessary input from the developing countries. But all attempts at constructing a new framework quickly would be overtaken by events.

In the United States, the entire apparatus of government became enmeshed in the Watergate affair and international economic and political problems took a distinct back seat to the widening scandal. Unfortunately, political events overshadowed the need for a coherent economic policy. Despite some significant foreign policy advances made by the Nixon administration, especially *rapprochement* with China, scandal continued to plague the White House, making international economic policy seem insignificant. In June 1972, what would become known as the Watergate affair began when five men were arrested for breaking into the offices of the Democratic National Committee in Washington, DC. In the spring of 1973, several key White House aids and advisers resigned as the scandal grew. In October 1973, Vice President Agnew resigned amid charges of tax evasion while he was Governor of Maryland. And at the same time that the OPEC export ban to the United States was announced, the US Attorney General, Elliot Richardson, resigned and the special prosecutor assigned to the Watergate affair, Archibald Cox, was fired by President Nixon.

In Britain, the aftermath of the miners' strike and the shortened working week seriously undermined the authority of the Heath government in dealing with crises and caused a deterioration of confidence in sterling. But during mid- and late 1973, the Committee of Twenty pushed on with its suggestions for reforming the exchange rate regime although as time passed it became more and more apparent that floating exchange rates would be the order of the day for the foreseeable future. Financial and economic concerns had given way to political crises and floating exchange rates became a *de facto* reality of economic life.

The oil price rise and the political problems in Britain and the United States gave the stock markets little cheer in 1973. And financial scandal crept into the picture as well, only adding to the markets' collective miseries. One of the better-known scandals took a full 3 per cent off the New York Stock Exchange's value on the day it was disclosed.

Beginning in the mid-1960s, a California-based insurance company called the Equity Funding Corporation began a phenomenal rise in price that resulted in its being traded as high as $90 per share with a fairly lofty price/earnings ratio as well. The company employed a British concept in selling life insurance that was little known in the US. Customers buying life insurance also purchased shares in equity mutual funds at the same time, the assumption being that the increase in the mutual fund's price in a rising market would help pay off the premiums due on the insurance policy. The novelty of the idea helped sell more and more policies. The company was considered a high flyer until a startling revelation was made by a financial journalist; a disgruntled employee had blown the whistle on the company's fraudulent practices.

During the later years of its relatively short history, the Equity Funding Corporation had been creating phony insurance policies, inflating its earnings records, selling the bogus policies to reinsurers and generally defrauding customers, its auditors and investment bankers alike. Most of its phenomenal earnings were obtained by cooking the books while the company was actually being looted slowly by its senior management. When the scandal eventually was disclosed, most insurance stocks fell dramatically in New York, dragging down the entire stock market. But the affair helped fuel a general trend that had more far-reaching effects in the financial markets.

47

The American press publicised the Equity Funding scandal well. Stories emerged of widows and orphans having invested their life savings in the stock only to see them become worthless as the courts wrapped up the company's affairs. Many well-known college and university endowment funds also lost money in addition to other institutional investors. Within the next two years, a clear trend away from investing by the individual (or retail) investor emerged. Individual shareholders declined from a peak of 30 million in 1970 to 25 million in 1975. The bear market that developed had taken its toll on the individual investor.[7]

But it was certainly more than scandal that curtailed the growth in stock prices as the price of oil began to rise in 1973. The stock markets, as society in general, were poised to enter a new period of volatility that would change the face of the industrialised world and cause severe problems for the developing countries, creating what was known at the time as the 'north–south' problem. Asset values and revenues were about to change in the wake of inflation and even the political leadership would have a difficult time persuading the growing doubters. When Richard Nixon remarked that market conditions after the OPEC price rises presented a good buying opportunity, he was probably correct, at least in the short term, but no one was listening.

Both the New York and London stock markets suffered between 1972 and 1973. In addition to the market indices falling, the number of new equity issues coming to market dropped substantially as did the number of new corporate bonds in the United States. As the picture of a new economic climate characterised by higher interest rates in addition to the new price of oil became more clear, companies began to adjust to capital investment in the new climate. The outlook was far from sanguine. The cost of both debt and equity capital had now risen substantially from the more halcyon days of the 1960s when a strong bull market had made new equity issues in particular quite popular.

Within a relatively short time, the idea of an equity capital 'shortage' began to make the rounds in the American market. As the stock market grew slowly, if at all, the major concern in market and corporate finance circles centred around potential future sources of capital funding. The new issues market witnessed a marked drop immediately after 1972 and planted the seeds for sluggish American and British capital investment for the next decade. In Britain, this marked the beginning of a decade of slow economic growth, while in the United States it helped fuel the debt explosion that would radically alter American companies' balance sheets for the foreseeable future.

The London Stock Exchange reacted poorly to the OPEC price rise. Also depressing stock prices was the continuing secondary banking crisis, which had only just begun in late 1973 when the Lifeboat was launched. Although the promise of the standby facility calmed fears of a market run or collapse it did little to assuage investors' fears over the knock-on effects in other parts of the economy. The Lifeboat operation would continue until 1975 with the bill rising for the rescue from month to month. The miners' strike added the political element by casting doubt upon the Heath government's crisis management abilities and fears resurfaced of Britain's long-standing problems of class struggle and general industrial decline.

The British and American experiences in the immediate aftermath of the OPEC price rise were similar but the reactions of policymakers and the private sector differed, in some cases substantially. The ability of the private and public sectors to react and respond to inflationary trends would determine how competitive Britain and the United States would be in the inflationary period and immediately after. The response from government was more immediate in Britain than in the United States. The Heath government, which had imposed wage and price controls in November 1972, allowed interest rates to rise but not to the sorts of levels that the market ordinarily would have dictated, partly in fear of putting home mortgage rates into double digits. The American response was more muted, because the Watergate affair was continuing to put pressure on the Nixon presidency.

But while the stock markets adjusted to the new environment, the bond markets began to develop new lifelines that would transform them from the sleepy backwaters they had been prior to 1970. Almost all of these developments occurred in the US domestic market and, at the time, to a lesser extent in the Eurobond market centred on London. Ironically, the major stimulus came not from the corporate sector but from social programmes passed during Lyndon Johnson's administration several years earlier. Quickly, noble ideas would be mixed with inflationary fears that would cast a cloud over one of the more clever developments in the financial markets.

In 1968, part of Johnson's Great Society programme was passed when the department of Housing and Urban Development was created as a cabinet department. Part of its original charge was to create 28 million new housing units in the country mainly to serve lower-income households. In order to finance the programme, the Government National Mortgage Association, or Ginnie Mae, was created to help provide a secondary market for government-sponsored mortgages.

During the same period, federal government borrowings increased due to the Vietnam War and a budget deficit. Treasury guarantees for new borrowings for the new housing programme would have been difficult since the new Ginnie Mae bonds that would have to be issued to support the financing would only have added to the growing amount of Treasury or Treasury-backed debt in the market. As a result, the new agency developed a technique that used the strength of a directly guaranteed federal agency with private collateral that was to become the standard for mortgage assistance agencies thereafter.

At a time when the stock markets were volatile and the bond markets under pressure, the new Ginnie Mae bonds became extremely popular. The better known of these obligations were referred to as 'pass-through certificates'. The proceeds of the bond borrowings were used to purchase mortgages from mortgage originators, which in turn became the collateral for the bonds. Each bond issue was supported by a pool of underlying mortgages and was known as a pass-through: each month, the interest and principal repayments (if any) by the mortgage holders were passed directly through to the bondholders. These became the only federally supported bonds that had ever been collateralised – a concept that would become quite common in the years following.

Conceptually, these types of bonds were known as mortgage-backed securities, or MBSs. More specifically they were the first examples of securitised mortgages. Essentially, this means that the underlying mortgages have been converted into securities, a concept that is broadly appealing but not entirely correct. The mortgages have been used as collateral for securities, meaning that they can be transferred, or sold, from the original owner (Ginnie Mae) to the bondholders. The agency then is said to be providing a market for mortgages by buying them up from the originators either to be used for pools or for other specified reasons.

Securitisation became something of an overnight sensation when it was first introduced, although it was actually nothing more than a form of long-term factoring of mortgage receivables. Because of the details, Ginnie Mae bonds paid interest monthly rather than semi-annually and that feature alone drew investors to the newly emerging market. But, more importantly, because of this factor the obligations would be considered off-balance sheet liabilities of the US government and not appear in the official indebtedness of the Treasury. The liability to pay interest and principal if necessary was not considered direct, only contingent.

This example of government assisted intervention in the marketplace for mortgages had been practised for over thirty years by the Federal National Mortgage Association (Fannie Mae). Ginnie Mae added more depth to the market by expanding the types of mortgages that were eligible for agency assistance and provided an example of how market developments can help what otherwise would be a stagnant sector of the economy. While interest rates were rising, mortgage money was still being made available in the United States due to the popularity of this new type of security among investors. The market for these new securities began to expand rapidly in the early 1970s.

On the back of Ginnie Mae's initial success, Congress established another agency to provide support for the mortgage market in 1971. The Federal Home Loan Mortgage Corporation, or Freddie Mac, was established to assist in purchasing mortgages from thrift institutions and also quickly established itself as a premier borrower in its own right. Unlike Ginnie Mae, Freddie Mac was never intended to remain a public sector institution and was quickly privatised although its broad functions were similar to those of Ginnie Mae and Fannie Mae.

In Britain, the opposite effect occurred in the bond markets. High inflation effectively made corporate bonds a rarity. The number of new issues, never particularly strong for an industrialised country, fell to almost nothing in 1973 and registered a negative number in 1974, meaning that redemptions exceeded new issues. Share financing also dropped dramatically in those two years before recovering in 1975. High gilt yields and fears of corporate bankruptcies effectively crowded many companies out of the market, a trend that was to last for the better part of the decade.

The housing market in Britain fell into a slump after the secondary banking crisis began and prices began to drop, in some cases precipitously. Mortgages in the UK were linked to bank rates, which the Heath government was desperately trying to hold down, but the floating nature of British rates had its effect on the housing market nevertheless. In the United States, the new mortgage-backed securities all bore fixed rates of interest for thirty years, reflecting the American penchant for fixed rate financings. Indirectly, Regulation Q was keeping a lid on rates and Ginnie Mae, along with Fannie Mae and Freddie Mac, was assisting the market. Without that combination, the housing market arguably would have fared much worse.

This convergence of market assistance and slavish adherence to interest rate ceilings in the US is the best example of the fundamental difference between American and British practice prior to the 1980s. British practice at the same time reflected less regulation but more concentration of oligopolistic power among the clearing banks in the form of the interest rate cartel, which made them sensitive to market rates, albeit slowly in some cases. While the two banking and market systems bore some similarities during the 1960s and 1970s, this functional difference separated them and caused different reactions to the same external pressures.

Agency intermediation between the markets and financial institutions is a function that never developed in Britain institutionally. In contrast, by the early 1970s, the United States had agencies devoted to mortgage assistance, student loans and farm loans and mortgages operating in the markets. In fact, the concept never became popular in Britain at all, although the UK would begin to amass contingent liabilities to the constituent members of the EC after it joined that body, as will be seen in Chapter 4.

The early and mid-1970s were the beginning of vast financial changes in the United States. But in Britain, change was much slower and that slowness began to hurt London's international reputation as a financial centre. The Eurobond market and the increased volume of foreign exchange trading helped maintain London's pre-eminent position as an entrepot market, recalling Lord Cromer's description, but the sterling sector of the financial markets began to fall behind.

The Americans reacted to the crisis of confidence in the markets by passing legislation to protect investors against shoddy brokerage practices. In 1971, Congress created the Securities Investor Protection Corporation (SIPC). This was an insurance programme designed to protect investors' holdings in their securities accounts with brokers. Any securities held by a brokerage firm on behalf of a client were insured, not against the market but against the broker. If the broker failed, as several did in the late 1960s bull market, the securities held were safe even if the broker misappropriated them. While the immediate effect of this legislation was not great because of the poor market in the wake of floating exchange rates, it did help restore confidence in the system once the equity indices regained some momentum several years later.

The market for mortgage-backed securities also continued to turn in a strong performance because of the securitised nature of the MBS. In 1971, Congress also chartered a similar organisation for supporting student loans, the Student Loan Marketing Association or Sallie Mae. The purpose of this organisation was to buy government-guaranteed student loans from banks and warehouse them until they were repaid. This helped banks with their liquidity as well as serving a social function by helping to provide relatively low-cost loans for students attending institutions of higher education. The student loan programme helped provide support for higher education at a time when the demand for tertiary education had risen substantially.[8]

SOCIAL EFFECTS OF FLOATING EXCHANGE RATES

During the 1970s, the collapse of Bretton Woods was considered just another economic event in a decade that eventually became full of momentous economic events. But it did not take long for the events of 1971–73 to make themselves felt on unemployment, productivity and the balance of payments in both the UK and US. As will be seen in the next chapter, the inflationary spiral also triggered a wave of optimism in Britain based upon oil discoveries in the North Sea. But that optimism was tempered somewhat by a decade of labour strife that carried with it all of the connotations of the class struggle revisited. Nevertheless, the effects of floating exchange rates and inflation clearly were felt very quickly.

Taken by themselves, the immediate effects of the events of 1971–73 were not necessarily negative. As inflation increased, so too did the performance of many economic factors, suggesting that floating exchange rates were having little immediate effect upon employment, investment and consumption. Because of the early, positive aspects of what was to become a new stage in the inflationary cycle, no one took much notice of the new exchange rate environment. That perhaps is why the breakdown of Bretton Woods only became a topic later in the 1970s and early 1980s, rather than in the immediate aftermath of August 1971.

In Britain, most economic indicators were favourable in 1972 and 1973 despite the large increase in the money supply. In that sense, the policies of the Heath government achieved their stated objectives. Average earnings increased, employment and wages and salaries also increased, as did disposable income and investment. The largest percentage increases were recorded in wages and import prices, especially for imported fuels. This latter price increase was particularly significant because it would lead the coal miners to demand higher wages in 1973, bringing the National Union of Miners into direct conflict with the Heath government, which clearly stated that the country could not afford the sort of increases being demanded.

Economically, the miners' position was not without foundation. In the latter part of 1972, continuing into 1973, retail sales increased, capital expenditure by manufacturing also rose, overtime increased and unemployment continued the downward trend established a year earlier. The boom triggered by the monetary expansion continued and Britain's continued reliance upon coal put the miners in the position in which unionised car workers often found themselves in the United States: being in the forefront of wage demands that would severely test government's determination to keep wages and prices from spiralling upward.

Interest rates became the most volatile indicator of all in Britain during this time. The Bank of England's minimum lending rate (MLR) rose from 6 per cent to 8 per cent by 1973 and continued upward to almost 14 per cent by the end of the year. Gilt yields also rose across the board, in the medium and long terms as well as the shorter dates. This was the culmination of all economic indicators that was clearly visible and showed that reaction to economic conditions in general would become a point of contention between organised labour and government. In a sense, a new era was being introduced slowly; interest rates had become more central to social affairs than they had in the past.

Because of the structure of British banking, the impact of changing interest rates was more quickly felt by the populace than it was in the United States. Neither country offered any financial alternatives to traditional banking institutions for individual savers and, as a result, whichever system posted changes in rates at banks was effectively notifying the public that either monetary conditions or policy had changed. In this respect, the UK was slightly ahead of the United States by raising mortgage rates and deposit rates, although it was the US that first developed the money market funds shortly thereafter.

The American experience in the aftermath of Bretton Woods was very similar to the British. Compensation and personal income rose, consumer expenditure increased, unemployment fell slightly, motor car sales increased, car imports decreased and personal savings declined. The inflationary trend also increased as the consumer price index (CPI) increased to 8.5 per cent in 1973 and wholesale prices rose by 10 per cent. And, as in the UK, short-term interest rates also increased – in fact doubled – from 3 to 6 per cent. But unlike the UK, long-term bond yields remained relatively stable at around 7.5 per cent. Long-term yields can be found in Figure 2.1.

Stable long-term interest rates did not prevent new housing starts from dropping in late 1972, lasting for almost a year. But the property boom/bust cycle that plagued Britain and the fringe banks never materialised because of the relative steadiness of long-term interest rates. Americans had not yet felt the nervousness that they would feel later in the decade and in the 1980s, as short-term interest rates rose to historically high levels. As a result, bond yields remained steady at the same time that British long-term gilt rates rose along with the short-term. British investors had already discovered that, when short rates rise, the long cannot be far behind.

In 1972, a drastic change in the way Americans viewed the future came about as social security payments to the retired became indexed to the inflation rate. In the thirty-seven years since social security had been instituted

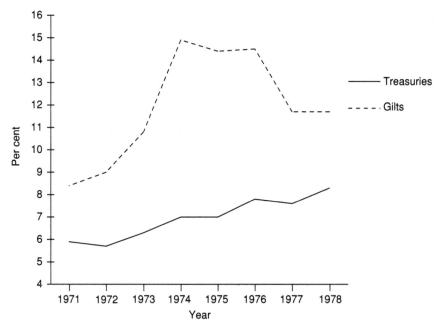

Figure 2.1 Long-term yields, US and UK

Source: Federal Reserve *Bulletin*, various issues and Central Statistical Office, *Financial Statistics*, various issues

during the Depression, indexing had never been attempted. Benefits paid to recipients were automatically indexed to the inflation rate, as were increases in the wage base for contributors. However, within five years it became apparent that the programme had several flaws as benefits exceeded contributions, putting the system under intense pressure. Further changes made in 1977 and 1980 finally helped correct the oversight so that the wage base (for contributors) was increased to keep abreast of payments.

This event was perhaps the best single acknowledgement that inflation had become entrenched and that if it was not recognised it would literally impoverish many who depended upon social security payments as their sole source of retirement income. It also helped unleash a flurry of activity among pension fund managers and those who would help develop new financial products, as will be seen in the next chapter. Within a relatively short period of time, it would also help establish defeating inflation as a political goal worthy of national attention.

The relative weakness of the dollar and the increasing import bill for oil set in motion a trade-related trend that would have a profound impact upon the American psyche. While the United States was quicker than Britain in abandoning coal as a primary fuel, its reliance upon oil was only increased by the inefficient, large American motor cars that dominated the highways. After the OPEC price rise had increased the cost of petrol, consumers began to seek smaller, more efficient cars. Since American manufacturers did not produce cars that fitted consumers' needs, imports began to gain more of a foothold in the American market.

Although not clear at the time, this paved the way for the Japanese invasion of the American car market. The traditional European-made small cars were losing ground in the United States and the void was quickly filled by Japan. But all of these cars were imported; none was yet produced in the US itself. In 1972, Japanese direct investment in the US was negligible, amounting to less than $1 billion. The relative (and continuing) weakness of the dollar against the yen would now provide a window of opportunity for Japanese firms that wanted to penetrate the American marketplace. Imports from Japan would be relatively cheap if Japanese firms were able to maintain prices in the wake of a declining dollar. But, more importantly, Japanese companies now would be able to purchase American assets relatively cheaply, enabling many to establish American manufacturing operations by the end of the decade.

By the end of the 1970s, Japanese direct investment in the United States would increase almost tenfold. High interest rates would cause many American firms to curtail capital investment and, as a result, many American manufactured products became outdated and acquired a reputation for shoddiness or unreliability. The scores of Japanese companies that set up shop in the US funded themselves with capital imported from Japan, where interest rates were low in real terms compared with those in the US. When combined with what was billed as the Japanese penchant for quality, many of those goods quickly gained a significant share of the American market, especially for electronic goods and (later) motor cars.

The effect upon Americans' perceptions of their own abilities to manufacture and maintain their reputation as the world's strongest economy was profound. For almost a fifteen-year period, from about 1975 to 1990, almost every American newspaper and magazine, not to mention the broadcast media, ran articles on the decline of American productivity and manufacturing. Many of the complaints about American competitiveness and corporate strength proved well founded. During the 1970s, the balance sheet of the American non-financial corporation became more heavily skewed in favour of debt. Liquidity declined on average and much capital expansion was financed through internally generated funds (retained earnings). Capital expansion could only be financed in that manner for so long because shareholders would naturally expect their stocks to rise in the marketplace. If they did not, then new equity financing would become less likely and many companies would be left with only debt financing, at higher and higher rates of interest. But perhaps the most disturbing part of this trend was the xenophobia that was developing against foreign investment.

Ever since it became apparent that the Arab members of OPEC now had vast resources at their command, the natural question of exactly where that money was being spent became an important issue to those who viewed that potential investment as a threat to American interests. This was part of the split personality that had developed in the United States concerning foreign direct investment. For most of the twentieth century, the majority of foreign investment in the US had been portfolio investment. Direct investment was substantial but was held by foreigners in countries not considered inimical to US interests, the main foreign direct investor in the US always had been, and still is, Britain. As mentioned previously, many of the brand names to which Americans had grown accustomed were in fact British-owned. Superficially, given the common language, no one ever suspected that these companies and their products were foreign.

The same could not be said of the *nouveaux riches* OPEC members however. Having only one product to sell on an export basis and possessing so much liquidity as a result, the suspicion became that many American companies were being bought up secretly by OPEC members. As a result, Congress passed legislation in 1974 and 1976 aimed at discovering whether vital American industries were falling into foreign hands. Both the Foreign Investment Study Act and the International Investment Survey Act required the Department of Commerce to study foreign investment in the US with more care than at some times in the past, but the motives were clearly political nevertheless.[9]

Later in the decade it would be discovered that fears of large OPEC investment were unfounded. The oil-rich sheikhdoms and Saudi Arabia preferred the deposit facilities of the major banks in the Euromarket and more liquid portfolio investments to direct ownership of American companies. But the tone was clearly set for a decade of American insecurity concerning the value of the dollar and the economic role of the United States in world affairs. Currency instability and inflation had caused Americans to look inward after almost two decades of internationalism and the perception was one of economic decline and inefficiency. Gone was the time when the American corporation had its way with the rest of the world. The Germans and the Japanese were on the rise although the increase in Japanese investment in the US was the most carefully watched.

Most annoying was the speed with which Japanese manufactured goods had improved in quality while American goods seemed to be on the decline. In the 1950s and 1960s, American–Japanese trade tensions centred mostly on Japanese exports of cheap cotton items that threatened the domestic American garment industry. However, the quality of those items was clearly poor and their main advantage was their low cost. Fifteen years later, trade tensions were springing up over electronic goods and cars that did not have a shoddy image and that had clearly come to threaten Detroit car makers especially.

Britain experienced much the same in the years immediately following 1971–72. Foreign investment in the UK private sector doubled between 1971 and the sterling crisis of 1976 as the pound gradually declined. Britain's entry into the EC made direct investments in the UK attractive to American firms anticipating a widening market for their goods and services using Britain as a base. Sterling's problems made this expansion possible. Cheaper British assets made direct investment in the UK more attractive to foreign companies although the numbers do not suggest that direct investment was considered highly attractive across the board. More proportionate investment was drawn to the United States rather than Britain, although the cheap pound did produce some positive benefits. At the same time, as would be expected, British foreign direct investments fell by sometimes sizeable amounts on a year-to-year basis. Although the British were, and remained, substantial direct foreign investors, each year after Bretton Woods collapsed witnessed liquidations of UK assets overseas. Whatever the destination of those repatriated funds, the declining pound had a somewhat beneficial effect. Despite complaints about low domestic British productivity and rebellious labour, the weak currency nevertheless compensated to an extent.

During the same period, the UK remained the largest direct foreign investor in the US by a sizeable margin. This was accomplished by keeping many of those foreign earnings in the United States rather than repatriating them, allowing equity on the US subsidiary companies' balance sheets to increase. As a result, the UK investment in the US remained sizeable, fuelled in no small part by the reluctance of many British firms to repatriate their American earnings into what was proving to be a declining pound.

Despite the problems caused by the collapse of Bretton Woods, both Britain and the United States found some solace in an increase in foreign investment. In fact, the increase in foreign investment illustrates how even direct foreign investment flows can be prompted relatively quickly by changes in the exchange rate when they might otherwise be expected to occur more slowly. However, as in the United States, the increase in foreign investment was not always viewed positively but, rather, in many cases as a form of foreign invasion against the British consumer and British industry as a whole. But when taken in context of the 1970s overall, the phenomenon was only one of a mass of changes occurring or about to occur.

3

RESPONDING TO INFLATION

By the mid-1970s, it had become apparent that exchange rates were permanently floating and that a return to the more orderly days of Bretton Woods was not on the horizon. The OPEC price rise had set loose a round of inflation that would increase in the next several years, only adding to the miseries already being experienced in the markets. Clearly, a corner had been turned in contemporary history. The only question now was how and when the markets and policymakers would react.

The years between the end of the Second World War and August 1971 appeared halcyon when compared with what was yet to come. In those twenty-five years, the United States had enjoyed an unparalleled trade advantage and become a major exporter of long-term capital to the rest of the world. The dollar had enjoyed remarkable stability and the United States had enjoyed an advantage in direct investments abroad against foreign direct investments in the US of about six to one. Yet within three years of the collapse of Bretton Woods, the dollar would decline about 10 per cent on a trade weighted basis while the yen would appreciate by almost 30 per cent. In a sense, the original Bretton Woods agreement had helped create a *pax americana* that had been shattered.

America's travail with the dollar paralleled Britain's troubles with the pound about ten years earlier. In the years following the Suez crisis, sterling underwent a series of devaluations in the mid- and late 1960s that seriously undermined Britain's international status and finally rent asunder any notion that Britain was still a first rank international economic power. The decline of the pound mirrored the loss of empire that began with the independence ceremonies of the former colonies in the early 1960s. The decline of the dollar also coincided with the loss of American *imperium* but in this case it was economic rather than political.

Reactions to the currency and interest rate turmoil varied. After American wage and price controls were lifted, the financial markets all weakened and the immediate reaction in the markets themselves was to fix what was wrong. As the political environment began to deteriorate because of the Watergate affair, official intervention in what appeared from the outside to be esoteric matters such as the dollar's value became more and more remote. So the markets themselves intervened. As a result of the turmoil in the markets following August 1971, innovations designed to combat the effects of inflation in the financial markets and declining investor interest began to appear after years of development. Most were American in origin. The American markets became a laboratory for new financial concepts. Many were developed and practised mainly at home while others developed offshore in the Euromarket and were imported only after the regulatory climate became more conducive.

At first glance, the financial markets in Britain appeared to be playing catch-up with the Americans. Beginning in the early 1970s, the Americans developed the traded options market and began trading new types of futures contracts based upon financial instruments rather than more traditional agricultural and industrial commodities. Within a decade, these new markets would develop into sophisticated financial markets challenging the more traditional capital markets for investors' attentions. Britain would also attempt to develop similar markets but with considerably less success. The reasons for the differences again can be traced back to the structural differences that plagued each country's institutions at different times. American markets, less clubby and less restrictive than their British counterparts, would be in the forefront of financial innovation and develop new products in what would become known as the new derivative markets. Conversely, British banking institutions, less regulated than the Americans, would provide more stability to the economic infrastructure when the banking crises began in the early 1980s. Each would begin to learn from the other slowly.

The thrust for new financial products in the United States was based upon competition to some extent. As seen in the last chapter, bonds began to make great inroads at the expense of stocks in both the primary and secondary markets. The great inflation of the late 1970s and early 1980s was not yet in evidence so fixed income instruments still appealed to investors' desire for safety of principal as opposed to traditionally volatile stock prices. If any sector of the marketplace would have to develop instruments designed to enhance trading or help protect against loss it was the stock sector, not the bond markets.

Equally, the currency markets lacked depth to some extent. The spot and forward markets had not had any competition in the twentieth century and continued to serve mostly large or multinational corporations and banks that were accustomed to their peculiarities. Small companies that did not require relatively large amounts of foreign exchange were excluded from the market and were necessarily exposed to additional currency risks if they ventured into the international trading arena. When Bretton Woods collapsed and the general currency float began, all types of business organisations would feel the aftershocks, not only multinationals. The financial markets were feeling the effects through both inflation and increased price volatility. Whatever organisation or market that recognised the problems and sought to provide some effective means of mitigating risks would undoubtedly begin to reap the benefits in the near future.

Early in the development of many of the first generation derivatives – options on shares and basic financial futures – loud cries were heard decrying them as speculative instruments being introduced at a time when financial conservatism was more appropriate. Options on shares had been available for years through various over-the-counter market makers but had never proven themselves to be more than an esoteric speculative tool. Although any new financial instrument could be designed on paper, it would take some convincing arguments to make them viable hedging tools. That battle was won relatively quickly in the United States but took considerably longer in Britain. As will be seen below, the UK markets would soon have oil to buoy their spirits; this was not the case in the United States.

PLANNING FOR FUTURE INFLATION

One of the financial lessons of previous decades not lost on anyone in the early 1970s was that inflexibility would lead to strains in the financial system and even its ultimate demise unless new methods were devised to cope with rapid change. Rigid adherence to the gold standard during the 1920s contributed to the market crash and the Depression and eventually to the Second World War. Even before the Bretton Woods system began to deteriorate, it was recognised that new financial volatility was just around the corner. Economic advancement was subject to the marketplace and any factors that frightened investors, causing diminishment of capital investment, had to be anticipated well before they caused a decline in economic standards.

Housing in the United States was but one example. No sooner than Ginnie Mae and Freddie Mac had entered the mortgage market, interest rates began to rise, threatening the purposes for which Ginnie Mae, especially, was founded. Long-term mortgage rates had become a commodity – as important as plywood or building materials in the expansion of housing. While certainly not a new idea, the days of relatively cheap, low real-rate mortgages was gone. In order to keep the market vibrant, methods would need to be devised to stabilise the rates or at least protect lenders of fixed-rate mortgages from loss.

The same could be said for small businesses. While the 1960s were best known in the United States as the decade of the conglomerate, small businesses were increasing the portion of business they did overseas but without much protection against volatile exchange rates. As devaluations increased with greater frequency, the risks of exporting increased. Traditional hedging methods in the forward market were not immediately applicable to many small businesses because they did not need, or could not afford, the amounts of money required for forward hedging purposes. As a result, they either took the risks to do business or shied away from the export market entirely.

While representing two different ends of the spectrum, both sides had a strong case for protection against the effects of interest rates and exchange rate movements. As a result, the first significant product development in decades in the financial markets began to develop rapidly. Ironically, the development did not come in New York, the home of the capital markets, but in Chicago, the home of futures trading.

The Chicago futures markets introduced the first futures contracts on both interest rates and foreign currencies. Currency futures appeared almost simultaneously with the demise of the Bretton Woods system, appearing first on the International Monetary Market (IMM) in 1971. These contracts were the first attempt to treat financial instruments as commodities and offer contracts on them. Until that time, only gold had a futures contract representing it but it was hardly a fully fledged financial instrument. But this new development changed the conceptual basis of futures contracts. Now contracts existed on commodities that were not agricultural, metallic or industrial. In fact, this new trading expanded the conceptual nature of the term 'commodity' itself. Clearly, no one could argue that long-term interest rates were as important to the housing market as was plywood or some other essential building material. The same was true of currency futures and the role of small business in the US balance of payments. Trading in currency futures began modestly but the timing was certainly right.

Small businesses were the prime targets for these new contracts, which allowed small traders to buy or sell forward for delivery at standard delivery dates. The contract amounts were relatively small, representing about $50,000 or the equivalents. Contracts in the forward market, on the other hand, were usually for dollar amounts (or equivalents) of about $1 million and the delivery dates varied from contract to contract. In theory, small businesses and traders now had access to the same information and potential trading possibilities that banks and multinationals had for years.

Currency futures contracts were bothered by myriad technical problems that hindered their development. Essentially, traditional commodities futures traders were now being asked to step up and trade currencies, something in which most had little experience. Rather than trade on fundamentals such as weather or the demand for agricultural commodities, the traders now needed to possess some knowledge of interest rates and the other factors that affected currency rates. It would take several years before the market grew enough in stature to attract all but the hardiest of outside traders and investors.[1]

The second major development of the decade in the futures markets was the introduction of interest rate futures on long- and short-term Treasury bills and bonds. This was perhaps even more radical than futures on currencies because the underlying instruments were themselves financial instruments, not tangible products or currencies.

Interest rate futures were introduced by the Chicago Board of Trade (CBOT) in 1975 on thirty-year Ginnie Mae mortgage securities. Originally designed and marketed as hedging instruments, the new futures were intended to be used by institutions that had originated new mortgages in unstable interest-rate environments. The future was designed to follow the price of the actual Ginnie Mae securities upon which it was based so an institution holding mortgages or actual mortgage securities could sell the futures against them for short periods of time to ensure price protection.

In theory, when the new mortgage-backed securities were considered as having new, parallel instruments that could be used to hedge them the mortgage market should have received a considerable advantage, especially at a time when interest rates were unstable. However, over the next decade, the Ginnie Mae future never developed as a particularly popular futures contract for technical reasons and was superseded by the futures contract introduced on the long-term Treasury bond instead.[2] The actual securities themselves continued to prove popular and held investor interest, although long-term interest rates would have to find another effective hedging vehicle.

A contract on the long-term Treasury bond did not appear until 1977. When it was introduced, it was based upon the twenty-year bond. The thirty-year maturity bond was not introduced until later in that year. When the long bond future did make its debut, it was apparent that the contract would not be used for hedging actual bond holdings, although that certainly was possible, but for hedging *exposure* to long-term interest rates. Rather than actually own Treasury bonds, investors could either buy or sell long bond contracts with an eye toward interest rates. Those with actual exposure to rates, of whatever sort, were considered hedgers. Those simply seeking a gain on short-term movements in rates were considered speculators.

Hedging exposure to long-term interest rates was not novel but previously was confined to professional bond traders. Many fixed-income institutional investors were still passive managers of their funds rather than active; they most often bought a bond and held it to maturity rather than actively trade it in the marketplace if interest rates rose or fell. Bond futures remained something of a novelty until about 1979 when long-term interest rates began a long, inexorable rise. The thirty-year Treasury bond had been introduced in 1977 and the additional years on the long bond's maturity added to its volatility, especially if a secular change in interest rates came about. In the interim, between 1972 and 1979, short-term interest rate futures were more popular.

Futures on short-term Treasury bills (T-bill futures) were introduced on the IMM in 1971. The inflation of the early 1970s had more of an impact on short-term rates than the long-term and the T-bill future was the first to be introduced. Vacillating money market rates had helped to underscore the need for protecting banks and others from unexpected changes in short-term rates. As a result, the T-bill future became the most popular in the nascent marketplace and was followed by futures on bank CDs and commercial paper.[3]

Futures initially were used only by professionals who understood the intricacies of the money market. The saving public, on the other hand, were still subject to relatively low rates of interest paid by their banks because of Regulation Q of the Federal Reserve. Because of the laggard nature of Regulation Q, it had been assumed for years that the average saver was indifferent to short-term market interest rate levels because he or she could not obtain them in any case. If and when that assumption could be proved wrong, the entire face of the banking and capital markets would change. The revolution was not long in coming.

In the early 1970s, several investment companies began offering a new type of mutual fund (or unit trust) called the money market mutual fund, or MMMF. Using the well-established concept of mutual funds, these new investment vehicles purchased money market instruments rather than common stocks. The shares they subsequently sold to the investor bore a rate of return almost equal to the money market rates upon which they were based. At the time, even the basic rates offered by Treasury bill funds were attractive since bill rates were usually higher than Regulation Q ceilings offered at banks and thrifts. While the funds grew in popularity enormously in the mid- and later 1970s, the initial reception was moderate. While attractive, they still offered less security to the saver/investor than bank deposits.

Bank deposits for the most part were guaranteed by federal deposit insurance for amounts up to $40,000. Unlike Britain (several years later) and other continental European countries, the total amount of the deposit was covered if it did not exceed the maximum amount. This protection had been in place since the Depression and had provided great security to savers even if the Regulation Q ceilings were a bit unrealistic at times. When the new funds came along, vying for savers' funds, the one feature of bank deposits that they could not compete with was the security of insurance. The mutual funds were not offered by banking institutions and as a result did not qualify for deposit insurance.

At the same time, they offered another element of risk. Investors and savers experienced a counterparty risk with the investment company itself because they bought shares in the fund which in turn distributed returns to investors by paying dividends. The fund was only as good as its management. Given that the 1960s had seen a good deal of widespread mutual fund fraud in Europe and the United States that was well publicised, investors were naturally wary of new funds, even as simply constructed as the MMMFs.

Rising interest rates became the best marketing tool that the new funds could have hoped for within several years of their introduction. Investors began to subscribe heavily to them as rates rose. For the first time since the 1920s, savers had demonstrated that they were not passive to changes in interest rates and would eschew some of the safety of deposit insurance if they could find a relatively safe, and higher, rate of return elsewhere. But even the funds themselves were shocked by their growing popularity. Between 1972 and 1980, they had attracted almost $200 billion of cash, equivalent to the deposits of the two largest American banks at the time. While savers could afford to smile, this massive shift in savings caused severe strains in the banking system that would require remedial action by Congress and the regulatory authorities.

The 1970s proved to be a decade of financial change, both functionally and structurally. Rising interest rates had caused more than just new products to be developed; they also created institutional change that would use these new products for new purposes. The American banks, heavily regulated and protected at the same time, were quickly becoming something of a relic as the new MMMFs would soon prove. Inexorably, the marketplace was placing strains on the banking system that would in the end make it look more British: accustomed to dealing with changing interest rates it would adjust its products and loans accordingly.

Inflation became an acknowledged fact when social security payments were officially indexed to prices, beginning in 1972. That link contributed to the individual's quest for higher interest rates. At the same time, stories of the inadequacy of the social security system to handle future claims became widespread. For the first time in more than a generation, the future became clouded due to the inflation nemesis. While most individuals were probably not willing, or competent, to speculate with their savings or retirement funds they apparently were more than willing to take an additional, but small, risk to pursue higher interest rates in the money funds.

The legal complement to the growth of money funds came in 1974 when Congress passed the Employees Retirement Income Security Act, or ERISA. This was the first major piece of legislation passed in the twentieth century aimed at curbing abuses in the pension fund industry. Prompted by abuses in certain industries' pension fund management, the ERISA nevertheless sparked a boom in MMMFs when it created the personal pension plan – a private plan that could be created by an individual planning for his or her retirement.[4]

The private individual retirement accounts, or IRAs, could be created by individuals putting aside funds each year to be liquidated at retirement. Any taxable gains in the accounts would be deferred until liquidated, presumably when the individual would be in a lower tax bracket. Because of the bad press received by the social security system and the general worry about purchasing power created by rising inflation, IRAs quickly became established at brokers and later at banks. Given that individuals were seeking ways to keep abreast of inflation it did not take long for the MMMF, with its floating rate returns, to find quick acceptance as the prime vehicle in which to invest an IRA.

This combination of new product development, an unrealistic regulatory environment and legislation helped change the face of American investing and financial intermediation. No longer were individual savers considered to be passive customers of banks. The growth in money funds alone proved that the individual was interest-rate sensitive and more than willing to invest in new financial products. But what was not foreseen was the effect that all of these rapidly moving developments would have on the banking system and the thrifts, both still protected by Depression era legislation at a time when inflation was beginning to increase rather than abate.

OPTIONS ON THE FUTURE

The other major initiative in financial product development in the 1970s was the introduction of exchange traded options on shares. As with interest rate futures, the concept certainly was not new but the idea of establishing an exchange on which to trade these new options was novel. The first of what was to become many options exchanges officially opened at the Chicago Board Options Exchange (CBOE) in the spring of 1973.

The development of exchange listed options was the market's way of responding to declining investor interest in common stocks in general. As in the case of futures, it would have appeared more natural for this market to develop in New York rather than Chicago, but options had a spotty history in the home of the equities markets and the home of the established futures markets was a better place for them to develop without the hint of interference from the stock exchanges.[5] Similar to financial futures, options were originally billed as hedging instruments designed to help share investors protect against unforeseen price movements.

Of the two types of standard options – calls and puts – calls were introduced first. As options to buy stock at a specified price for a specific time period, calls allowed buyers to take an option on potentially rising prices. But that alone was hardly a standard hedging technique. Unlike futures, which allowed investors to go 'short' by selling a contract and potentially benefiting from a price fall, selling calls did not achieve the same result. Although billed as hedging products, the early history did not quite fulfil the marketing claims. The real hedging instrument, the put option (an option to sell a specified number of shares at a price for a specific time) developed much more slowly because of fears of stock manipulation and investor misunderstandings.

Puts, as options to sell, appreciate when the price of the stock they represent falls in price. The buyer of a put option will profit if the under-lying stock falls in price, whereas the buyer of a call would profit by a rise. Put buying is therefore tantamount to selling a stock short but with less risk and expense for the short seller. Originally, puts developed slowly, being introduced slowly by the CBOE with permission from the Securities & Exchange Commission (which has authority over options markets). Investors coming to options for the first time found the put concept con-fusing; professional traders knew of puts' intrinsic strengths but unfortu-nately they had a long history of being used to manipulate the price of stocks in the past.[6]

Although the hedging concept and actual product development were not necessarily well timed, options got off to a very fast start in the market-place. Debate began almost immediately concerning their overall impact on the capital markets. One of the original issues centred around options' ability to divert money that otherwise might have been intended for the new issues market for smaller capitalised companies in need of new or addi-tional capital. Equally, concerns were raised that calls might divert cash that would have been invested in actual shares of more mature companies. Speculators might choose the easy way out by putting up only a fractional value of the shares' value in options, thereby depriving the secondary stock markets of needed liquidity at a time when the market indices did not show any sound underlying strengths.

While concerns continued to be voiced, the options markets grew in volume and the number of options listed on exchange traded stocks also grew. The new market experienced success based upon the same principle that had benefited the futures markets for years – price volatility. As the stock markets continued to experience volatility, the options market also experienced the same volatility. Speculators enjoyed the rapid price move-ments in many options, and wide price movements only helped underscore the need for hedging, despite the limitations.

Because of conditions in the financial markets, the options markets became successful very quickly and experienced prosperity at a time when the capital markets were suffering. Arguments that the derivatives markets were little more than organised gambling facilities continued to be heard but did not deter the markets expanding year after year. Calls were con-tinually added to the outstanding list along with puts. While not helping the capital markets directly, options helped prove that business expansion was possible when economic conditions were less than ideal. Unfortunately, the same could not be said for Britain's experiment with listed options.

As in the United States, options had been used in Britain for years on an over-the-counter basis. In 1977, listed options were introduced on the London Options Exchange that were similar to American-style options for the most part.[7] The original listings were somewhat meagre given the number of stocks listed on the London Stock Exchange. For the first several years of its life, the exchange experienced moderate interest but nothing on the scale of options' success in the United States. The reasons for the lack of interest were twofold: the account period used by the London Stock Exchange played a major role and the Inland Revenue board added a fairly bizarre twist with its interpretation of options gains and losses.

The account period used by the London Stock Exchange allowed investors to pay for purchases of shares at the end of the period, sometimes a period of as long as three weeks. In effect, a speculator (or punter in market parlance) could anticipate a price rise and bet on a stock's appreciation by deferring payment although for only a short period of time. This form of delayed payment was well entrenched among speculators and listed options, although different sorts of investment vehicles, would have to compete with this sort of practice if they were to make any inroads in the marketplace.

The Inland Revenue's interpretation made it doubly difficult for options to gain a foothold in the marketplace. Treating options as diminishing assets, the tax authority required investors to calculate a true value based upon amortisation rather than simply calculate gains and losses based upon the original price at which a deal was struck. The calculation effectively made it difficult for an investor to realise a gain in a simple manner. When combined with the practices used during account periods, it made it doubly difficult for options to succeed and for the next decade options remained in the background, never achieving the success they enjoyed in the United States.

Equally, interest-rate futures got off to a slow start in Britain and did not become popular until the mid- to late 1980s. Again, traditional market practices militated against bill and bond futures in the early years. The practice of trading gilts on a partly paid basis gave investors a tool with which to speculate, especially if interest rates fell within the partly paid account period. A newly issued gilt's price could rise if rates fell and the investor who had only invested a fraction of the original issue price could stand to gain by the final payment date, set a month or two from the original issue date. That sort of practice, as the account period for trading common stocks, made it difficult for gilt futures to achieve a reasonable level of success until the market matured and trading volume increased in the latter 1980s.

In the 1970s, comparisons between the London and New York markets helped to underline the shortcomings of the UK market in favour of New York. When the specialist system, employed on the US stock exchanges, was compared to the single capacity system used by jobbers on the floor of the London exchange, the differences between the two market systems became even more pronounced. Within ten years, the comparisons would uncover less differences as London changed many of its procedures and became more advanced than New York in many respects. But the 1970s quickly proved that many existing market practices were becoming dated as the trend toward institutional intermediation by mutual funds and pension funds on behalf of the individual investor picked up speed. The exchanges still adhered to practices that were developed in a previous generation, when individuals accounted for much more direct stock market activity than they did after the collapse of Bretton Woods.

'MAY DAY' 1975

Major reform came to the US stock exchanges when the Securities Acts Amendments of 1975 were passed by Congress. The oligopolistic power exercised by stock exchange member firms over the commissions charged to customers had become a major bone of contention in the early 1970s, as institutional trading became more prevalent. The large institutional investors began arguing for economies in the commissions paid to their brokers, claiming that the fixed commission structure being charged was too high. That complaint, plus the increasing use of computers in reporting prices executed on the exchanges, made reform necessary if Wall Street was to maintain its legislatively granted power over securities dealings.

The immediate threat to Wall Street's hegemony came when many large institutions threatened to buy their own seats on the stock exchanges so that they would not have to pay high brokers' commissions. In effect, the investors were claiming that they would add to the competition and reduce transactions costs, something that was in their own investors' favour. Congress reacted by passing the bill, which abolished the fixed commission rate charged by brokers and also prohibited the institutions from buying their own seats.

The abolition of fixed commissions came on 1 May, 1975. Wall Street applauded the idea as its own, showing that it was ready to compete in the new national marketplace envisaged by the legislation. The new structure revolutionised the way many brokers did business thereafter. Some began to offer extensive research services to their clients in return for commission business ('soft' dollar commissions) while others began to specialise in a narrow range of products that did not rely upon such intense price competition.

One of the major products of May Day was the rise of the discount broker, a broker offering 'bare-bones' brokerage services for its (mainly) retail clients. These firms were able to lure clients away from the larger 'wire house' brokers by not factoring research or other ancillary services into their commission charges. As a result, these brokers captured a relatively large number of traditional wire house clients, forcing the larger firms to keep their commissions low or offer enhanced services to justify charging the client more.

The same competitiveness did not extend to Britain, however. It would be another eleven years before the London Stock Exchange took similar measures to ensure its own viability in the face of international competition. During the 1970s, the financial markets in Britain remained remarkably free of reform, although the Wilson Committee would examine banking and financial markets later in the decade. Part of London's lassitude could be attributed to persisting exchange controls which distinguished between sterling and non-sterling investment areas as well as the investment premium required to be paid by some investors. Again, foreign exchange related problems had a direct bearing upon the financial markets and individual companies' ability to raise external capital.

Yet it is noteworthy that while the American markets developed and tested new concepts and products, the British were only begrudgingly willing to play catch-up. Part of the reason was due in no small part to the discovery and rapid development of the North Sea oil fields. While the United States needed to import a good deal of its oil and was suffering a short-lived embargo of sorts from the Arab OPEC members, Britain was faced with the pleasant prospect of being theoretically self-sufficient in petrol for the next twenty-five to thirty years. The North Sea was to provide a windfall that would temporarily change the face of British life, at least in the short term. With the excitement created by oil discoveries, reform receded to the background in London and would only surface again when international pressures began to force the London Stock Exchange to reconsider its methods of doing business.

PROBLEMS DESPITE NORTH SEA OIL

Shortly after the Phillips Petroleum Company discovered significant oil reserves in the Norwegian section of the North Sea in 1969, the economic cloud that had hung over Britain since the Second World War seemed to have temporarily lifted. British Petroleum discovered oil on the British side in 1970 in the Forties field. Other than the prospect of self-sufficiency, the discovery potentially meant that a declining industrial and manufacturing economy would again have something to export other than its traditional mainstays, financial services. But Britain's newfound liquid asset did little to prevent the sterling crisis that was developing in the mid-1970s nor did it do much to instill confidence in Britain's economy or its financial markets. More than a decade of self-doubt and theorising about the 'British disease' would provide a damper to the markets despite the prospects raised by petrol.

In the mid-1970s, when oil production was just beginning, the outlook for Britain was fairly sanguine. The Organisation for Economic Cooperation and Development (OECD) estimated a positive impact upon Britain's balance of payments in the medium-term and self-sufficiency in oil by

70

1980. In fact, production was projected to increase astronomically, from only about 5 million tons in 1975 to over 110 million tons by 1980.[8] The major reason for the optimism was that most production was estimated for use within the UK rather than being exported. Thus, the balance of payments would benefit not by export sales but by diminished imports.

But the lack of fresh capital investment in industry and inflation continued. By 1975, inflation was well into double figures and interest rates remained high as the post-Bretton Woods recession began to take its toll. The pound weakened despite high interest rates and labour problems normally culminated in higher wage settlements. The Conservative government was replaced by the Labour government of Harold Wilson in March 1974. Although the pound was little affected, within the next two years it would drop below $2.00 for the first time. Despite its good fortune, Britain seemed destined to suffer the consequences of a diminishing industrial base and declining international competitiveness.

On the surface, the decline of the pound seemed all the more unlikely since many international investors were seeking alternatives to the dollar. But unlike the dollar, which was free of capital controls and always effectively had been despite the presence of the IET between 1962 and 1974, the pound increasingly became a tool of Labour in dealing with industrial production and employment. Britain's problem remained somewhat unique: the service industries for which it was well known contributed relatively little to general employment. Those industries most likely to contribute were rapidly declining. When the manufacturing sector especially was able to increase productivity it was only at the cost of leaving more workers redundant. North Sea oil was not able to fill the gap by providing new jobs nationwide, although workers in Scotland did benefit. In order to make exports grow, government seemed faced with little choice except to allow the pound to depreciate.

This was part of the analysis of Bacon and Eltis (1978) who demonstrated that Britain's economic problems in the 1970s stemmed from the fact that non-market sector employment gained at the expense of market sector employment during the period 1966–75. During that period, the labour force as a whole remained constant while those employed in market sector jobs (to which tangible economic benefits could be attributed) declined by 1.5 million. The non-market sector grew by about 1.2 million so the net contribution to unemployment was about 300,000.[9] Since non-market sector jobs normally pay less than those in the market sector, this would spell a decline in purchasing power among the employed but would raise the productivity of those in the market sector since fewer workers presumably were producing the same or more products than previously was the case.

This did not necessarily mean that Britain's international competitiveness would improve however. During the Heath government and after, during those of Harold Wilson and James Callaghan, wages continued to increase helping to offset any gains made in productivity. The Heath government, Conservative though it was, entered into a tripartite agreement with the Confederation of British Industry and the Trades Union Congress in order to achieve a consensus over economic policy. This was taken to mean that the government had endorsed the continuing demand for higher wages by British industry. The result helped to push certain inflation indicators as high as 20 per cent during mid-1975.

Under these conditions, it is easy to see why the pound did not fare well despite continuing dollar weakness. And the wave of British 'industrial decline' psychology did not help sterling's prospects either. As the Americans would experience ten years later, all sorts of reasons were offered as explanations of how Britain had gotten itself into such a sorry state. True to British self-perceptions, the answers tended to be mostly historical. Unlike the Americans, who tended to view the problem of declining American manufacturing in the 1970s as a problem that could be reversed if they practiced less benevolent policies toward trading partners, on the one hand, while borrowing intelligent industrial policies and practices from them, on the other, the British viewed the problem as almost (but not entirely) insoluble. Little England was lost in a world of behemoths with which it was no longer able to compete. The process had begun at different times, depending upon the analysis: in some cases it dated back to the last decade of the nineteenth century, while in others it dated from the end of the Second World War or the retrenchment from Suez.

But once notions of that sort became fairly widespread, they did little to aid the pound or instil faith in British governments, Labour or Conservative, in the 1970s. Britain already had a track record of using devaluations to shore up its declining international competitiveness and it would be natural to suspect that it would be attempted again if domestic prices got out of hand. As investors shunned the dollar in some cases, sterling therefore did not become a viable option because it was susceptible to politicians who might use it to maintain the appearance of prosperity at home. In addition, it had links to the dollar that will be examined shortly. When taken together, sterling was relegated to a tertiary role among international investors.

After the dissolution of the Bretton Woods system, the idea of devaluations lived on but in a new form. Since the general currency float, informing one's major trading partners or the IMF of a desire to devalue was of far less importance than the notion of letting the market take its natural course. This could not be accomplished without giving the foreign exchange markets a little help, however. But the idea that a currency could depreciate according to market views and trends was much more politically appealing than having to lose face by officially devaluing. Britain's decline in the 1960s was made all the more embarrassing by the round of sterling

72

devaluations. Now, under floating exchange rates, the policy might still be pursued under the guise of natural market depreciation, with no one visibly to blame.

When the dollar depreciated after August 1971, many Europeans and the Japanese were alarmed about the consequences that the action might have for their own trading positions. Henry Kissinger recalled that President Pompidou had stressed the importance of a long-range solution rather than a short-term cosmetic political deal when he met with President Nixon in the Azores in December 1971.[10] Although that meeting led to the short-lived Smithsonian Agreement, and despite the fact that the Committee of Twenty laboured on, no effective alternative to fixed parities was ever devised and that now meant that fears of political devaluation were on the rise again. But the uncertainty of currency values was not without its political benefits in the brave new world of floating rates.

The effects of inflation and wage demands made Britain a prime candidate to test the waters in the new environment. The results would be less than promising however. Stagflation became the norm and did nothing to enhance Britain's reputation as a vibrant economy. Bacon and Eltis recalled that when the following question was put to Oxford undergraduates in 1965, 'Can economies have simultaneously, zero growth, rapid inflation, substantial unemployment and a balance of payments deficit?', the answer overwhelmingly was only in an underdeveloped country.[11] Ten years later, the irony would not be not lost at home. The description now also fitted Britain quite well. But while that sort of thinking plagued Britain in the 1970s, the UK certainly was not alone. By the end of the decade, many industrialised countries would be suffering the same problems but most were viewed as temporary. In Britain, the symptoms were considered terminal.

Put more simply, as exports fell, unemployment increased and the non-productive sector gained jobs, only North Sea oil seemed capable of pulling Britain out of its straits. And oil did help the stock market substantially at times in the mid-1970s although almost everyone recognised that the reserves were somewhat limited. But more importantly, if the original fields were capable of producing enough for domestic use but not enough for a substantial export trade, did this effectively mean that Britons would have enough petrol for a Sunday drive while still being relatively unproductive in the work place? Oil notwithstanding, the endemic problem remained with no serious long-term solutions in sight.

As the recession of 1975 set in, both Britain and the United States were suffering with their respective economic problems. While both governments were short of political solutions to their growing economic problems, the Americans were far in front of the British in financial innovation. By itself, innovation would not provide a cure for the underlying problems that were causing shares to be extremely volatile and sending bond prices lower, but it did help investors and traders cope with the problems to some extent. North Sea oil replaced innovation in the UK as the short-term answer to economic problems and created a new atmosphere of optimism. Unthinkable for a prime minister during the miners' strike of 1973, North Sea oil had Harold Wilson musing in the mid-1970s whether he could actually establish himself as the head of OPEC by 1980.[12]

ANOTHER STERLING CRISIS

By 1975, the Labour government found itself with few alternatives for curing Britain's mounting economic problems. North Sea oil gave the appearance of new-found wealth and cosmetically helped stop Britain's decline in international prestige but, ironically, the group of oil producers with which it was now associated were distinctly Third World countries with little other obvious means of revenues. But Britain would be able to employ oil as a weapon of its own in an attempt to stimulate spending in the face of the recession that was developing in most of the developed countries.

Although early estimates concluded that the North Sea discoveries would enable Britain to become self-sufficient in oil, many of the same conservative predictions did not envisage that it would become an exporter of any note. Yet within five years of the first significant drillings, its contribution to the UK balance of payments rose from almost nothing to approximately £2.3 billion by 1977.[13] This occurred initially at a time when Britain had among the highest short-term interest rates in the OECD and an exchange rate that was somewhat strong against both the EC snake and the dollar. A lower pound exchange rate would obviously have helped Britain's trading prospects.

The pound exchange rate was given a significant nudge downward in March 1976 in what became one of the best-publicised central bank operations for some time. The Nigerian government informed the Bank of England of its intent to sell sterling in favour of dollars. Rather than accommodate the Nigerians directly, the deal was done through the foreign exchange market where it would be made very public. At the same time, the Bank of England itself also sold sterling, giving a clear sign to the market that it wanted to see sterling drop. When combined with falling UK interest rates, the effect on the pound was swift and pronounced. Within a week sterling had lost over 5 per cent of its value against the dollar in what amounted to a mini-devaluation.

Equally important was the pound's decline to below the $2.00 barrier for the first time. By September 1976, it had fallen to $1.64 in what amounted to a 32 per cent depreciation since 1971–72 (see Figure 3.1). The precipitous fall apparently was more than the UK authorities had bargained for; sterling was quickly becoming viewed as a weak currency not

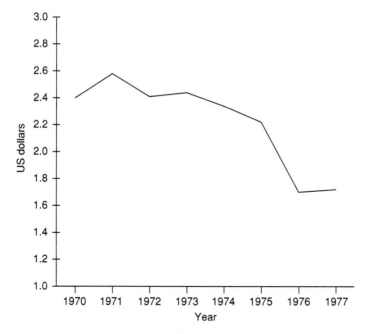

Figure 3.1 Pound v. dollar, 1970–77

Source: Federal Reserve *Bulletin*, various issues

deserving of international investment for fear of its continuing value. The blatant manner in which the Bank of England showed its willingness to let it depreciate would begin to instill panic in the hearts of international investors who began to realise that the UK was more than willing to use the exchange rate to offset declining domestic productivity and competitiveness. Even the relatively high yields offered by gilts could not offset the losses that investors had incurred in the first three quarters of 1976.

During this period, the Bank of England had actively used lines of credit from the United States in a vain attempt to shore up the pound. The Treasury had apparently shot itself in the foot by its policy of deliberate depreciation and soon the entire line of credit was used. Reserves were also being used, but to no avail: despite the fact that Britain used about 20 per cent of its foreign exchange reserves the pound still plunged to new lows. This forced the government of James Callaghan to what detractors considered new depths of despair: Britain applied to the IMF for a loan to bolster the currency.

Contrary to popular opinion, that particular loan application to the IMF was not Britain's first nor was it the first loan made to an industrialised country. In fact, Britain had used IMF facilities avidly in the post-war period, paying substantial amounts of interest on the facilities that were drawn down. As one commentator put it, the new headquarters building that the IMF built and occupied in Washington, DC in the early 1970s could easily have been paid for with British interest on previous loans alone.[14] Britain was no stranger to IMF facilities but its previous loans did not receive the attention that the latest one in 1976 did.

The attention that the loan attracted was not well timed. There was a general fear in the Labour Party that IMF assistance would require Britain to tighten her monetary belt or submit to conditions that the party found unacceptable. With the surfeit of OPEC money flooding the world's financial markets, Britain needed to attract international hot money flows, not discourage them. The reason for the loan application was to shore up the pound without substantially raising interest rates, which would have made recovery from the recession more difficult. But the unwanted publicity made the psychological side of attracting funds more difficult.

The results of the IMF borrowing were successful for the UK. Within two years, reserves increased dramatically and the exchange rate of the pound stabilised. Britain also began to repay much of the foreign debt it had incurred during the mid-1970s. But the psychological impact of the borrowing did not do much to enhance Britain's stature in the international financial community. This particular IMF borrowing was too visible and gave the investment community the distinct impression that Britain was resorting to tactics normally associated with Third World countries.

The loan required Britain to submit to IMF scrutiny of its books and gave the impression that the IMF was dictating Britain's monetary and fiscal policy. As with all loans, the IMF made suggestions to Britain to curb public spending and maintain a target for its exchange rate but those conditions were not applied in the same way that they might have been to a developing country. Nevertheless, the connection was made and, when combined with the overall discussion about Britain's unproductive economic malaise, did little to dispel the notion that the country had sunk to the level of a third-rate economic power.

After the pound settled at about $1.70 following the crisis, it gradually began to rise again toward the end of the decade. But strangely absent from discussions about the new sub-$2.00 level were any serious complaints about how far the pound had sunk since the Bretton Woods system was instituted. The value of the currency seemed to be of less emotional value than it was in France, where the level of the franc was often tied to national honour and influence. But practicality overtook prestige in this case and, again, North Sea oil was at the heart of the matter.

Being denominated in dollars, North Sea oil benefited the UK regardless of the value of the pound. As export revenues increased, so too did the amount of dollars coming into the coffers. If the pound declined further, then the dollars would purchase more pounds, making an even greater contribution to the balance of payments. A strong pound would not have the same benefits. In this case, Britain could benefit from the best of both worlds by allowing the pound to weaken while drawing in export dollars on the other side. But this sort of policy would only be short-lived at best. North Sea reserves were not as large as those of many OPEC members and were not projected to last beyond the end of the century. The IMF facility and oil together signalled a new phase in Britain's exchange rate management. Practising benign neglect on behalf of the pound was not feasible any longer in the age of increasing amounts of volatile hot money and petrodollars. The pound was coming uncoupled from its long-standing relationship with the dollar as the EC began to put demands upon Britain to join the European Monetary System.

But the ideal situation whereby sterling declined and increased petrodollar revenues offset it did not quite pan out as hoped. The dollar was also declining in the foreign exchange markets so the simple case of one currency offsetting the other was not actually realised. The general period of dollar decline, due mostly to continuing OPEC price increases, allowed the UK (notably the British National Oil Corporation, or BNOC) equally to raise its prices along with the OPEC members. While petrol revenues certainly increased, they were bringing in dollars that continued to decline in value while the pound remained relatively stable against the dollar at the same time.

THE DECLINE OF THE DOLLAR

Inflation, the rising price of oil, jittery financial markets, and the shift in investor preferences toward other hard currencies had a pronounced effect on the dollar throughout the 1970s. Financial innovation on its own could not prevent long-term financial losses in otherwise volatile markets. But the weakening dollar did act as a magnet for foreign direct investment, as mentioned above. The inflation cloud had a bit of a silver lining in a sense, although it would not be realised for some time. Dollar weakness would be seized upon by foreign investors as a cheap way in which to penetrate the American market.

The decline of the dollar during the 1970s was pronounced but some currencies fared better than others. As Figure 3.2 shows, the Canadian dollar and the pound did not appreciate much at all as the dollar declined and did not match the European currencies or the yen. In fact, the Canadian dollar was the one hard currency to actually decline against the dollar during the period. And the Swiss franc outperformed all the rest, rising by over 100 per cent during the 1970s to late 1980.

In general terms, the rise of most currencies is understandable but the rise of the Swiss franc and the fall of the Canadian dollar cannot be explained by dollar weakness alone. But if matched against political events of the decade, especially the OPEC price rises, it becomes apparent that

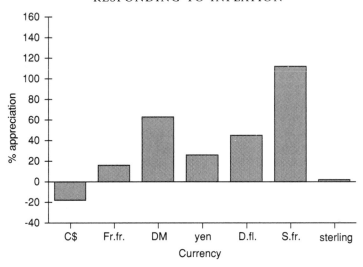

Figure 3.2 Depreciation of the dollar, 1972–80

Source: International Monetary Fund, *Financial Statistics*, various issues

the movements were mostly the products of hot money flows. The Swiss franc's largest appreciation of the decade came in the third and fourth quarters of 1974 (appreciating almost 6 US cents), the second and third quarters of 1978 (appreciating 11 cents) and in the second and third quarters of 1979 (appreciating 5 cents). Upon closer examination, it appears that international political events inspired these hot money flows to a great extent.

In 1974 during that period, the Herstatt Bank of West Germany failed due to large foreign exchange losses. At the end of the summer, President Nixon resigned causing speculative pressures against the dollar. In 1978, the Shah of Iran was under increasing pressure from Moslem fundamentalists and his regime appeared more shaky than at any other time in the past. In 1979, the Shah abdicated his throne and a shortage of petrol forced the market price above the fixed price to all-time high levels. And in all cases, currencies appreciated against the dollar with the exception of the Canadian dollar – but the Swiss franc's movement was certainly the largest of all.

The attractiveness of the Swiss franc was not difficult to explain in fundamental terms. Short-term interest rates were the lowest in the industrialised world during the 1970s and the consumer price index showed the slowest rate of change. But there was still a price to be paid for Swiss francs. Foreign investors buying francs for domestic investment were often paid negative rates of interest by banks which were not that keen to receive deposits in francs from foreigners. The atmosphere in which foreigners nevertheless clamoured for Swiss franc investments gave the currency the

78

aura of a 'dream currency'. Nevertheless, Swiss francs may not have been the ultimate destination of the hot money flows because Switzerland is also home to many gold investors and the funds were destined for bullion rather than Swiss francs in many cases.[15]

Yet as Figure 3.2 shows, the two currencies which did not appreciate against the dollar were the Canadian dollar and the pound. The Canadian dollar's depreciation was steady while the pound proved more volatile but ended the period with little gain. In fundamental terms, the explanation is simple: both countries had higher short-term interest rates, inflation rates, and consumer price increases than did the United States, despite the fact that both had proven oil reserves. Along with smaller economies such as Sweden, the oil bill became a significant factor when foreign investors determined which currencies to buy or hold. But another reason may be offered which has more to do with trade and investment patterns. The United States, Canada and Britain were all the largest direct foreign investors in each others' economies.

Traditionally, Canada has been the recipient of most American direct investment abroad, followed by Britain. In return, Britain has always been the largest direct foreign investor in the US, while the Canadian investment has been substantial but does not match that of the larger European countries. The American investment in Britain should not be understated: in many years, it has been valued at about 15–20 per cent of the total American direct foreign investment. In some years, it has almost matched the US investment in all of Latin America, an area that the US has been long assumed to dominate.

The numbers are much the same in reverse. British direct investment in the US has generally hovered at around 15–20 per cent of the total invested while the Canadian has been about 7–12 per cent. These investment links form strong ties that had direct consequences in the foreign exchange markets. The more closely related countries are in foreign investment, the more closely aligned their currencies will be in the foreign exchange market. But this does not necessarily mean that the currencies will move in tandem.

The short history of exchange rate movements since 1972 illustrated that investors did not have a clear preference for Canadian dollars or pounds over the US dollar. In fact, sterling's movements closely paralleled the US dollar with the exception of the sterling crisis of 1976 despite the fact that Britain was a member of the EC snake for a short time after its entrance in 1972. Given its history, investors were treating sterling as a surrogate for the US dollar. The Canadian dollar, on the other hand, could not be considered quite the same because the Canadian financial markets were smaller and provided less liquidity than those in Britain or the US. The link for this premise lies in the strong direct investment links between the three countries. If the US dollar weakened, British direct investors in the US would have little choice but to ride out the storm because long-term direct investments are not subject to hot money flows as are portfolio investments.

Since the investment links between Britain, the United States and Canada were both long term and long standing, exposure to one currency necessarily gave international investors exposure to the others in turn. This can be seen in Table 3.1. The Canadian dollar would be expected to be the laggard performer because of the sheer size of the American investment in Canada plus the relatively small size of the Canadian stock and bond markets as opposed to those in the US and Britain. Portfolio investors operating under the principle of diversifying internationally would thus need to find another currency not directly within the dollar's orbit, normally the Deutschmark, yen, guilder or Swiss franc. When deciding to sell a currency, international investors often try to reduce their exposure to a currency's orbit, not just the single currency itself. On that basis, the Canadian dollar was the most vulnerable of the three for most of the 1970s.

Economic and political developments did not help the dollar in the 1970s and the depreciation did much to change the face of American economic dominance. When combined with the Watergate affair, the resignation of Richard Nixon and the continued rise in the price of oil the United States found itself in a position to which Britain had become accustomed since the Second World War: inflation, high nominal interest rates, declining productivity and a loss of international prestige. The Americans were shaken even further when the Lockheed Corporation announced in February 1976 that it routinely made payments to foreigners in order to entice them to buy their aeroplanes. Although not uncommon in international business, the bribes became widespread news and gave the impression that American firms had to pay off customers in order to compete. All of these events

Table 3.1 US, UK and Canadian direct foreign investments, 1971–79 (billions US$)

	1971	1972	1973	1974	1975	1976	1977	1978	1979
US d.f.i in Canada	24.0	25.7	28.1	28.4	31.1	33.9	35.3	37.1	41.0
US d.f.i in UK	8.9	9.6	11.1	12.5	14.0	15.2	17.3	20.4	24.3
Historical total	86.2	94.3	107.3	118.6	124.0	136.4	149.0	168.0	192.7
UK d.f.i in US	4.4	4.6	5.4	6.1	5.3	5.8	6.4	6.2	7.0
Canada d.f.i in US	3.4	3.4	4.0	4.8	5.3	5.9	6.0	6.2	7.0
Historical total	13.6	14.3	17.7	21.7	25.6	27.4	34.6	42.5	52.3

Source: US Department of Commerce, *Survey of Current Business*, various issues

meant that within a short period of time, both Britain and the United States would have to make adjustments in their financial institutions in order to make them more flexible to rapidly changing economic events.

The Americans reacted first by providing for new stock market practices and protection for investors. But oddly, the banking system was equally in need of reform but would not receive any serious legislative attention until 1980. British banks, in relatively better structural condition than their American counterparts, would also be reformed and the corrective legislation would be similar in some respects to what the Americans would pass a year later. In many respects, hindsight suggests that the corrective measures came somewhat late on both sides of the Atlantic, but the effects of the collapse of Bretton Woods were still working their way through the financial system. It was only when it became apparent that exchange rates were permanently floating and that volatility in the financial markets had increased substantially from years previous that reform got underway. But the reform itself did not necessarily provide a panacea to the problems in the financial system: in some cases, it only exacerbated them, signalling the need for even more deregulation and regulation in a dizzying cycle of measures and countermeasures designed to protect the banking system.

4

RISING INSTITUTIONALISM

Political reaction to the economic turmoil of the 1970s would come toward the end of the decade. In Britain, the Conservatives would be returned to power in 1979 as public dissatisfaction with the Labour governments of the previous five years finally produced a victory for Margaret Thatcher in the general election. In the United States, Jimmy Carter would be turned out of office after one term as persistent inflation and a series of bungled political and economic policies led to a large victory for Ronald Reagan and the Republicans at the polls. Both were conservative reactions to the turbulence of the post-Bretton Woods period and the connection with what was perceived as ineffectual political leadership, unable to cope with OPEC, inflation and growing unemployment.

Another of the major products of the turmoil that followed the collapse of the Bretton Woods system was a marked shift toward an institutional concentration of economic power coinciding with the political shift to conservatism. As inflation rose, markets became more volatile, unemployment grew and individuals began to eschew the markets in favour of intermediaries who would invest for them. Politically, voters would demonstrate the same tendencies by voting out of office any politician who appeared incapable of effectively dealing with all of the bewildering changes, especially when those changes were perceived to put their economic welfare at risk.

Both reactions were predictable but the financial reaction was not often seen. In the past, savers and investors had few viable alternatives to banks or the stock market: investing or speculation meant either one or the other. But in the latter 1970s, these rather limited options caused a furore that eventually became translated into changes in the regulatory atmosphere in both Britain and the United States. Savers began to ask more of their banks and investors became disenchanted with the stock markets, demanding growth without undue risk attached.

While public reaction to markets and institutions was the most visible form of unrest, other relatively obscure developments also picked up momentum that caused profound changes in the nature of risk and reward. Both the United States and Britain began to accumulate significant amounts

82

of off-balance sheet liabilities to entities unknown to most of their voting publics. Usually, these contingent liabilities were considered fairly harmless, posing little risk to the governments that partially or fully guaranteed them. But, as time wore on, the liabilities began to amass in even larger amounts. By virtue of their sheer size, they could no longer be ignored.

As will be seen below, the reason that these off-balance sheet liabilities were undertaken in the first place has to do with the volatility of the 1970s and the strains it imposed upon the financial system. While many were vital to international economic development and the spread of market capitalism, they nevertheless posed (and still pose) serious questions of moral hazard to their governments. This trend first developed in the United States in the domestic credit markets and also became prevalent in Britain when it entered the EC, assuming many of the obligations that membership required.

Because of the increasing institutionalism that developed in the 1970s, the banking systems and markets of Britain and the United States came closer together than at any time in their histories. The market structures of the two became similar and more integrated while the banking systems, disparate for many years, also began to take on similar characteristics. These developments between the two rapidly developed into a greater inter-nationalism in the marketplace than at any time in the past, and by the mid-1980s it could certainly be said that the major financial markets of the world had truly become internationalised. But it was the British and American markets that led the way to this phenomenon by adopting each other's practices at a time when their institutions were under stress for similar reasons.

Although the investor's side of this phenomenon took about fifteen years to develop and mature, it began with the disappearance of the small investor from the marketplace in the early 1970s. While a decade and a half is hardly an historic trend in itself, small investors, on aggregate, took with them a substantial amount of savings that potentially would be used for investment in new financial vehicles. Once the flight had begun, institu-tional developments would quickly follow, turning those fifteen years into what seemed a century for regulators and market professionals.

THE FLIGHT OF THE SMALL INVESTOR

Institutional dominance of the financial markets has been taken for granted for the last two decades although the trend only dates from the early 1970s. The dominance has been best seen in the stock markets. Money and bond markets have always been institutionally dominated and when individual investors are present it is usually the exception rather than the rule. Traditionally, the buyers of bonds have been money managers who have acted as intermediaries for pension funds, life insurance companies and mutual funds. Stocks have also had heavy institutional interest over the years but in past decades individual investors had a much more significant impact than they have had in the past twenty years.

In previous chapters, the events that began to chase away individual investors from the American stock exchanges in the late 1960s and early 1970s were mentioned. The Equity Funding scandal, the failure of several brokerage firms after the 1960s bull market and the rise in interest rates all had a negative effect on the markets in general. The development of options exchanges and futures exchanges were early attempts to persuade the individual investor to remain active in the markets. Their basic design and trading characteristics were tailored for small investors, although it was institutions and professional traders that eventually came to dominate those markets as well. Originally, the concepts and mechanics proved difficult to sell to the uninitiated. As the population grew, the number of small investors remained steady in overall numbers but their influence as a percentage of all investors involved in the markets began to decline, in some cases notably.

In many cases, intermediation produced positive effects for the individual investor that he or she could not achieve when acting alone in the markets. Mutual funds were the best example of this. Building upon the basic investment principle of diversification, the stock mutual funds were able to offer small investors with several thousand dollars or pounds to spend more protection than their purchasing power would have suggested by investing in a group of stocks rather than in one or two positions. Less likely to lose large amounts of capital, investors began to favour mutual funds in the late 1960s and early 1970s, especially after the principles of modern portfolio theory became more popular. Although mutual funds control vast amounts of investment monies, they are still considered investments made by the individual in the United States, not indirect investments such as those made through insurance or pension funds. In Britain they are considered a separate investor category.

By offering small investors opportunities only afforded to larger investors, the mutual funds were able to amass vast amounts of money and exercise significant influence over the market. But their political influence could not match that of the pension funds and life insurance companies that managed long-term contractual arrangements. These investors are true conduits of institutionally intermediated funds invested for the individual rather than by the individual. This became underlined in the later 1980s and 1990s as pension funds began to exercise more of a political conscience than in the past – a topic that will be taken up later in this chapter. But the beginning of a distinct trend was already becoming clear shortly after the collapse of the Bretton Woods system: investors were handing a significant amount of power to the funds and their managers, which would later be translated into political as well as economic influence.

The flight of the small investor in the United States can be traced to the turbulent bear market following 1971–72. Between 1970 and 1975, the number of individual American investors active in the stock market declined to about 25 million from over 30 million. The trend was certainly accelerated when the Federal Reserve Board raised margin requirements both in 1971 and 1972 to a final level of 65 per cent; matching the level reached in 1970 when the marketplace also was in disarray. Adult shareowner incidence in the adult population fell from one in four to one in six during that time, while the average age of shareholders rose from 48 to 53, suggesting that only those who had been investors for a relatively long period of time remained during the exodus.[1]

Equally, the largest defections came from investors in the age group 21–44 years who were either classified as having professional and technical occupations or clerical and sales jobs. The income group apparently the hardest hit was those in the household income bracket $5,000–$15,000, representing modest to average salaries at the time. Retirees and those in the higher-income brackets suffered smaller defections from their ranks, either because they understood market techniques better or could not afford to get out quickly.[2] In any event, the market lost most heavily among the largest demographic group of investors.

This lack of interest in the stock market was one of the major forces behind the construction of money market mutual funds by the same investment companies that also marketed equities funds. As seen in earlier chapters, Regulation Q in force at the banks and thrifts also helped market the new funds. While the success of the new funds helped the investment companies prosper, the effect upon the major market indices was predictably negative. But the independence displayed by the individual investor would have even more profound consequences upon the banking system within a few years: the effect upon the stock market was only the first in a chain of events.

Investor reaction in the UK was similar to that in the United States. After 1972, stock exchange turnover in ordinary shares declined substantially. The miners' strike and the OPEC-induced turmoil took their toll quickly. Overall market turnover declined, found a new lower level and began to rise again only in the later 1970s when gilts accounted for most of the slack created by ordinary shares.[3] Ordinary share trading remained at 1972 levels for almost the remainder of the decade. And, as in the US, small investors abandoned equities in large numbers, leaving the market to institutions.

As can be seen in Table 4.1, shares as a proportion of the personal sector declined substantially between 1972 and the sterling crisis of 1976, being replaced mostly by bank accounts and building society accounts. Unit trust units (mutual funds in the US) also declined while equity in life insurance and pension funds increased, giving additional buying power to those institutional investors. The flight to quality, evident by the increase in gilts

Table 4.1 Financial assets of the UK personal sector, 1971–76 (billions pounds)

Type	1971	1972	1973	1974	1975	1976
Cash	2.9	3.3	3.6	4.2	4.9	5.5
Bank deposits	10.7	12.5	15.9	18.8	19.0	20.0
National Savings	9.0	9.8	10.0	10.1	10.7	11.6
Building Society deposits	12.0	14.2	16.6	18.4	22.5	26.1
UK gilts	4.1	3.3	3.5	2.5	5.4	7.0
Unlisted shares	4.9	6.6	6.8	5.7	7.1	7.3
Unit trusts	1.6	2.2	1.5	0.9	1.7	1.7
Life insurance and pensions	24.3	28.1	28.3	25.2	32.2	37.1
Ordinary shares	24.9	29.7	18.7	7.3	17.0	15.5

Source: Central Statistical Office, *Financial Statistics*, various issues

generally, also applied to the personal sector although, as in the United States, individuals do not form a substantial number of bond buyers. Also interesting to note is the individual's preference for cash and bank deposits. In times of financial upheaval, the preference for cash rather than riskier market accounts can be clearly seen.

The increase in the shares and deposits in building societies in Britain is noteworthy because, in the 1970s, many of those societies were still mutual associations, that is, technically owned by their depositors. Some life insurance companies fell into the same category. The move toward savings can be viewed as a clear move toward savings/investments that had strong proprietary overtones. In theory, the individual owned his or her building society, so the individual's deposit represented both savings and ownership at the same time.

As a result of negative economic factors, the long-term trend became entrenched by the early 1990s. By the end of 1992 when a major benchmark study appeared, institutional investors, mostly pension funds and insurance companies, held about 57 per cent of UK common shares, valued at about £350 billion, as opposed to 20 per cent for individuals, amounting to £126 billion. Individuals were the heaviest investors in the newly privatised industries with those shares amounting to about 25 per cent of their holdings. Institutional holdings of the privatised industries were proportionately less, illustrating that the Conservatives' policy of privatisation was successful with the small shareholder, as intended.[4]

Gilt turnover was greatly helped by tax concessions which proved very attractive for those investors who did brave the market. In the 1970s, the capital gains tax on ordinary shares sold for a profit was about 30 per cent on average. Gains on gilts, on the other hand, were not taxable if the holding period was longer than one year. That clear advantage could not even be offset by the advance corporation tax (ACT) instituted in 1973, which provided some relief for companies paying corporate tax on their profits. Investors were still not affected by the tax and clearly showed more interest in safe deposits and life insurance and pension contracts. But again, the economic reasons were very clear: taxpayers could deduct any personal contribution to an approved superannuation scheme and therefore used the pension plans to save, avoiding tax. A variation of this technique would be seen in the United States about a decade later.

While investor interest in intermediated investments was natural, the concentration of financial power in the pension funds and life insurance companies was not without its problems. As inflation continued to climb higher, the assets of the institutions began to decline in balance sheet terms in the later 1970s, continuing into the next decade. As far as the individual was concerned, the contractual relationship between him- or herself and the intermediary was inviolate; what he did not realise was that contractual institutions were capable of losing money as well as the individual. In reality, however, the fiduciary investors also began to suffer badly as a result of the inflationary trend and the balance sheets of money pension funds and insurance companies began to decline along with the financial markets. The trend toward intermediation left the investor sleeping better at night but not necessarily the money managers.

The growth in institutional holdings in the United States was nothing short of astonishing. Life insurance company holdings in common stocks more than trebled between 1965 and 1975. This was a reflection of the growth in life insurance overall. In both the US and Britain, individuals taking out life insurance contracts increased dramatically during the 1970s as financial turmoil prompted many to increase their coverage as inflation continued to rise. If measured against the end of the Second World War, the insurance companies' holdings increased over twenty times. Mutual funds increased their stock holdings more than twice during the 1960s and 1970s and pension funds recorded a similar gain. Even though mutual funds are considered a direct stock investment by the individual in the US, the amount of institutional holdings in them also increased considerably. Between the end of the Second World War and 1975, institutional stock holdings rose from 14 per cent to 34 per cent.[5] Those increases, evident throughout the latter 1970s as well, show that even the hardy individuals remaining in the market decided to place more and more of their money with funds rather than brave it alone.

Even though equities were falling as a percentage of capital market financings in the United States, they still occupied a large portion of capital market activity in both the primary and secondary markets. In Britain, the case for equities was a bit more bleak as gilts carved out a larger and larger share of stock exchange turnover. New issues of common shares in the UK rose sporadically in the early and mid-1970s but never matched 1975, when the market caught up with several previously poor years for new issues. At the same time, the value of ordinary shares turnover showed the same problem, with little net increase. This can be seen in Figure 4.1.

The shift toward intermediated investments was the one major change brought about by the collapse of Bretton Woods. But, as seen in previous chapters, the stock market was not the only casualty of the investor flight. The MMMFs in the United States were attracting funds from both the stock market and bank deposits that began to have repercussions for the commercial banks, thrifts and the Federal Reserve as well. Trapped by the strictures of Regulation Q, the banks and thrift institutions searched for ways to compete for investors' deposits, but had little hope of offering higher deposit rates. One area that had potential to compete with the money market funds and the burgeoning money management accounts being offered by securities brokers was the traditionally unexciting cheque (current) account.

Some banks and thrifts began to offer current account facilities to their customers that offered a rate of interest along with the chequing privileges. At first glance, this appeared to be clever marketing of an old service that allowed the banks to offer new products to customers in what remained a plain vanilla business. But even offering interest on current accounts ran into strong opposition because it was not specifically allowed by the Glass–Steagall Act. According to the 1933 legislation, only commercial banks were allowed to offer chequing facilities; thrifts had to content them-

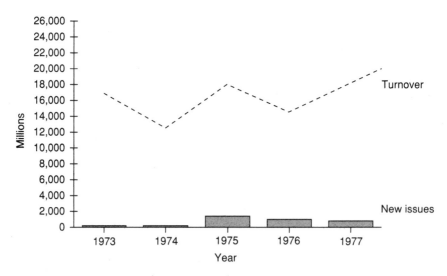

Figure 4.1 Common share activity in the UK

Source: The Stock Exchange

selves with offering only savings accounts. The idea of offering this new type of current account ran into strong opposition from the regulators, who quickly realised that current accounts with interest would probably require new reserve requirements on this sort of account and perhaps even a new definition of the basic money supply.

The banks had strong reasons to fear the new money market funds. By effectively competing for bank deposits, the funds were siphoning money away from the banks and raising their costs in the money market at the same time. As commercial banks searched for loanable funds, and retail deposits shifted toward the funds, the banks began to use the commercial paper market (when applicable) and the money market to raise negotiable certificates of deposit (CDs). When they ventured into the money market, their borrowing rates were certain to rise above Regulation Q ceilings. The great irony was that many of the buyers of their commercial paper and CDs were the money market funds, searching for high yields for their own investors. The money funds were adding insult to injury both by disintermediating the banks and raising their costs of capital at the same time.

The commercial banks began to feel the full effects of the power of the money market funds in the latter 1970s when savings deposits grew at a slower rate than the money supply (M1) in several years. In the earlier part of the decade, deposits increased at annual rates of change in excess of money supply growth when the competition for those funds was less intense. But the financial power accumulated by the money funds in such a relatively short period of time created severe problems for the Federal Reserve. The facilities offered investors by them and the money management accounts being developed by the large brokers challenged the way in which monetary policy was administered. Traditionally, if the Federal Reserve wanted to dampen credit creation, it would raise the reserve requirements on member banks and/or raise the discount rate. That in turn would signal the banks to begin making fewer loans. When combined with Regulation Q ceilings and the lack of alternatives for savers, that sort of monetary policy would usually cause a slowdown in consumer activity, encouraging savers to tighten their belts and save even more. But the new funds effectively linked savers and investors to the inflation rate, helping them keep abreast of the consumer price index by at least helping them preserve their purchasing power. In short, consumers could continue to spend in inflationary environments without fear of a real loss. This change in the traditional climate would cause the Federal Reserve to react severely to money creation in the early 1980s.

In addition to liberating savers from interest rate ceilings, the money funds had the net effect of helping to quickly destroy some of the Federal Reserve's power to pursue effective monetary policy. Although there was little the central bank could do to control the funds, it did include the amounts invested in them in the definition of the money supply beginning in 1980.

The traditional definitions did not include them, so to avoid even further embarrassment they had to be included even though no reserve requirements could be imposed. The markets were changing very quickly and the Federal Reserve was playing catch-up, not for the first or last time during the post-Bretton Woods era. In the case of the changes forced upon banks, the money funds and disintermediation were prime examples of consumers exercising rights in the post-Bretton Woods environment. The money funds were proof that consumers would not sit idly by while inflation and artificially low rates of interest ate away at their savings.

Inflation and disintermediation began to take an even greater toll on the thrift institutions. The American thrifts were perhaps the most simple and protected of all financial services. Their product base consisted of simple deposits on the liability side and mortgages on the asset side, quite similar to the mix of their brethren, the British building societies. Raising funds in the money markets was not possible for the overwhelming majority of them because of their relatively small sizes: most thrifts were local institutions with assets smaller than those of even the small regional banks. Issuing CDs was not feasible for them so they relied mainly on deposits. And they, too, were constrained by Regulation Q ceilings.[6]

But as they began to experience the competition for savers' funds, many of them began to offer current accounts that offered a basic rate of interest, dubbed negotiable order of withdrawal, or NOW accounts. Although in violation of the 1933 Banking Act, the Federal Reserve was slow in reacting to this marketing because the thrifts' financial positions were declining as interest rates rose. Since the Federal Reserve was not the regulator of federally chartered thrifts (the Federal Home Loan Bank Board performed that function), the central bank had to adopt a careful stance in dealing with a breach of the Glass–Steagall Act. But the thrift industry was also on tenterhooks as the 1970s progressed. Most of their mortgages were fixed-rate assets for thirty years. As interest rates rose, these assets became less profitable, even when the cost of funds was protected by Regulation Q but still losing them customers in the process. If the industry as a whole became unprofitable (as it eventually did in 1980–81), then the entire American mortgage market would be placed in jeopardy.

The new environment was not the sort that the American banking institutions were accustomed to dealing with after so many years of virtual protection by the Federal Reserve regulations. After having been institutional powers in their own right, the banks now found themselves playing catch-up with the money market funds and the other fiduciary investors that benefited from the new uncertainty. Years of becoming accustomed to fixed interest rates both at the banks and in the mortgage market did not seem to dissuade the individual savers and investors, who showed a spirited dexterity in quickly adopting new methods of behaviour as interest rates rose. The depository institutions were much slower in adopting new strategies, due in no small part to the bureaucratic inflexibility of large institutions attempting to come to grips with changing economic times.

British banking institutions did not suffer the same problems although they too lacked a broad product base to offer their customers. Exchange controls until 1979 helped to keep all but the largest investors' funds at home and the ability of banks to adjust the MLR and deposit rates accordingly insured that disintermediation on a large scale would not occur. The repercussions of the fringe banking crisis were still being felt in the mid- and latter 1970s, but again, the clearing banks benefited by being viewed as safe when compared with their marginally capitalised, smaller brethren. Most of the problems associated with fixed interest rates were non-existent in Britain although other problems would surface, causing the Banking Act of 1979 to be passed.

The dominance of stock exchange turnover in the UK by gilts was enhanced by the UK Treasury, which began to attach bells and whistles to its new issues in order to market them more effectively. Partly paid issues enabled many investors to 'stag' new issues in a similar manner to shares traded within the account period and, when combined with tax incentives, led many more conservative investors into the gilt arena, shunning equities. Similar to US Treasury issues, the secondary market for gilts was, and is, highly efficient (meaning a relatively small spread between bid and offer prices) and that added another incentive for investors. Although the equities business in the UK would recover in the 1980s, gilts continued to dominate stock exchange trading even after the Financial Services Act of 1986 was passed.

OFF-BALANCE SHEET LIABILITIES

Just as the financial turmoil of the 1970s began, both the United States and Britain rapidly began assuming increasing liabilities that have long remained invisible to the outside world. Over the next twenty years, these liabilities became substantial but have remained little understood even by those who have helped assume them in the first place. The principles under which they were assumed remain theoretically defensible but the amounts involved may not always be so.

The contemporary concept of governmental off-balance sheet liabilities originated in the United States during the Depression. In 1968, it was developed further into the practice that is common today. Originally, Congress created specialised agencies over the years designed to provide economic assistance to certain parts of the economy during periods when the markets and private capital could not be relied upon. Housing and the mortgage markets were two of the early beneficiaries. In broad terms, an agency would buy loans of whatever type from private originators, borrowing the money needed to do so from the bond market. Investors were content to buy bonds from the agency because originally the securities had the backing of the US government in the event of default.

Over the years, the idea proved so popular that agency intermediation was expanded into other areas, such as student loans. But the amounts guaranteed by the US Treasury began to mount. When securitisation was developed shortly after the founding of Ginnie Mae, agency intermediation took a different turn. Agencies, public or private, would use the loans purchased to collateralise the borrowing. Technically, the bond issues did not require Treasury backing. In the case of many agencies that were privatised over the years, however, the question of the guarantee persisted. The assumption always remained that if those agencies ever experienced operational problems and reached default the Treasury would come to their aid. By being in such a position, the indebtedness of those many agencies became implied contingent liabilities of the US Treasury, although in strict legal terms, the government could adopt a somewhat different interpretation.[7]

The same idea was never employed in Britain because of the nature of the unitary (non-federal) central government. But when the UK joined the EC in 1972 the complexion of Britain's debt began to change. By joining the community, Britain had to guarantee its share of community borrowings, many of which were assumed by entities similar to the government sponsored enterprises in the United States. But in this case, those institutions were international, in keeping with the fundamental nature of the community.

The United States also had its share of international off-balance sheet liabilities in addition to the domestic. After the Second World War, the US became a signatory to the Bretton Woods Agreement and as a result also became the major contributing member of the World Bank. When that institution began lending to developing countries and funding itself through the international bond markets, the US as well as Britain and other major developed countries assumed an indirect responsibility for the World Bank's borrowings in the event of default. Although the World Bank and other major international institutions such as the Inter-American Development Bank (IADB) and the European Coal and Steel Community were designed to stand on their own and service their own debts in the marketplace, the ultimate guarantee of their operations in the markets lay with the governments that had established them in the first place.

In this respect, the United States has more off-balance sheet liabilities than any other government. In addition to the borrowings of the domestic assistance agencies, it also carried an implicit guarantee to back the borrowings of the World Bank and the Inter-American Development Bank as well as portions of the Asian and African Development Banks. It was not alone in this respect since the borrowings of the World Bank, the largest of the development banks, had all of the developed countries as members.

If the World Bank actually defaulted on one of its obligations, the member states, including Britain, would share the responsibility of assuming the debt in proportion to their annual contributions. As a result, any default would have an impact on the members but probably not a material one given the diversity of the bank's membership.

Guarantees to development agencies are based upon the same diversification principle that is found in those institutions' lending policies. By lending to a broad spectrum of developing countries, a default in any one of them would not have a serious impact upon the lender. And if third-party guarantees are also required by the lenders then the risk of default by a developing country borrower is reduced even further. This reduces the overall institutional risk to the point where the major problem for most development banks and intermediary agencies is operational: how to manage interest rate exposure effectively while performing basic lending functions at the same time.

That does not imply that these disparate institutions do not present risks. Lending agencies can diverge from their original principles as well as present a moral hazard to those who helped capitalise them in the first place. When they do, arguments can be heard for tighter control so that the guarantees provided by governments are not diverted for purposes that are secondary to the institutions primary reasons for existing. Essentially, intermediary agencies rely upon investor confidence in order to perform their functions effectively. If confidence wanes so too does the agencies' effectiveness in performing basic borrowing/on-lending functions.

The American agency function has been viewed from many angles over the years. Fannie Mae provides one example. This agency borrows on the bond market and uses the funds to purchase eligible residential mortgages from lending institutions. The mortgages it purchases are normally guaranteed by a government agency which will pay Fannie Mae if the mortgage holder defaults. Fannie in turn imposes restrictions on the mortgages it purchases. The investor buying Fannie's bonds assumes that the payment of interest and the repayment of principal is guaranteed by the federal government, although the agency is no longer government-owned: it is now known simply as a GSE, a government sponsored enterprise.

Fannie Mae's operations can be viewed from the angle of fiscal policy. The additional purchase of mortgages helps keep the economy more resilient than it may be without that assistance. That overlooks the fact that Fannie is not government owned but the same interpretation could be applied to Ginnie Mae, which is a part of the Department of Housing and Urban Development. Interpretations such as this date from the Depression when government agencies were viewed in Keynesian terms. But others also exist that are a bit less grand.

The social side centres around how much assistance Fannie is able to provide indirectly to potential homeowners who are less well off than the average home buyer. If the agency lowers its criteria for eligible mortgage purchases, then more potential buyers will be able to arrange financings that can be bought by the agency. This makes the banks more willing to originate them with the intention of selling them shortly thereafter. The looser the criteria, the wider the group of homeowners who will seek mortgages supported by Fannie Mae or one of the other mortgage-assistance agencies.

Those more concerned with interest rates can view these agencies ventures into the bond market as an attempt to establish a national level of mortgage rates, which they have effectively done over the last twenty years. The mortgage rate is marginally higher than the bond coupon rate that the agencies pay investors. While long-term interest rates will naturally vary, it can be assumed with some certainty that the mortgage rate will be somewhat higher but uniform nevertheless; a uniformity that was not evident before the agencies began their activities.

The same sort of interpretation can be given to development bank borrowings. At the same time they provide long-term loans for countries badly in need of fixed-rate money and stimulate their local economies in the process. If the contractors with whom those countries do business are from the developed countries then the loans also help stimulate international trade and services. But in all cases, the foundation upon which their stability rests is the guarantees of the governments that contribute to their capital. Even though development banks are intended to stand on their own and operate as any other commercial enterprise, without the guarantee of their member states no investor would buy their bonds. If they did, they would naturally demand a much higher coupon rate than the development banks would be accustomed to paying.

Britain entered the arena of development bank guarantees by first signing the Bretton Woods Agreement and then later joining the EC. Within the original EC, several institutions existed that performed development bank activities within Europe and in the Third World as well. The European Coal and Steel Community (ECSC) provided for the integration of the coal and steel industries within the member states, while the European Investment Bank (EIB) made development loans within the EC and in the Third World as well through the Lomé and Yaounde Conventions. Equally, the European Atomic Energy Commission (Euratom) also borrowed in the bond markets for developing nuclear power facilities and its borrowings were also guaranteed by EC members. Those borrowings were all in addition to the external borrowings of the EC itself, which floated bonds in the major international markets for a variety of purposes.

EC members shared the responsibility of paying off these borrowings in the event of default. In this manner, they had something in common with the US Treasury, which had assumed the ultimate liability of paying off any of the debt of the directly owned agencies or the GSEs that might default. In the case of EC members, they assumed liability to the extent of their strength in the EC itself, based upon GNP. Although that portion may have varied from year to year, the majority of these off-balance sheet liabilities would have been assumed by the West Germans, French, Italians and British in the 1970s, at that time the strongest economies in the community. The same principle applies today.

Table 4.2 illustrates the total bond indebtedness of the EC and the other agencies affiliated with the European Union (EU). Of the total, Britain's share of the debt is approximately 19 per cent, or ECU17.52 billion, the same as that of Germany, France and Italy. This is based upon the UK's share of the capital in the EIB, roughly the same amount that it contributes to the EU's budget, which includes the ECSC and Euratom. Britain's share of World Bank capital is about 5 per cent of a total of $170 billion, making it accountable for $5.3 billion.

Table 4.3 shows the total indebtedness of domestic agencies of the US government or the GSEs that borrow in the public bond markets for the

Table 4.2 Outstanding debt of the European Community

Borrowing/lending operation	Amount outstanding 31.12.92 (millions ECUs)
European Coal and Steel Community	7,701
European Investment Bank	75,713*
European Communities	8,831
Total	92,245

Note:* Includes ECU2,089 guaranteed by general budget of European Community
Source: European Communities, *Financial Report*, 1992

Table 4.3 Contingent liabilities of the US Treasury, 1975 and 1993, government sponsored enterprises (billions US$)

Enterprise	1975	1993
Farm Credit System and related institutions	27.0	53.1
Federal Home Loan Bank and related institutions	20.6	141.5
Fannie Mae	28.2	201.1
Freddie Mac	6.3	50.0
Sallie Mae	0.2	39.7
Total	82.3	525.5*

Note:* Includes other agencies, including Refcorp, founded since 1975
Source: Federal Reserve *Bulletin*, various issues

same period. World Bank borrowings and IADB borrowings are not included nor are those of the Asian Development Bank and the African Development Bank, of which the United States became a shareholder in the early 1980s. While the domestic side of these borrowings is more significant than the international, other agencies are included in the total figures that are not borrowers in the public bond markets for which the United States also has assumed responsibility.[8]

If these international agencies' portion bearing a United States government guarantee is included, the total is increased by some $24.5 billion (see Table 4.4). Britain's responsibility to the non-EC group adds $8.8 billion more to its off-balance sheet liabilities. This means that in 1993, Britain's total bill for off-balance sheet liabilities was $28 billion while the United States had some $550 billion. For both Britain and the United States, the possibility of actually having to provide cash in the event of a default by one or more of these institutions is quite remote. As long as the agencies prudently manage their mandates, the indirect sovereign guarantee should remain in the background. But the real problem is one of moral hazard: by insuring that the institutions will remain viable, have the member governments given them license to exceed their bounds without fear of accountability?

This question seems remote but not quite as remote as it might have seemed only ten years ago. The savings and loan crisis in the United States was caused in part by two factors – deposit insurance at the banking institutions and liberalised regulations surrounding the sort of assets in which thrift institutions could invest. When the thrifts began to extend their assets because of the provisions of the Garn–St Germain Act of 1982 into commercial real estate and junk bonds, they assumed that deposit insurance would protect depositors in the event of crisis.[9] Although the assumption was correct, the bill to the taxpayer for both guaranteeing those deposits and disposing of insolvent thrifts proved to be great. The imprudence excercised by thrift bankers translated directly into a government-led bailout, until then unprecedented in American banking history.

Table 4.4 Outstanding debt of international development banks (millions US$ equivalents)

Institution	Indebtedness, 31 Dec 93
World Bank	$106,811
Asian Development Bank	$13,519
African Development Bank	$8,788
Inter-American Development Bank	$23,424
Total	$152,542

Source: Annual Reports

The problem of moral hazard is also present for the international lending agencies as well as the domestic agencies supported by governments. As demands have grown for the expansion of their services, most of these institutions have responded by having their capital bases expanded and the range of their lending activities widened. As their capital increases so too does their ability to lend, since lending is usually calculated as a multiple of capital, as it is for commercial banks. And that is where the risk of overextending an enterprise's mandate arises. Whether the enterprise be domestic or international, the government's guarantee compounds the problem by providing an incentive for the enterprise managers to take far greater risks than otherwise might be the case without the guarantee. If only shareholders' funds were at stake, lending would be much more prudent.[10] And there is a material difference here in the nature of the potential risks faced between a domestic agency and an international one.

The risks faced by these agencies may be either operational risk or interest rate risk. Operational risk is that faced when performing everyday business such as lending and collecting interest due. Interest rate risk refers to the problem of mismatching between rates of interest received and those paid to bondholders should the interest rate environment change or funding needs change. Of the two types, the operational risk is the greater of the two because it is less visible to the outside and more open to abuse. If a domestic mortgage agency lowers its standards to imprudent levels and agrees to purchase very risky mortgages then the chance of a default to the bondholders increases. Similarly, if an international agency begins lending to very risky projects and the borrowing country subsequently defaults, the lender will have to seek aid from its paid-in country members in order to avoid a default in the bond market. In either case, the hazards become apparent only after the fact.

Putting all international agencies and US domestic agencies in the same category is only convenient when underscoring the problem they pose as a group. The domestic American agencies serve an infrastructure purpose as do the World Bank and others but on a different level. Without the developing country loans made by the World Bank and the regional development organisations, the quality of life in the Third World undoubtedly would be more harsh than it is today. The private credit markets would not provide the money necessary for most of the poor countries to undertake development projects because of the fear of default or the mismanagement of funds. Without the assurances of the lending institution and its guarantors, money for those projects would be available on a much smaller scale and at a much higher cost of interest to the end-borrowers.

The arguments for entering into these off-balance sheet liabilities are certainly worthy, especially when they involve aid to the developing world or to sectors of the domestic economy in need of intermediary assistance. But the price of a default has the potential to be substantial. In this respect, the United States is in a more precarious position than Britain because of the wider range of its commitments, both domestic and international.

These off-balance sheet liabilities have added significantly to the trend toward financial institutionalism in the post-Bretton Woods period. Most of the debt obligations issued by the borrowing agencies are backed by governments and purchased by institutional investors, mostly avoiding public scrutiny in the process. While the process is relatively understood in the United States by some in the investment community it is less understood in Britain because agency intermediation is rarely practised domestically in the UK. But the two major examples of institutionalism described in this chapter remain at different ends of the spectrum.

Although the rapid accumulation of international off-balance sheet liabilities apparently benefits developing nations, the trade that should ensue can have a positive trade effect upon the developed country lenders, especially if they provide the expertise and materials for Third World infrastructure projects. Quantifying the business engendered by the lending is difficult but clearly needs to be done in order to offset the criticisms that would eventually surround the contingent liabilities, especially if mismanagement creates a problem of moral hazard.

The shift toward institutional investing, on the one hand, and contingent government liabilities, on the other, only helps underscore how the investment community in general has drifted inexorably toward a centralisation of power. In the latter 1980s, carrying over to the present, some of this power has been put to new and effective purposes. Both British and American institutional investors have pressured the companies whose stock they hold to divest of their South African operations in the later 1980s, put pressure on companies to pay their chief executive officers less and have raised a score of environmental issues unheard of twenty years ago. In this respect, they are raising issues and forcing changes that individual investors would be powerless to address. However, these trends are still relatively new, so it remains to be seen whether the long-term social benefits of the new institutionalism will continue into the future.

Leaving the socio-political power of institutional investors aside, their day-to-day power in the marketplace also has a profound effect upon individuals and companies. As will be seen in Chapter 6, the stock market collapse in 1987 was mainly caused by institutional selling of equities in most of the major stock markets. When institutional investors decide to sell bonds of a company or international institution, enough selling will cause the cost of funds for that entity to rise, making capital investment or development lending more expensive. The centralisation of financial power leads to a centralisation of investment information that can have a significant impact far beyond what any individual investors could ever accomplish in the marketplace.

The interest rate and exchange rate volatility of the last twenty years has forced the small investor to the sidelines in the stock markets except in the instances of very strong bull markets, which attract many to mutual fund (unit trust) investments. At the same time, the same volatility has caused Third World borrowing to explode, requiring assistance from the developed countries in the form of development banking lending. While the more sophisticated consumers in developed countries demand assistance in the mortgage markets or additional consumer credit in order to maintain their standard of living, their counterparts in the Third and Fourth Worlds are beginning to ask, with increasing frequency, about what can be done to help develop infrastructure so that they too may legitimately address the question of living standards. Twenty-five years ago this was referred to as the 'north–south problem', but it has quickly become universally recognised as the clash of two different stages of consumerism.

CHALLENGES TO STATE SOVEREIGNTY

These two trends toward the institutionalism of financial power helped to bring about a subtle yet profound change in the complexion of sovereignty unknown only twenty years before. As the financial world became more complex and hot money was free to cross national boundaries, many political decisions were forced upon governments that would otherwise have been left to their own discretion. The marketplace was beginning to intrude into once purely domestic matters of policy. The reactions to economic policies in the financial markets became a contemporary chronicle that directly affected consumers by demonstrating an immediate reaction to politicians and their policies.

Politically, Jimmy Carter became the first casualty of volatile financial markets in the United States. Financially, the most notable casualty of the new environment was fixed interest rates. For years, mortgage rates and most consumer borrowing rates were fixed, encouraging home and consumer purchases because of the certainty involved. Investors in mortgage-backed securities and long bonds were in a different position, assuming most of the risk in those financings if rates rose precipitously. But as institutional investors become more powerful in the market, floating rate instruments became more popular as investors sought to hedge themselves against rate rises in the future. The popularity of the floating rate mortgage shifted risk from the investors in floating rate mortgages to the holders of the mortgages themselves. As the United States became more anglicised in this respect, it also became more institutionalised as a result.

By the mid-1980s, the political aspect of these influences was evident. Ever since Harold Wilson devalued the pound and Richard Nixon devalued the dollar, both blaming international speculators as the cause, domestic monetary policies were no longer solely in the realm of politicians and regulators. The best that could be done was to react to correct the trends developed in the markets; leading them was never a part of stated public policy. The old market adage that the markets lead the Federal Reserve (and the Bank of England by default) had now been extended to the entire spectrum of economic and financial events. The foreign exchange market made demands upon central banks that, if left unanswered, would cause considerable upset across the board. The stock markets had already proven that they were quite capable of uprooting presidents and prime ministers. The bond and money markets were a major factor in the defeat of Jimmy Carter in 1980 and the foreign exchange market helped unravel the Callaghan government in Britain, paving the way for a decade and a half of Conservative governments to follow.

Ironically, these events put many developed countries at the mercy of the markets in much the same way as developing countries were at the mercy of the IMF in some cases. Many countries, including the United States, were drawn into the 1980s version of Hobson's choice: either allow hot money to flow unimpeded across borders through the banking system and the financial markets, or risk missing the benefits of those flows, especially when the domestic markets needed an infusion of capital. The influx of foreign investment into the United States was one positive post 1971–72 benefit as was the massive foreign investment that would be attracted to the stock and bond markets after 1982.

After the Conservative and Republican governments assumed power in 1979 and 1981 respectively, contemporary consumer democracy became entrenched. After having made itself heard politically, consumerism was ready for a new era and any government not responding to its demands would not survive. The monetarist leanings of both the Conservatives and Republicans and the Federal Reserve provided a golden opportunity for both parties to become entrenched with voters. As will be seen in the next two chapters, a strong dollar created by the Federal Reserve's monetary policies and a pound supported by a government commitment to prudent spending helped create the conditions that would lead consumers to take heart and become an active force again, more so than at any time since the early 1970s.

While power was accruing to both institutional investors and governments alike, governmental control over exchange rates was becoming more distant in the United States and Britain. This was actually an erosion of state sovereignty as traditionally defined because both countries had maintained for years that control over their own monetary affairs was solely within their respective realms. Britain's traditional reluctance to embrace the monetary aspects of the EC and the Federal Reserve's central role in international monetary affairs since the First World War are evidence of this. But when inflation would force interest rates higher, affecting exchange rates in both countries, then the best that both governments would be able to do would be to accept the new exchange rate regime of the first half of the 1980s and attempt to accommodate themselves to it. By 1981, any pretence of returning to a Bretton Woods system would be gone forever as both governments realised that nimbly accommodating exchange rates was better than fighting them.

5

BANKING REFORMS ON BOTH SIDES

As the 1970s drew to a close, the banking systems in both Britain and the United States were in need of reform. Of the two, the American banking system was in much more need than the UK's. The Americans were operating a banking system created in the 1930s to prevent abuses from a past era. While priding itself on its economic record and status among the industrialised nations, the United States nevertheless was hobbled by its balkanised banking system, which was seriously out of step with the rapidly changing financial environment. Banks were slowly losing their natural monopoly over many financial services because of a great irony: the rules once intended to regulate and protect them now seriously hampered their competitiveness.

At the same time, the British banking system was also equally outdated but in a different way. As many of the industrialised countries moved closer to the regulatory/deregulatory phenomenon that characterised the 1980s especially, the UK was still mired in an earlier era as well. Although the Lifeboat operation by the Bank of England and the clearing banks had proven successful, the British banking system was still regulated by winks and nods from the Bank of England. British banking legislation was the opposite of the American: a patchwork of previous legislation defined banking *per se*. As commentators put it, the 'governor's eyebrows' became a gauge of how the central bank felt about banking topics. Furled brows meant the Bank did not agree with a clearing bank's methods or tactics in the marketplace, usually because no specific regulations existed that could guide clearing banks or others. In more traditional banking terms, the eyebrows were a metaphor for what both the British and Americans called moral suasion: the tendency for a central bank to convince its banks of the proper road to follow rather than enforce it by regulation or fiat.

That system would be severely tested in the late 1970s and early 1980s. It could be argued that in an international trend toward deregulation of financial institutions and markets, the UK system was well positioned because the Bank of England's informal rules had never been cast in stone to begin with. As a result, the UK should have had a flexibility to react to events in the marketplace that the Federal Reserve did not possess because of the bevy of laws and regulations that surrounded American banking practices. But the problem was still clear: banking in Britain, especially on the wholesale level, was becoming more and more competitive as foreign banks continued to be attracted to London because of the Euromarket and the other parallel markets that many of them sought to enter. Loose regulations would only lead to trouble if the new banks could not decipher the traditional UK banking metaphors, or if they simply decided to circumvent them.

The one single factor affecting banks on both sides of the Atlantic in the latter 1970s was the continued growth of the Euromarket, both the Eurodollar market for deposits and the Eurobond market. The deposit market was estimated to be about the size of American M1 by the beginning of the 1980s while the Eurobond market was issuing about one half the number of bonds appearing annually in the US corporate bond market. The impact on the American marketplace was significant. The Euromarkets in general served as a laboratory of sorts for new ideas and market practices. When these new ideas proved successful, they were quickly exported to the US domestic capital markets where some proved successful while others failed. One of the successful concepts that crossed the Atlantic in that fashion was that of dollar floating interest rates, an idea that had never been successfully used in the US domestic markets because of Regulation Q. However, it would not be long before the concept would prove to be an allure too strong to resist, especially after the Americans dismantled interest rate ceilings in the early 1980s.

The Euromarkets also had a pronounced effect upon the UK markets, although the pound sterling was not a major Eurocurrency. Even though the Bank of England had successfully weathered the fringe banking crisis with its reputation intact, the presence of so large an unregulated market on British soil would eventually put pressure on Parliament to regulate the domestic markets more than had been the case in the past. Fears of Euromarket problems spilling over to the domestic sector had been a concern when the Lifeboat was launched in 1973. The problem was simple but still somewhat vague: there were admitted links between the Euromarket and domestic markets although they were difficult to quantify. The presence of so many Eurocurrencies in banks based in Britain meant that some leakage could be expected to occur between them and the domestic UK market.

The UK credit markets were changing rapidly but appeared on the surface to be about fifteen years behind the Americans, at least in terms of consumer credit. Credit card use only began to become popular in the latter 1970s and early 1980s as the clearing banks adopted the American credit card franchises for their own customers. The cards quickly changed the face of British retail banking and consumerism. Many of the same discussions that were prevalent in the United States ten years before began to surface.

103

Namely, were credit cards to be considered money and, if so, did they pose any threats to monetary policy? When combined with the consumers' preference for contractual long-term financial assets, discussed in the last chapter, it was apparent that the UK financial services sector was in a state of change that would continue throughout the 1980s. The UK was in a state of transition between being a traditional cash and carry consumer society and one characterised by easy access to consumer credit. As a result, demands would be placed upon the banking system that would be hard to resist.

DEFINING BANKING IN THE UK

The 1970s were no less turbulent for the UK than they were for the United States. Adjustable rates of interest helped banks maintain a relatively stable course although the consumer ultimately paid the bill for escalating interest rates. The revolution in British banking would not only come because of bank failures and general dissatisfaction of the commercial banks with the central bank, as in the United States. The true revolution would come when Britain finally joined the rest of the industrialised nations in giving more form to the Bank of England, which had previously been somewhat amorphous, while at the same time finally defining what was meant by banking in the Banking Act of 1979.

Critics of the British manner of banking often pointed to the loose way in which banking was defined and regulated prior to 1979. There was no one piece of legislation that defined British banking: what the banks could and could not do. Commercial banks had accumulated their various functions over the years in a patchwork fashion, many times by applying to the Bank of England to perform a specific function, such as deposit taking or dealing in foreign exchange. The London and Scottish clearers all performed the major banking functions (except investment banking) but it was difficult for new banks to break into the field quickly as full service institutions. That sort of oversight had enabled the fringe banks to carve out a significant amount of wholesale business for themselves in the 1960s although they only performed limited functions. But after the changes of the 1970s, even banking in the traditional manner needed more definition and regulation.

The foreign exchange problems brought on by the collapse of Bretton Woods and Britain's entry into the EC brought pressure on Parliament to rectify the situation by finally defining British banking. Most of the pressure that culminated in the Banking Act of 1979 was international in origin. Britain no longer had the luxury of operating a system where everyone was supposed to understand the rules of the game without having them written down. EC directives and London's central location were attracting more foreign banks to Britain than ever before and it could not be assumed that they would all play fairly without a well-defined set of rules.

The role of the Bank of England in the new banking legislation would be vital to London's continued pre-eminence in international finance. While directing the Lifeboat had shown that the loose British system did work well in bad circumstances, the point was to ensure that situations like the fringe crisis never occurred again. The Bank of England had always operated as a central bank that knew well what the clearing banks and others were doing in the marketplace: it had acted as a referee with a player's knowledge of the game.[1] The idea now would be to codify that power, define banking and set out a set of regulations controlling it all under one bit of legislation.

Despite the fact that new regulatory powers were embedded in the Banking Act of 1979, the powers themselves were somewhat different than those found in the United States or the EC countries. The idea of gentlemanly powers exercised by the Bank of England was still found in the Act, meaning that moral suasion was still a tool of monetary policy well worth practising. While all central banks practised it to some extent, moral suasion continued to mean reading the 'governor's eyebrows'. Now the eyebrows had been to the cosmetician for greater definition.

The Banking Act required all banks in the UK to be authorised by the Bank of England while distinguishing between a bank *per se* and a licensed deposit taker. It also established the standards for authorisation and created a deposit protection scheme for depositors. According to the legislation, only 'recognised' institutions were able to accept deposits, a bow to the troubles caused by the fringe banking crisis. However, the Act did differentiate between banks and licensed deposit takers. The former were able to make loans while the latter were limited in what they could do with deposits. Ordinarily, they were placed in the money market at a higher rate of interest. The Bank of England was the obvious regulator of these banking institutions and it set up several new departments within itself to ensure that the new regulations would be complied with. Essentially, the guidelines brought the UK closer to EC guidelines, envisioning the day when the European Community would have an integrated banking system within its borders.

The similarities between the broad guidelines of the Banking Act and the Glass–Steagall Act in the United States are striking. Both defined commercial banking in their respective countries despite being enacted thirty-six years apart. The Banking Act was not as specific concerning non-permissible activities since they had already been proscribed in the patchwork of legislation preceding 1979. But the fact that both pieces of legislation sought to define and re-establish the authority of the central banks in times of financial instability were noteworthy, as was including depositor insurance schemes in both acts. When exchange controls were finally dismantled in 1979 and foreign banks continued to open offices in the City, it was clear that deposit insurance would be necessary because of the intense competition UK banking was undergoing. Although this was a different reason from that which prompted the Americans to establish deposit insurance in the 1930s, the similarities were nevertheless unmistakable.

The deposit protection scheme was closer to American-style retail banking than it was to the European. The Act provided for deposit insurance for amounts up to £10,000 but only insured 75 per cent of an account's value. At the time, American deposit insurance covered 100 per cent of an account for a maximum of $40,000 per account at either banks or thrift institutions. As in the United States thirty-six years earlier, the insurance was the least popular proposal because strong banks felt they would be penalised by subsidising weaker banks when paying premiums to the scheme. But some sort of depositor insurance was necessary in order to allay customers' fears in times of financial instability.

As Peter Cooke of the Bank of England put it, the depositor protection scheme 'was never intended to serve as an arrangement for the comprehensive underpinning of the institutions covered by the legislation'.[2] There was an assumption that more comprehensive insurance programmes such as those in the United States could effectively underwrite a bank's imprudent actions when lending deposits because of the lassitude that the insurance plans could create among depositors and even shareholders. Bankers assuming that insurance would protect them from imprudent lending would then began to lend imprudently. That particular criticism would reappear a few years later, especially in the United States, during the Third World lending crisis and then shortly thereafter during the savings and loan crisis that effectively destroyed the thrift industry. Although the topic was not raised for another decade, it had always been assumed that full deposit insurance for relatively large amounts of money raised significant problems of moral hazard.

Although the Banking Act went a long way toward bridging the gap between tradition and the growing internationalisation of financial institutions in Britain, it would be superseded by another act within the next eight years. The new deposit insurance scheme was tapped several times within five years of initial operation by failed banks but, for the most part, the new environment worked tolerably well with a few exceptions. The most notable was the distinction made by the 1979 Act between banks and licensed deposit takers, the latter being less than a full-service lending institution that operated in the shadows of the banking industry, much as the fringe banks had before them. That distinction finally would be eliminated in 1987, as will be seen in Chapter 6.

RE-DEFINING BANKING IN THE UNITED STATES

Banking problems in the US were more complicated than those in Britain and would required much more attention in the 1980s. Although the domestic credit markets were showing signs of stress by the late 1970s, most of the legislation passed in the same time period centred on international banking developments. The reason for what appears in hindsight to be an unnecessary preoccupation with the international sector was the perception that the US banking system was under attack by Euromarket practices that were inimical to the health of the domestic banking system.

As the Euromarket grew in power and influence, many banks found it a convenient method of avoiding domestic US banking regulations. American banks and foreign banks with branches in London could make loans in dollars to domestic US customers from overseas without having to create reserves against deposits. This was especially enticing to American banks since their required reserves did not earn interest at the Federal Reserve banks. Although Eurodollar rates were marginally higher than domestic US rates, the opportunity savings were especially valued by American banks before Congress passed legislation effectively putting a halt to this round-tripping activity. The borrowers themselves were American multinationals and other businesses that came to view Eurodollar borrowing, based on a spread over the London Inter-Bank Offered Rate (LIBOR), as more flexible and often cheaper than loans based on the prime rate of interest.[3]

Despite the slowdown in round-tripping effected by the International Banking Act of 1979, the explosion in international lending activities continued unabated. The major depositors in the Euromarket were OPEC producers while the major borrowers were developing countries. As both the supply and demand for Eurodollars continued, most banks were realising strong profit margins on syndicated loans, regardless of where their borrowers were located. When Eurodollar lending by American banks to domestic customers slowed, lending to developing countries picked up the slack. This was the sort of diversity that the banks sought in light of the geographical restrictions they faced at home. The international lending boom was in full stride in October 1979 when the Federal Reserve changed tack on monetary policy, using open market operations to force interest rates higher. Within two years, Eurodollar rates were the highest interest rates on US dollars recorded in the twentieth century as borrowers faced the full brunt of the restrictive monetary policy without the benefit of caps of any sort on their borrowings.

Throughout the 1970s, loans at the major American banks increased while equity on their books declined as a percentage of assets. This created the potentially dangerous situation where more risky loans were being made in the international market while driving down the equity capital on the books of many large American banks. Although it could not be seen due to the general euphoria of the time, within several years high US dollar interest rates, the declining capital ratios and the number of loans made to marginal borrowers would all collide to create the Third World debt crisis among the banks not only in the United States but in most industrialised countries.

The outdated American banking laws were again coming home to roost. One of the major reasons that American banks sought overseas business in the Euromarkets was because of a panoply of restrictions at home. One of the most notable was the prohibition against branching across state lines. Banks had to remain in their home states, meaning that those which desired to expand and diversify their businesses domestically were unable to do so.[4] Many were also confined to certain parts of their home state by state banking authorities. But opening branches in foreign countries was permitted and, when combined with the benefits of the Euromarkets, that made Eurodollar banking extremely attractive. Once the banks expanded their horizons internationally beyond their multinational American clients operating abroad they increased their exposure to risk substantially, despite the fact that many of their new clients were sovereign states in need of funds.

Despite the plunge into the Euromarket, many banks were still less than enamoured with the Federal Reserve's handling of inflation and adherence to the rigid policies of the past. Interest-free reserves at the Federal Reserve were a contentious matter, causing many banks to withdraw from its system, opting to return to their state charters instead. Between 1975 and 1980 about 375 banks turned in their Federal Reserve charters, taking with them the Reserve's authority to dictate reserve levels at a time when inflation was increasing. This embarrassing situation was another problem that could be attributed directly to the outdated banking legislation in effect at the time.[5] The crisis in American banking was increasing along with inflation, consumer prices and bond yields.

The most critical point in post-Bretton Woods American financial history occurred in October 1979 when the Federal Reserve, under its new chairman, Paul Volcker, announced its change in monetary policy. Beginning in that month, the Federal Reserve actively began to target the amount of bank reserves available in the money market. In order to eventually curtail inflation, the Federal Reserve would subsequently use its open market operations to raise the federal funds rate, making reserves more expensive for the banks requiring them. While the markets generally applauded the move, the new volatility that followed in the markets was not anticipated as American interest rates were on a course to historic new highs.

One of the first victims of the new interest rate environment was the first bond issue ever floated for the IBM Corporation. Announced earlier the same day that the Federal Reserve announced its new intentions, the issue fell dramatically in price, providing an inauspicious debut for IBM and the new thrust of monetary policy. Both short-term and long-term interest rates were affected almost instantly by the emphasis on bank reserves, and the upward spiral in interest rates had officially begun a new stage as the Federal Reserve was intent on raising the federal funds rate as high as necessary to choke off inflation. Prior to 1979, the American bond markets were relatively quiet places where traders were not accustomed to quick price changes and the concomitant changes in yields. Within a year, the bond markets would match the stock markets for price volatility, causing almost equal disillusion among investors accustomed to holding debt securities rather than trading them quickly.

The new monetary policy became the straw that broke the camel's back in the banking world. By using open market operations, especially reverse repurchase agreements, to put upward pressure on interest rates, the Federal Reserve was ensuring that the panoply of banking laws would be strained even further.[6] Money market mutual funds grew even further as interest rates rose and general disillusionment with the Carter administration began to grow. The financial markets were not as disheartened as the general public since President Carter's selection of Volcker to head the Federal Reserve was warmly applauded on Wall Street because of his wide experience in central banking and general popularity in the financial community. But the public reaction was not as understanding. High interest rates and inflation, accompanied by a low rate of economic growth, all led to disillusion with the administration and contributed to the growing perception that the United States had lost its way in the world.

The problems in the markets in general only helped underline the structural problems that the banking industry in particular faced. Despite the size of the economy, the United States banking system's archaic nature came to the surface because of rising inflation. The largest economy in the world had a central bank that could only effectively regulate those commercial banks that were members of one of its regional banks. Reserve requirements were only binding on the same institutions although they were the nation's largest. But regulations did not apply to the state chartered banks that were now increasing as the federally chartered were leaving the Federal Reserve in large numbers to protest the inability of the central bank to pay interest on reserves. Equally, although many of those banks that were federally chartered traditionally bore the name 'national', outdated banking laws forbade them from crossing state lines so they were in fact oversized state banks, many of which were drawn into the international sector seeking diversification that they could not find at home. The direct results of the collapse of Bretton Woods were apparent not only in the economy in general and in the banks in particular but also at the Federal Reserve. Without legislation enabling it to respond, the entire banking system and its chief but partial regulator were doomed to obscurity.

Responding to the structural banking crisis, Congress passed the Depository Institutions Deregulation and Monetary Control Act (DIDMCA) in 1980. The most ambitious piece of banking legislation since the 1930s, the DIDMCA had two sides as its name implied – deregulation and monetary control. On one side, it sought to dismantle Regulation

Q, enabling banks and thrifts to become more competitive in the market-place when paying interest on accounts. On the other, it sought to give the Federal Reserve extended powers so that many deposit taking institutions did not escape its authority over reserve levels and other supervisory matters.

Unfortunately, gradualism was adopted concerning Regulation Q. The Act set up a committee made of the top regulators from different government agencies and the Federal Reserve, mandated to eliminate ceilings over a six-year phasing out period. But market conditions continued to deteriorate as interest rates climbed steadily higher and it quickly became apparent that a gradual approach to deregulation was not enough to prevent the disintermediation plaguing the banks. But before Congress could act again, another relic of the past was employed by the Carter administration in an overtly political attempt to intercede in the credit markets in the late winter of 1980. Time was running out on the administration because 1980 was an election year and inflation showed no signs of abating.

The Carter administration invoked the Credit Control Act at that time, a vestige of the Nixon administration that harkened back to controls often invoked after the Second World War. The controls were aimed chiefly at extensions of credit from existing levels and were aimed at consumer spending as well as wholesale lending at banks. The Federal Reserve was at first reluctant to go along with the President's plan, feeling that politics was interfering with the course of monetary policy. In the end, however, it was decided that to go against the President would be imprudent and the Federal Reserve helped design and administer the anti-inflation plan.[7] The Federal Reserve was authorised to be the agent for controlling credit, which included licensing persons or transactions that involved credit use. Temporary controls were also placed on the use of credit cards and increased reserve requirements were placed on certain types of bank accounts. On the face of it, the controls looked like a strong political attempt to bring down inflation by cutting the demand for money. While not attacking the underlying causes of inflation, they did nevertheless succeed as a temporary palliative. But the restrictions on consumer credit, not particularly effective, did cause the administration political problems because it was one of the rare attacks on consumption and would quickly become associated with what was generally believed to be an ineffective Democratic administration.

The controls returned some order to the credit markets but proved to be short lived. By the end of the summer, they were lifted and the markets returned to their inflationary behaviour and bond prices began to drop again. The economy also came to an abrupt halt and the recession of 1980 began. In this instance, a stagnant economy was beset with inflation at the same time, evoking the term 'stagflation'. The pattern of both American and British inflation at the time can be found in Figure 5.1.

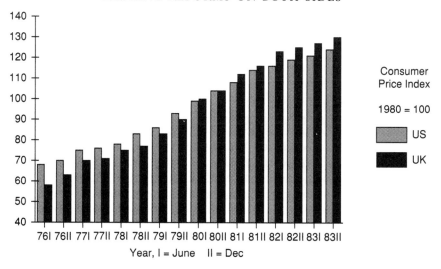

Figure 5.1 US and UK inflation

Source: IMF, *Financial Statistics,* various issues

As interest rate and currency markets again became unsettled, political events followed hard on their heels, helping to seriously damage the reputation of the Carter administration. When domestic economic conditions were coupled with American frustration over the Iranian hostage crisis, the fate of the Democratic administration was sealed and a Republican victory in the November 1980 presidential election was almost guaranteed. However, by the autumn of 1980, the banking system was still not free of its restraints, despite the DIDMCA. Deposit rates were not free to follow the market and until they were the banking system, including the thrifts, was still in jeopardy.

THE RISE OF THE DOLLAR

In the nine years since the Bretton Woods system had disintegrated, most financial events had no precedents in the post-war period. Interest rates had climbed inexorably higher and the currency markets had displayed unsettling conditions not seen since the 1930s. Both British and American interest rates, along with the Canadian and the French, were now all poised to rise to even higher, unprecedented levels within a year that would severely test all governments that had the misfortune to be in office as these events unfolded. The financial horizon was filled mostly with clouds, but one actually had a silver lining that was not expected in 1979, when the Federal Reserve changed the course of US monetary policy.

Although most investors had been registering serious losses on their positions in stocks and bonds, some currency speculators began to detect a new trend developing in the early 1980s. On the face of it, this trend should have proved more disturbing than it did at the time although its longer-term consequences for the United States were hardly healthy. But when the new trend began, it appeared as a moral victory for the Americans because, after so many years of relative currency decline, the dollar was showing healthy signs of life as the 1980s began. This development flew in the face of many time-worn (if not proven) theories of currency fluctuations and general movements.

Before the dollar began its phenomenal rise to post-Bretton Woods heights, sterling also showed unusual signs of life after almost a decade of volatility and the well-publicised IMF package in 1976. Upon entering office, the Thatcher government announced a strong commitment to bring down public spending and eventually interest rates by adopting monetary prudence. In the autumn of 1980 at a dinner in the City of London, Mrs Thatcher stated that 'We shall take whatever action is necessary to contain the growth of the money supply. This government, unlike so many of its predecessors, will face up to economic realities.'[8] That sort of sentiment, plus the concomitant rise in interest rates announced by the government in the autumn of 1980 (MLR was raised to 17 per cent) gave the markets heart since it sounded much like the pronouncements from the Federal Reserve, which was attempting the same thing by allowing interest rates to rise on the back of its open market operations. Ideologically, Mrs Thatcher acknowledged Keith Joseph's 1976 paper *Monetarism is not Enough*, stating that public spending cuts and borrowing cuts would also be necessary in order to curtail inflation and promote economic growth.[9] The Federal Reserve's new policy was not mentioned although this particular action marked the beginning of a convergence of both views and policies by the Bank of England and the Federal Reserve.

Whatever the origins of the Thatcher government's leaning toward monetarism, the concentration on controlling money supply growth was the first in a series of similar policy adoptions that would bring the two banking systems closer together over the next decade. But the immediate effect of the announcement about better monetary control and high interest rates was a substantially higher value for the pound. In dollar terms, the pound rose from its $1.75 level in 1977 to $2.45 in 1980, a level not seen in ten years. Many reasons were given for the rise. Most prominent was sterling's role as a petrocurrency, which was vastly overdone. The main impetus for the rise was high interest rates, especially since they were being viewed as being part of an aggressive monetary policy. Even before the Federal Reserve would prove the point conclusively, the Thatcher government proved that foreign exchange values can be increased dramatically by adopting a tough monetary policy and pursuing it by tightening interest rates.

However, the strong pound proved ephemeral. By mid-1980, sterling began to decline against the dollar as the US currency began its somewhat meteoric rise against all currencies. In sterling's case, economic fundamentals had come home to roost. British productivity and competitiveness were still suspect since there was no fundamental reason for sterling to rise to its highest dollar value in ten years.

The rise of the dollar between late 1980 and March 1985 was even more puzzling on the face of it were it not for the clash of Fed policy on interest rates and the Treasury's abandonment of foreign exchange market intervention after 1981. This can be seen in Figure 5.2. Like Britain, the United States was plagued with a stubbornly unacceptable unemployment rate, declining competitiveness and stagflation. Nevertheless, the dollar began to rise against all of the other hard currencies on the back of high interest rates. The rise was even more peculiar when taken in context of textbook theories of how and why a currency should appreciate. But the currency markets adopted a different view, betting on the Federal Reserve's monetarist stance and the ability of the economy to recover in the face of adverse domestic and international pressures. The US Treasury seized upon this stance and quickly abandoned its foreign exchange market intervention that had been actively pursued since the Carter administration in order to shore up the dollar. Now the Fed was doing the Treasury's job for it.

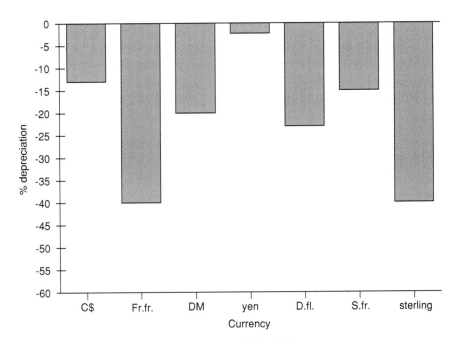

Figure 5.2 Appreciation of the dollar, 1980–85

Source: Federal Reserve *Bulletin*, various issues

The rise of the dollar was quickly seized upon by the Reagan administration as a means whereby consumption could be maintained in the face of high real interest rates and slack economic activity. Not responsible for the rise in interest rates, the administration nevertheless used it to its best advantage. Consumers would be able to continue, and increase, purchasing foreign goods as long as the dollar remained strong. The Treasury could take the opportunity to fund the increasing budget deficit, brought about by the Economic Recovery Tax Act of 1982, by borrowing from foreign investors who were attracted to the high yields on US Treasury securities. In 1983, Martin Feldstein, Chairman of the Council of Economic Advisors, stated that in the face of a choice between a lower dollar, meaning a loss of capital inflows created by foreigners, and a loss of exports, the latter would be preferable because financing imports should be given priority. Conversely, a 'weaker dollar and smaller trade deficit would also mean less capital inflow from the rest of the world and therefore a lower level of domestic investment in plant and equipment and in housing'.[10]

Also buried in the mountain of economic arguments surrounding high interest rates, a strong dollar, increasing deficits and domestic investment was the matter of consumer expenditure. Arguments about official or unofficial exchange rate policies could not afford to ignore the effect that a lower dollar would have upon consumers' ability to continue purchasing, even if those purchases came to be centred more and more on imports. When balancing a lower dollar and what was thought to be a temporary increase in the budget deficit Feldstein came down firmly in favour of an increase in the deficit behind a strong dollar because domestic investment and 'interest-sensitive consumer spending' should not have had to be reduced. It was better to allow exports to temporarily suffer.[11]

Early in the five-year history of the dollar's rise, that position was speculative at best but began to look far better as time wore on. With inflation and short-term interest rates about even in late 1980, the fundamental outlook for the dollar was problematic. But politically the outlook was somewhat more sanguine, although it was too early to tell what the new Reagan administration's economic policies would be. American self-esteem was at a low point, hindered by perceived failures in foreign affairs (despite the Carter administration's negotiating an Israeli–Egyptian peace treaty) along with rising inflation and the decline of the basic smokestack industries. But a more popular president and stimulants such as the Economic Reform Tax Act and the Garn–St Germain Act gave the market heart until the Mexican debt crisis emerged in August 1982.

When the Mexicans informed the Federal Reserve that they were technically broke and could not afford to keep maintaining their debt payments to the international banking syndicates that had loaned them more than $60 billion over the previous decade, the debt crisis officially began. The Federal Reserve's first reaction was to lower short-term interest rates temporarily and encourage the banks to form a committee to work out new arrangements for Mexico. A default would have been unthinkable for both sides for it would have meant economic chaos in the banking systems of the developed country lenders and a collapse of economic development in Mexico itself. But the crisis served as a catalyst, bringing the UK and US banking systems even closer since they now shared both similar and common problems.

The rise of the dollar did not hinder the foreign investment trend that had developed in the United States after 1972; if anything, it helped accelerate it. While American assets began to become increasingly expensive for direct foreign investors, foreign firms nevertheless continued to acquire American assets at a record pace. The dollar itself continued its steady rise, the real rate of interest was high until 1985 (suggesting a low return on capital for hard asset investors) and the mood in the country was turning sour toward visible foreign investment, especially from the Japanese, the most publicised group.

The rise in direct foreign investment in the 1970s had caused enough concern in Congress that two separate acts had been passed calling for studies to determine the extent of foreign ownership of American assets. The result was numerous Department of Commerce studies through the 1980s attempting to determine who owned what. They also led to a new definition of what exactly constituted direct foreign investment; after 1980 any company that was 10 per cent or more in foreign hands was deemed under foreign control.[12] Clearly, the United States was worried about the effect of a low dollar in the 1970s but after the dollar began to rise the fears became more intense. That was because a shift had occurred in foreign investment patterns.

The amount of direct foreign investment in the United States increased significantly after 1980 despite the high value of the dollar. This was partly due to the increased values of those existing investments already in the country. Inflation and the desire of many parent companies to keep their retained earnings in the United States rather than repatriate them helped increase the value of the foreign owned companies. Once the stock market began to rally in 1982, equity prices increased and many companies with only partial foreign ownership were also marked higher in value. But foreign companies also continued to pour money into direct American investments. After the recession of 1980–82 ended, many foreign firms, especially the Japanese, wanted to be well placed to capture sales in the US once consumers began to spend more freely again.

The influx and higher valuation for foreign investments plus the lower threshold for determining the number of assets under foreign control gave the appearance that the United States was being bought up by foreign investors. In reality, the Japanese were the largest net investors since the breakdown of Bretton Woods, while the other traditional direct investors

– the British, Canadians, Dutch and Swiss – all managed to keep their relatively influential positions by investing fresh capital or retaining earnings at the American companies they controlled. But the purported Japanese threat was the one seized upon by the press as symbolic of American industrial decline. One part of the singling out of the Japanese was because of cultural differences, the other simply because the invaders were '*nouveaux riches*'.

Japanese products sold in the United States, whether as imports from Japan or as the products of transplant operations manufacturing in the United States, were much more visible than British goods or services. Because of the common language and years of foreign investment experience in each other's countries, many British goods and brand names were assumed to be American and vice versa. The same could not be said of Japanese goods, whose names were distinctly foreign. As a result, as the number of Japanese goods sold increased so too did the perception that American civilisation (consumer civilisation) was on the decline.

While the British remained at the top of the league tables for the amount of foreign direct investment in the United States, despite the surge from Japan in the 1980s, even the increasing amounts from the traditional investors was interpreted as a sign of American economic decline. For example, Graham and Krugman (1989) viewed the increase in investments from all industrialised sources in the 1980s as a sign of the 'general decline of US economic preeminence rather than a by-product of the trade deficits of the 1980s'. But to avoid misinterpretation, they attributed the increase in foreign direct investment as a consequence of the decline, not a cause of it.[13] This trade-related interpretation is consistent with the general notion that US industrial performance was in serious trouble in the 1980s, but is much less consistent with the interpretation that the increase in investment was the product of a strong dollar, on the one hand, and the desire to penetrate the American marketplace, on the other.

The increased foreign investments can be taken as something of a compliment in the United States given the lack of incentives given to foreign direct investors, at least by the federal government. Unlike Britain, where tax incentives have gone hand in hand with stipulations about using local labour and supplies, the American policy has been to leave the matter of incentives to state governments since it is the states that are the primary beneficiaries of direct foreign investment. Although the British policy had its successes as well as its fiascos, the UK policy has always sought to encourage foreign direct investment while the Americans have seemed to take an ambivalent position.

A stronger case can be made for bullishness on the foreign portfolio investment side where many trade-related and manufacturing factors do not enter the equation. In this respect, the British and the Americans have run neck and neck throughout most of the twentieth century. Encouraging foreigners to purchase domestic portfolio investments, mostly shares until the 1970s, the financial communities in both countries realised early that the expectations of foreign investors toward domestic investments was a particularly good gauge of both expectations for the domestic economy and the currency at the same time.

Both governments benefited greatly from foreign investment in their respective government bond markets beginning in the 1970s. Floating exchange rates freed up a good deal of hot money seeking a temporary home and efficient, liquid bond markets became the favourite of international investors; they became places where the securities could be sold on short notice at a reasonable price so that the currency could also be sold in order to invest elsewhere. The narrow spreads and sizeable volumes in the Treasury bond and gilt markets made both magnets for international investors, both speculators and longer-term investors.

Turnover in Treasury bonds increased dramatically on the part of foreign investors. During the period of the dollar's rise, gross foreign turnover increased eight times. By 1986, it had increased almost twenty times. But this turnover should not be attributed to net demand alone, for many foreign investors were actively trading bond positions the same way that many speculators traded stocks. Basically, the original interest in Treasuries had to do with a vote of confidence in the Federal Reserve's new monetary policy. The continued trading meant that the same investors were not adverse to trade their positions actively, attempting to profit on the Federal Reserve's successes.

A good deal of the demand for government bonds in most of the hard currency countries came from Japan. After the Ministry of Finance liberalised yen movements in 1980–81, institutional money was released providing much demand for American, British, Canadian, Dutch and German government securities. Japan had become a net exporter of capital in its own right, and Japanese demand for Treasury bonds actually exceeded the amount of direct foreign investment in the United States by Japanese companies. This clearly was the result of the unusually large trade balances held by Japan against the United States, but also could be interpreted in hedging terms. By placing their large balances in US dollars, the Japanese were hedging against the probability that the yen would decline against the dollar. In the early to mid-1980s, this proved to be a poor bet. But for the first half of the decade, the Japanese were traders more than investors.

The same was true of the British. Along with the Japanese, they accounted for about 50 per cent of all Treasury market turnover attributed to foreigners.[14] Their net figures were less impressive, however, lagging behind the Germans, suggesting that the Japanese and the British were among the largest speculators in Treasuries. This phenomenon was one of the first functional proofs of the internationalisation of the world's financial markets

117

in the 1980s, providing proof that money would flow quickly from one market to another in the absence of barriers to capital movements. But again, the British activity was much more muted than that of the Japanese, who attracted a good deal of attention with their activities in the market.

While usually considered to have occurred for different reasons, the increase in US investments of both types by the British and the Japanese can be attributed to the same reason – currency hedging. Graham and Krugman (1989) demonstrated that about 80 per cent of the equity of US subsidiaries was held by single foreign parent companies in the mid-1980s while about 80 per cent of the debt was provided by US sources.[15] This means that subsidiaries were subject to infusions of debt capital from the bond markets, public or private, while equity continued to be provided by the parent company. This appears logical from a hedger's point of view in that if the dollar declined so too would the parent company's long-term liabilities for translation purposes. Profits in the subsidiaries could be retained (kept in dollars) or repatriated into the parent's currency depending upon market conditions.

The same was true of portfolio investments. As long as the dollar increased in value, purchases and sales of Treasuries were subject to the foreign exchange market as well as to local credit market conditions. The increased foreign investment in government bonds demonstrated a risk that had not been witnessed before in international investing since the days of the gold exchange standard – domestic credit markets were subject to influences originating in the foreign exchange market. Increasing internationalisation, on the one hand, had created something of a black box hazard, on the other.

Because of this very real risk, the securities authorities and banking authorities of many of the major industrialised countries began to allow foreign securities dealers/banks access to their local market for government bonds. Dealers which were members of the primary dealers group in the US or a recognised gilt dealer in the UK were important to regulators in two respects: first, they would receive the lion's share of business from their domestic clients in the host countries' bonds; and, second, they would be easier to regulate than if they remained outside the recognised circle. While cross-membership has always been touted as a sign of increasing internationalism among the world's leading markets, it was not without its more practical, security-conscious side as well.

COMPETITION AND TRADE PROBLEMS

While the strong dollar was attracting foreign investments and helping to finance the expanding budget deficit, it also helped purchase a vast amount of imported goods creating an enormous trade deficit, especially with Japan and Germany. For the exporters, increased sales to the United

States helped to offset their weak currencies and some of the capital exports attracted by the dollar. But few would have been able to foresee the Americans' penchant for foreign manufactured goods. When they did realise it, the strong demand only strengthened their desire to set up shop directly in the United States, attempting to satisfy both demand and political considerations at the same time.

Americans had developed a strong preference for Japanese and German manufactured goods within the previous fifteen years. American motor cars and electronics, on the other hand, had acquired a reputation for shoddiness that caused considerable distress in manufacturing generally as consumers began to vote for foreign goods with their dollars. Ford's near bankruptcy in 1980 and the decline of smokestack and manufacturing industries were all cited as examples of the lack of American competitiveness. Leaving the managerial and quality control issues aside, however, the lack of competitiveness could also be attributed to the effects of high real rates of interest and their effect in turn upon the value of the dollar. Simply put, why bother to develop a better mousetrap at home when one can well afford to buy a better one from abroad?

The relative decline of American manufacturing industry in the late 1970s and early to mid-1980s is usually interpreted as a decline of the American worker and management no longer hungry enough to compete with their major industrial rivals. In this respect, the Americans and the British fell into the same category. While the analogy is generally valid, it is not for that overly simple reason. The decline of both countries' manufacturing industries in the post-Bretton Woods era can be attributed to high real costs of capital that put a serious damper upon capital investment. Without that investment, new product design began to lag at a time when consumers were demanding newer and better products and showed a marked willingness to pay for them.

Table 5.1 shows capital activity in the manufacturing sector for both the United States and Britain. In both cases, it can be seen that when interest rates were at historic post-war highs in both countries capital investment declined as borrowing and raising of equity capital also declined. The erratic performance in both countries provides a non-subjective answer as to why American and British manufacturing competitiveness declined in the late 1970s and early to mid-1980s. Interest rates were too high in nominal and then in real terms, and price/earnings ratios were low in the stock markets. Under those conditions, the best that British and American companies could do was to wait: unfortunately the price paid was high. Both fell behind in research and development and their products fell on the list of consumer choices behind German and Japanese imports. Interest rates were lower in both of those countries and Japanese price/earnings ratios higher, translating into a cheaper cost of equity capital.

At the same time, high interest rates were taking their toll on British

Table 5.1a Capital issues and investment in manufacturing, USA (billions US$) total amounts

	1978	1979	1980	1981	1982	1983	1984	1985
New common	7.50	7.75	16.85	23.55	25.45	44.30	18.50	29.0
New bonds	36.80	40.10	53.20	45.10	53.60	68.50	109.7	165.7
New capital investment	67.30	98.60	115.8	126.7	119.6	111.1	138.7	153.4

Source: Federal Reserve *Bulletin*, various issues

Table 5.1b Capital issues and investment in manufacturing, UK (billions £) increase from year to year

	1978	1979	1980	1981	1982	1983	1984	1985
New common	0.924	0.96	1.98	1.835	0.965	2.289	1.422	4.23
New bonds	-0.127	-0.276	-0.20	0.67	0.58	0.98	0.87	0.527
New capital investment	1.983	1.743	1.518	1.900	2.907	4.675	3.562	2.300

Source: Central Statistical Office, *Financial Statistics*, various issues

and American companies' balance sheets. Table 5.2 illustrates the liquidity problems that non-financial firms in both countries were finding themselves in the late 1970s and early to mid-1980s. Higher costs of debt service, declining sales due to the 1980–82 recession and declining exports (especially in the US) began to corrode companies' liquidity positions and the quick ratios of many began to decline as a result. Faced with this problem, many firms did not use the markets for fresh financing for fear of poor acceptance by investors or that credit ratings would decline. Manufacturing, one of the industries most reliant on long-term capital investment, had little chance in the face of stiff foreign competition even from high wage countries such as Germany.

The decline in American competitiveness cannot be attributed to high interest rates and a strong dollar alone but they were nevertheless the major factors. As mentioned in earlier chapters, Britain's lack of competitiveness

Table 5.2 Liquidity of non-financial companies (quick ratios, in per cent)

Year	1977	1978	1979	1980	1981	1982	1983	1984
US	0.96	0.92	0.88	0.88	0.86	0.87	0.91	0.90
UK	0.93	0.93	0.92	0.92	0.94	0.85	1.15	1.01

Source: Federal Reserve *Bulletin*, various issues and Central Statistical Office, *Financial Statistics*, various issues

had already been established for several decades and now the Americans found themselves in the same situation. Part of the solution came with the increasing establishment of many more service industries that were less reliant on long-term capital. But for those industries that did rely on a steady supply of long-term funds, the outlook was not optimistic. Unlike foreign firms that could raise debt capital in the US dollar markets when costs were tolerable, US firms had fewer options. Those markets that could have supplied lower-cost funds – the German and the Japanese – were not easily accessed by foreign firms, so the choice was to borrow high-cost dollars or to wait until interest rates fell. The wait would prove costly in many respects.

The strong dollar certainly aided consumers but the cost became apparent in both the merchandise trade deficit and the federal budget deficit. What was thought to be a temporary phenomenon quickly became entrenched as the combination of the dollar's strength and lower-income tax rates made the importing of foreign goods and capital necessary. Between 1980 and 1986, the merchandise trade deficit increased from a deficit of about $12 billion to almost $170 billion. During the same time, the budget deficit increased from around $75 billion to over $220 billion. But the twin deficits had a message for policymakers that was often overlooked, as absolute against real numbers were argued over when discussing long-term trends. The high dollar exchange rate was telling industry that consumers preferred high-quality foreign manufactured goods. But the budget deficit, when coupled with the exchange rate, suggested that financing new capital ventures to make industry more competitive would be difficult because of the high interest rate regime. Real rates of interest on long-term bonds remained stubbornly high during that period, requiring much short-term roll-over financing and reliance upon stop-gap measures by many companies to remain competitive in the face of stiff foreign competition.

A BLUEPRINT FOR DISASTER

The banking industry appeared to be one place where legislation could prove an effective remedy to national economic problems. But one of the provisions of the DIDMCA was to prove disastrous for the thrift industry. Since thrifts, as building societies in Britain, were limited purpose banks, they were exposed to the long end of the yield curve. By traditionally holding about 80 per cent of their assets in mortgages, they were severely exposed if long-term interest rates began to rise, leaving them with low yielding assets for which not even a mortgage assistance agency would pay nominal value in the market. In order to alleviate this stress on the savings industry, the DIDMCA allowed thrifts to purchase corporate bonds up to 20 per cent of their assets. Logically, corporate bonds yielded more than traditional mortgages or mortgage-backed securities so as expanded assets they seemed to be a viable remedy for low yielding mortgages.

The impact of that particular provision would take some time before making itself felt in the marketplace. But within two years, Congress passed another piece of legislation intending to liberalise the deposits and investments of thrift institutions even more. In 1981, the thrift industry as a whole lost money over the previous year and assets continued to be marked down in value as interest rates climbed higher. Congress then took quick action to allow depository institutions to offer accounts that were competitive with the money market funds. The new accounts were called money market deposit accounts. No sooner was the ink dry on the bill than the thrifts began offering the new products with high rates of interest, in some cases almost 20 per cent initially. Unfortunately, there was no eligible asset that the thrifts could book as a profitable asset. This was the earliest warning sign that some thrifts were more than willing to play the yield curve and future expectations by offering such high returns to their depositors.

The second bit of deregulatory legislation – the Depository Institutions Act of 1982, better known as the Garn–St Germain Act – also allowed thrifts to begin offering commercial mortgages in addition to their traditional residential mortgages. In theory, this allowed thrifts two new assets that they could create. There were several other areas that were also deregulated for the thrifts but it was the commercial mortgage and the corporate bond that would produce the most trouble for the savings industry over the next several years. In order to cope with their high costs of deposits, thrifts were naturally drawn into the two most risky areas of investment of the 1980s, junk bonds and commercial mortgages. Neither would provide the anticipated return after the market collapse of 1987.

Most of these factors were helped immeasurably by tax incentives provided to investors by the Economic Recovery Tax Act of 1982. That one event, more than any other, helped trigger the bull market of the Reagan years before the market dropped precipitously in 1987. The capital gains rate for assets held longer than one year was dropped from 40 per cent to 20 per cent, providing a supply side remedy for the ailing markets. When coupled with the fall in the price of petrol and a momentary drop in interest rates, the factors converged to provide a note of investor optimism that had not been seen in several years. On the back of that optimism, investors eagerly greeted new issue junk bonds and zero coupon bonds. But the thrift institutions showed the greatest enthusiasm for junk bonds that would cost them dearly in many cases.

According to the DIDMCA, thrifts were now permitted to hold up to 20 per cent of their assets in corporate bonds rather than simply residential mortgages. In their rush to acquire as many high yielding assets as possible, many of them began to purchase the newly fashionable original issue junk bonds. The deregulation introduced the thrifts to the capital markets for the first time. Akin to their British counterparts, most thrifts were relatively small institutions, local or regional in nature. They had not been borrowers in the credit markets before nor had they any need to invest in securities because of the limited nature of their charters. But on aggregate, their total assets were substantial and 20 per cent of them represented a potentially huge market for the junk bond issuers and their investment bankers.[16]

Within the next five to six years, thrifts became avid buyers of junk bonds along with a full array of other investors, from bond funds to insurance companies. But the glaring problem of moral hazard remained: thrifts were being allowed to use insured deposits to buy speculative, less than investment grade, securities without any constraint. When the stock market collapse of 1987 occurred, many of the bonds began to lose a significant portion of their values as investors began to sell them *en masse*, realising that many of them were so risky that they resembled equity investments more than bonds. As market values declined so too did the balance sheets of many thrifts, which realised too late that they had purchased illiquid assets with little chance of repayment. In this case, as in the case of commercial real estate investments, the thrifts had been irreparably harmed by investments in which they had too little experience or sophistication to trade well. As will be seen in the next chapter, this experience again underlined the problem of moral hazard that deposit insurance had created at federally insured depository institutions.

The Garn–St Germain Act allowed thrifts to increase commercial mortgages from 20 to 40 per cent of their assets, also attempting to help liberalise their previously narrow asset bases. During the property explosion of the 1980s, this helped many to enjoy profitability after several poor years at the beginning of the decade. However, when the property market began to wane after the stock market collapse and these recently acquired portfolios began to default, the thrifts' problems were only compounded further.

Although the DIDMCA and the Garn–St Germain Act were necessary in order to deregulate the financial institutions, they were too soft in some places, allowing oversights to occur which literally destroyed the thrift industry within a decade. The American experience with thrifts was not unlike that experienced by the British with their own class of non-commercial bank depository institutions – the fringe banks – a few years earlier. However, both experiences did underscore the need for further legislation so that all depository institutions would be treated more or less the same, depending less on name than on actual function. But the road toward that further legislation would not prove to be a smooth one despite the experiences.

Adjustable interest rates

More significant than the actual legislation itself was the adoption of adjustable rates of interest in the United States after 1982. Once the Garn–St Germain Act had effectively put an end to Regulation Q, thrift institutions and other mortgage lenders were able to adopt adjustable rate mortgages, or ARMs. Although a simple concept well known in Britain, ARMs began a revolution in American mortgage financing that was quickly adopted by consumers tired of the constraints of thirty-year conventional (fixed rate) mortgages, especially when interest rates were relatively high.

By allowing lenders to constantly adjust the mortgage rate charged to customers with the interest rate paid to depositors, the new mortgages helped mortgage lenders avoid the classic mismatch in interest rates that borrowing short and lending long could create. When the American yield curve was negatively sloped in the late 1970s and early 1980s, the traditional long-term mortgages on the books of lenders were not yielding enough of a return. In addition to the disintermediation caused by high short-term rates, the mortgage problem drove many thrifts to the brink because they were unable to manage their interest rate exposures. The new instruments gave them a fresh opportunity to correct the mismatching.

Consumers approved of the new mortgages. By 1985–86, when the ARMs were being contracted on a large scale, interest rates were still relatively high in real terms but the yield curve had returned to a positive slope. Borrowers preferred ARMs to conventionals by a margin of almost two to one, especially since the new instruments had interest rate caps attached. Critics claimed that most mortgage applicants would neither understand nor tolerate variable payments on their mortgages but consumers soon proved that contention unfounded. Homebuyers showed that they were as astute with their liabilities as they had been with their assets several years before when they began investing on a large scale in money market mutual funds.

The rapid acceptance of ARMs brought the British and American banking industries closer than at any time in their histories. The flexibility offered by the ARMs certainly helped many mortgage lenders out of the difficult financial straits of the previous several years. When the mortgage assistance agencies agreed to begin buying them in the secondary market, the industry was provided with an additional fillip. But despite the increased flexibility ARMs infused into the thrift industry, it would not be enough to save them from the next crisis, which was already in the making.

Second-generation derivatives

During the debt explosion of the late 1970s and early 1980s, many borrowers had accumulated debt, both bank loans and bonds, that bore floating rates of interest rather than fixed rates. The second round of interest rate rises in US dollars after 1982 made many of those borrowers vulnerable again to escalating coupons on their debt. When interest rates had risen well into double digits in 1980–81, many floating-rate borrowers were faced with coupons adjusted at greater than 20 per cent interest based upon six-month Eurodollars. Many of those floating-rate debt agreements did not provide caps on the amount of interest to be paid so the borrowers were technically faced with unlimited debt payments if interest rates continued to rise. Although rates did fall in the wake of the Mexican debt problem, the lesson was driven home painfully. Floating-rate debt payers needed a method of mitigating further interest rate rises without calling their debt, depriving themselves of capital funding.

The same sort of exposure could be seen on the foreign currency side as well. The rapid rise in the dollar meant that any non-US company needing dollars was paying more and more for them after 1981. That created potentially damaging translation and transaction exposure on balance sheets and income statements that could lead to disastrous consequences in the stock markets for companies with volatile quarterly reports due to foreign exchange fluctuations. Interest rates were having their effect on foreign exchange values and for many companies with extensive foreign operations that were heavily indebted the potential consequences were quite serious.

These corporate needs led to the development of the currency swaps and interest rate swaps market in the early 1980s. Investment banks and commercial banks began to offer their corporate customers the ability to swap their currency or interest rate payments with themselves or others, effectively changing their exposure. A borrower could swap floating rate debt with another possessing fixed-rate debt.[17] By doing so, the borrower could change the payments for the life of the swap, avoiding potentially escalating costs of debt service in the future.

Currency swaps also became popular. Two counterparties could swap the principal amounts of their currencies at a fixed rate of exchange, removing doubts about the future value of spot rates. This technique would have served many US and British companies well just several years before when the cost of capital in dollars and sterling was prohibitively expensive. But rather than coming too late, the swaps market exploded exponentially in size and by the end of the decade had become the fastest growing financial market ever devised.

The market was not able to grow without a significant shift in financial risk. When two companies agreed to swap their currencies or interest coupons, a third party guarantor was required in order to insure that the deal would be honoured in the future in the case of a potential default. The natural guarantors of these swaps were the commercial banks, which guaranteed the deals by either being counterparties to the actual swaps or third parties brought into the deals for expressly that purpose. The banks were eager to accumulate this sort of business because their loan portfolios were suffering at the time. In the process, they helped to significantly shift financial risk from securities markets investors to themselves, at least in the case of interest rate swapping where the traditional risk had rested upon bond investors. In the case of currencies, they added to their own natural risks in that market by becoming counterparties to swaps, a form of forward market arrangement that was extremely limited before the swaps market developed.

The early 1980s became a period of financial innovation because of the endemic problems that high interest rates and deficits had created in the American economy. Swaps would also become popular in Britain for many of the same reasons since British companies were also faced with an economy that was growing slowly. While not a panacea for fundamental economic problems, the development of new markets and products illustrated that the investment banking industry was reacting to changes in economic policies by adapting. In this case, the adaptation was done with much success. Commercial banks would succeed only when involved with market developments. On the regulatory side, the reforms passed to help them would only create more problems than solutions over the course of the decade.

6

BIG BANG AND BEYOND

After the recession ended in 1982, the stock markets began a long bull market phase initiated by favourable tax legislation in the United States and an abating of inflation from the previous year. Oil prices continued to fall and a general commodity price deflation occurred which, while good for consumer and wholesale prices, proved ruinous for the export earnings of many developing countries. By 1985, the major economic problem plaguing the developed world was the strong dollar.

In March of that year, the dollar had reached its post-Bretton Woods highs against many of its main competitors. Sterling had touched an all-time low of $1.10 and no end to the dollar's strength appeared in sight unless the G5 nations decided to act in concert to bring the currency down. The enormous American trade deficit that had resulted made Congress restive and talk of trade retaliation against Japan in particular become more pronounced as some were willing to blame America's trade problems on foreign competition rather than on the purposeful neglect that had surrounded the currency for the previous four years.

The trade problems created by the strong dollar were exacerbated by the fact that foreign portfolio investment in American securities, especially Treasury securities, was increasing. Foreign direct investment in hard US assets had remained popular despite the possibility of a massive currency depreciation. Between 1980 and 1985, foreign direct investments had grown substantially and the strong bull market and declining interest rates had lured many foreign investors, including the British, to make increasing purchases of all sorts of equities and fixed-income securities, especially after the withholding tax on foreign purchases of new Treasury securities had been lifted in 1984.

For most of the decade to date, the Federal Reserve had not intervened in the markets to lower the value of the dollar. The only visible intervention occurred the day of the assassination attempt on President Reagan in order to calm the markets. Otherwise, the dollar had been allowed to rise unabated. This policy of benign neglect certainly helped fund the growing budget deficit and allowed consumers to purchase foreign goods, but has often been criticised for contributing to the growing trade imbalance and unemployment, and the decline of American industry (at least temporarily) by raising interest rates to historic highs. But on the positive side, there was little that the Federal Reserve could do in the markets by itself, especially if traders realised that the intent was to bring down the dollar. That exercise would only have cost the Federal Reserve foreign exchange reserves with no guarantees of success unless the action was co-ordinated with the other major central banks.

But the strong dollar did have positive benefits that are mostly overlooked. As interest rates increased in the US beginning in the late 1970s, foreign capital was attracted to the US, helping to offset the fears of a capital shortage first mentioned in Chapter 2. That capital helped many US corporations continue profits, partially helping create a reliance upon internally generated funds (retained earnings) rather than fresh equity raised in the markets for capital investment. But the combination of the two did supply capital to American industry although a large portion of it was debt capital rather than equity when raised in the markets. Thus, the idea of an equity capital shortage was still alive and well in the early 1980s but its ramifications were mitigated by the fact that large amounts of debt capital were available.

However, it was the political ramifications of the dual deficits and the possibility of Congressional reaction that prompted the G5 to meet at the Plaza Hotel in New York in the autumn of 1985 to plan for the dollar's systematic decline. Acting in unison, the G5 nations' central banks sold dollars so that by early 1986 the currency had fallen almost 20 per cent in value. That was in addition to the original losses recorded when the G5's intentions were first announced. The intervention continued into 1987 after the Louvre accords in Paris, although part of that agreement was dedicated to ensuring that the dollar stabilised and did not fall any further. By the end of that year, the total depreciation measured almost 30 per cent. Almost true to form, the yen rose the most of any of the major trading currencies – almost 50 per cent – despite the fact that it would have appeared that Japanese trade with the United States would have been hurt the most by the dollar decline.[1]

In the aftermath of the Plaza and Louvre agreements, the dollar decline was welcomed by the United States and its major trading partners. After fifteen years of currency instability and governmental inaction, the agreements were the first indications that the Group of Five could act in concert, albeit slowly, to remedy imbalances in the international financial system. That concern alone helped the dollar to depreciate after its historic rise but proved to be somewhat short-lived, and it was certainly not a surrogate for official governmental intervention on a more permanent basis.

Nevertheless, the concerted actions of the G5 finally provided a postscript to the effects of the collapse of the Bretton Woods Agreement some fifteen years before. During the intervening period, the developed countries collectively practised a policy of benign neglect toward currency movements by never resurrecting any sort of international agreement or system other than the European Monetary System (EMS). On an individual basis, they were more concerned and intervened frequently on behalf of their own currencies but mostly shied away from suggestions that a new international monetary system of some sort be constructed. The political side of currency movements had won the day and consumer democracy had made itself felt, albeit indirectly. But the multilateral decision to bring down the value of the dollar grew from a consensus that the enormous American merchandise trade deficit could not be tolerated any longer and that a realigned currency market would be the best method to curtail potential international tensions based upon trade patterns.

But as the dollar fell and the yen appreciated, a wave of Japanese buying of American Treasury securities ensued, illustrating that the United States was still partially benefiting from the depreciation. The period of dollar strength also bolstered consumer democracy in the United States and demonstrated to the Republican administration that the currency markets had unintendedly aided its fortunes. The period of the trade deficits introduced consumers to even more foreign goods than usual and the sheer diversity of choice raised American consumerism to new heights. This development was originally a bad sign for American manufacturers, for many surveys indicated a clear consumer preference for foreign manufactured goods over their American competition.

During the mid-1980s, it was becoming more difficult for the British to ignore the call to finally join the EMS and allow the pound to become a fully fledged member of the currency grid. The success of the EMS until that point was another sign that the direct consequences of the Bretton Woods collapse had finally ended and that a new era had dawned in the currency markets. The dollar/pound rate was of less significance than in the past and sterling's fall against the dollar, culminating with the historic low rate in 1985, did little to enhance sterling's role as a major international reserve currency.

The Plaza and Louvre agreements signalled that floating exchange rates were finally accepted and that currency volatility would be the order of the day in the markets, not just for the foreseeable future but permanently. The industrialised nations were willing to intervene in the markets on a massive scale only when serious adjustments needed to be made in currency alignments and, given the potential political ramifications, only when they were drastically needed. While the desire for some sort of fixed parity system lived on, floating rates had won the battle *de facto* and governments could only acknowledge it by intervening in times of crisis well after the fact. Again, the markets had succeeded in leading the regulators and central bankers. The political establishment quickly was won over, however, recognising the benefits that could accrue from either strong or weak currencies if those movements were anticipated and could be accompanied by political orchestration.

The wide and often bewildering array of new derivative financial products being constantly developed helped traders and companies cope with floating exchange rates in ways not imagined in the 1970s. The intrinsic volatility of the floating currency markets proved ideal for the swaps market. Seizing upon the volatility of the markets, banks were willing to make markets in interest rate and currency swaps, commodity swaps and options in order to help their customers hedge or speculate against market risks. The revenues derived from creating and trading these instruments provided much-needed revenues for banks during the middle stage of the Third World debt crisis. As banks shied away from making loans to developing countries, thereby avoiding booking assets, the revenues from trading the new derivatives originally avoided capital requirements of their respective central banks.[2]

The great irony of this situation took some time to be understood by regulators. Traders were now profiting from the very volatility that fixed parity exchange rates had once sought to prevent. Until the central banks caught up with this trend, commercial banks survived the debt crisis partially by creating new products. The original window of opportunity for the commercial banks without regulatory interference was actually quite long: derivatives exposure was not discussed until 1988 and the exposures were not included in capital requirements until the 1990s by most central banks. Effectively, that meant that the new market had gone unregulated for almost a decade. During that time, the markets developed the second generation of hedging instruments in response to the Mexican debt crisis in much the same fashion that options and financial futures had been developed a decade before in response to the breakdown of Bretton Woods. On the currency side, the reasons were much the same. Volatile interest rates had re-entered the picture after 1982 and continued product development produced more and more exotic versions of swaps and other derivative instruments.

But the benefits derived by commercial banks in both Britain and the United States from swaps and derivatives was not necessarily extended to other depository institutions. Thrifts and building societies remained outside the orbit of derivatives products because most were too small or unsophisticated to deal in them. In fact, many small savings associations were excluded from most forms of interest rate hedging and continued to conduct business in much the same fashion as in the past except where allowed to expand. But for the most part, expansion meant booking new assets to complement the old, not finding new ways to generate revenues without being in the loan business. As a result, American thrifts especially remained in the traditional spread banking business although now they had the flexibility to vary the rate of interest paid to depositors.

While it would take several more years for the savings associations to show signs of strain, the markets became increasingly international in the mid-1980s. This was due mostly to the foreign exchange market which remained as volatile as ever, even after the massive dollar depreciation following the summer of 1985. When many of the major market centres lifted withholding taxes on foreign investors in the summer of 1984, capital began to flow from one government bond market to another, enhancing flows between them and bringing their respective governments closer than ever before when considering monetary policies. But, for the most part, the internationalisation was accomplished by traditional over-the-counter markets, namely the foreign exchange market, bond markets and the derivatives markets. The stock exchanges, being more structured and heavily regulated, would need more time to catch up.

But the internationalisation that characterised the financial markets had some serious offsetting factors in the United States. Two developments challenged the assumption that the relative prosperity of the 1980s had cured economic problems in the United States. The first was the agricultural crisis of 1985–86 that prompted the Agricultural Credit Act of 1987, illustrating that the high exchange value of the dollar in the previous years had not been a blessing to all. Little known outside the financial community, Congress was required to restructure the Farm Credit System, that GSE responsible for providing farm mortgages and loans through federal land banks. The high interest rates and value of the dollar several years before had drastically reduced the amount of American agricultural exports, causing a crisis among farmers because a large portion of their income was derived from exports. As a result, several land banks became insolvent and Congress was forced to re-structure the entire system to keep it afloat. The provisions of the act became the first restructuring of a GSE since the Depression although it was billed at the time as a means of enhancing credit to farmers. Part of its provisions helped create a new financing arm for the Farm System that would borrow to cover the losses of the previous years. This new entity, dubbed Farmer Mac, required a direct, partial guarantee of the US Treasury. The 1987 legislation became the forerunner of the thrift bail-out that would occur two years later.

The provisions of the Tax Reform Act of 1986, passed by Congress as a means of providing more equitable treatment to taxpayers, would have the most profound long-term effects of any legislation passed during the decade. While attempting to provide more simple marginal tax brackets and cutting down on the number of tax deductions, the act also attacked some of the fundamentals of American consumer democracy. It abolished the preferential long-term capital gains tax that had been the cornerstone of investing and had fuelled the bull market that began in 1982. At the same time it provided for a phasing out of the consumer interest deduction, except for home mortgage interest. After several years of reduced deductions, consumer interest for personal loans or credit cards could no longer be deducted and when the phasing out period finanlly ended, the recession of 1990 began. A considerable gamble by Congress, the abolition of the deduction was inspired by the budget deficits of the 1980s and ended indirect government subsidies of consumer credit. The home mortgage interest deduction, however, was left intact although, unlike Britain, it covered 100 per cent of interest paid to mortgage lenders.

BIG BANG

Despite the relative prosperity of the mid-1980s, the London Stock Exchange was falling quickly out of step with the general internationalisation of markets. While always a home for foreign stocks as well as foreign investors, the market system itself began to show signs of being outdated. While the New York stock markets remained the world's largest, Tokyo was rapidly closing on second position. In the mid-1980s, the American equities markets were becoming increasingly popular with foreign companies seeking listings. In the face of the stiff international competition, London had no choice but to revamp its trading system or face being relegated to an even more rapidly declining position.

Experience with reform in the United States since 1980 had shown that gradualism was not particularly successful in the rapidly changing market environment. The slow process by which the DIDMCA had originally intended to lift interest rate ceilings imposed by Regulation Q had not proved successful and the Garn–St Germain Act had to be passed as a result only two years later. Gradualism in financial reform had only proven successful in the past when exchange rates and interest rates were much less volatile. When the Americans switched to a negotiated fee system for determining brokers' rates in 1975, the change was mandated to occur immediately rather than gradually and, while the marketplace lost some of its smaller houses that could not compete as a result, the change was relatively calm. Consequently, keeping those cases in mind, British market reform would come quickly rather than slowly.

The London stock market was fundamentally different from those in the United States in several respects. The jobbing system was different, as mentioned in earlier chapters, and the market actively listed and traded gilts. In contrast, Treasury issues in the United States traded on the over-the-counter bond market among market makers. In bad times, traders in Britain could always rely upon the gilts market for constant turnover whereas the American exchange members had to rely solely upon equities. One of the fundamental reforms of the British market was to allow foreign market-makers more access to the market. What attracted them was the gilts business in many cases rather than UK shares. Many of the American securities houses already traded large quantities of UK shares on an over-the-counter basis in New York, avoiding UK stamp tax in the process.

Although gilts became a primary allure, common shares also reached new levels of popularity. After Big Bang, foreign ownership of UK shares rose to about 12–14 per cent of the total and remained constant through the end of 1992. Americans were the largest investors in UK common shares, accounting for about 47 per cent of the total. That was almost three times the amount held by EC investors, who held about 17 per cent.[3] The Americans' attraction for common shares explains why many of the foreign firms applying for dealing licenses were from the US investment banking community.

Big Bang was intended to make the London Stock Exchange more international and responsive to movements in international capital flows. Fixed commission rates were abandoned in favour of negotiated commissions, more foreigners were admitted to the dealing ranks and the single capacity system was jettisoned in favour of an American-style dual capacity system. Improving upon the single capacity system, the new floor trading system allowed a trader to trade either for his own account or to deal for the public. Even the name of the exchange itself was changed to reflect the new international environment. The new International Stock Exchange, with more market-makers and lower commissions, hoped that the manner in which business was conducted would be radically changed with greater economies for investors as the ultimate objective.

Table 6.1 shows the changes in market statistics before and after the adoption of the new trading rules and procedures. As can be seen, turnover in both gilts and common shares almost trebled after the legislation was introduced. In this respect, Big Bang was highly successful although the new, lower commissions eventually led some foreign market-makers to withdraw, citing lack of adequate commission revenues.

Although the Financial Services Act helped modernise the stock market, another 1980s phenomenon had already become established and was well embedded in market practice even before the reforms were in place. Because of the increase in foreign investment and the increasing volatility of hot

Table 6.1 London Stock Exchange before and after Big Bang
(£ millions)

	Turnover		
	Shares	*Gilts*	*Total*
1986	181,210	424,416	646,263
1987	496,101	1,148,358	1,757,493
1988	400,000	1,129,112	1,602,804
1989	560,000	975,211	1,627,265

Notes: Excludes preference shares
Source: Central Statistical Office, *Financial Statistics*, various issues

money in the 1980s, many market-makers now quoted prices in securities away from their home markets on an almost continual twenty-four hour basis. Thus, there was a European market for US Treasury securities before the US markets opened. There was also a limited market for UK stocks in New York. Slowly, the securities markets were becoming round-the-clock operations, just as the foreign exchange market had been for some years.

Many of the American securities houses in New York as well as the British continued to quote prices in UK listed securities on an over-the-counter basis for customers in order to avoid stamp tax as they had in the past. In fact, the new market-making system adopted in London fitted perfectly with this practice since it fitted the general over-the-counter pattern quite well. This particular practice would add to the problems experienced in October 1987 when the world's stock markets experienced their largest collective price falls since the Depression. But, while the stock market received a much-needed dose of reform and liberalisation, the UK banking system was again in need of reform. The distinctions made in the Banking Act of 1979 were causing problems in the banking sector – not from foreign banks, but from UK banks which, as their American counterparts in the thrift industry, had spied a window of opportunity in the distinction between 'bank' and 'licensed deposit taker'.

UK banking legislation again

Although the Banking Act of 1979 was the first comprehensive piece of banking regulation passed in Britain, events quickly were proving that, as with the DIDMCA in the United States, it needed further legislation to tighten up certain oversights. The debt crisis, inflation and the continued flow of hot money around the globe all continued to put pressure upon financial institutions not imagined even five years before. A major British banking crisis erupted in 1984 with the failure of Johnson Matthey. By making somewhat dubious loans on liberal terms, the bank had managed to lose approximately £250 million, more than 50 per cent of its total loan portfolio. Again, the Bank of England had to come to the assistance of a bank despite the Banking Act of 1979. This followed hard on the heels of the failure of Continental Illinois, the American bank that was bailed out by the regulatory authorities with the help of a syndicate of commercial banks as well. As a result, the Banking Act of 1987 was passed, superseding the 1979 Act.

The new legislation finally came to grips with the distinction between 'bank' and 'licensed deposit taker' by eliminating the latter, calling all institutions by the generic name 'bank'. Eliminating the two-tier distinction was necessary because the fringe banks were operating, as they always had, as non-bank banks still on the fringe of regulation. This cumbersome term was used by central bankers to describe an institution that could accept deposits but not make loans or which did not accept deposits but did make loans. In either case, the funding or lending was accomplished in the money market, meaning that the institution was not operating as a commercial bank *per se*. While some non-bank banks were able to generate credit, they were not under the eye of the central banking authority. As a result of the 1987 legislation, all came under the regulatory wing of the Bank of England so the new act was actually expanding the Bank's powers.

In 1980, one of the DIDMCA's important provisions included an increase in deposit insurance from $40,000 to $100,000 per account. The Banking Act of 1987 would follow suit and increase deposit insurance from £10,000 to £20,000 per account although the partial coverage of insuring only 75 per cent of any account up to that amount remained in force. Critics maintained that increasing the amounts of deposit insurance coverage only acknowledged inflation while the usual public-relations oriented response was that such moves served to provide increased saver protections. In reality, increases helped to protect depository institutions against disintermediation by savers who had already proved that they were willing to take their savings elsewhere if bank accounts fell behind acceptable rates of interest or levels of the deposit insurance itself.

At about the same time, the building societies were the subject of new legislation that extended their asset bases in much the same way that the Garn–St Germain Act had done for their American counterparts. Passed in 1986, effective in 1987, the Building Societies Act greatly enhanced the potential profit centres for building societies in response to the strong growth for mortgages in Britain in the previous five years. Being limited banking institutions, the societies, as American thrift institutions, were vulnerable to downturns in the mortgage market and rises in interest rates. Accordingly, the new legislation enabled the societies to lend for second mortgages, provide insurance services, extend unsecured loans, and provide brokerage services for customers. Deposit insurance was also extended to their customers although the amount was limited to £10,000.

A new regulator for the industry was also created in the Building Societies Commission, akin to the Federal Home Loan Bank Board in the US for federally chartered thrifts. Traditionally, the building societies had seen little effective regulation since the Bank of England only oversaw the commercial banks and even that definition was becoming more broad as the deposit-takers were to be included in the new Banking Act of 1987. But the Building Societies Act was meant to make the societies more competitive with the clearing banks that were rapidly encroaching on their traditional preserves by making more and more residential mortgages, especially in the boom years of the mid-1980s.[4] Recognising the role of building societies in the mortgage process, Parliament needed to expand their scope lest they fall into the same trap that befell American thrifts in the late 1970s.

The Building Societies Act will best be remembered for enabling those institutions that desired to convert their charters to that of a commercial bank. When the Abbey National Building Society did so in 1988, it became the largest defection from the rank of building societies until that time and set a precedent that also would be taken up in the United States within a couple of years, when many thrift institutions changed their charters to become banks after the entire industry was shaken by the thrift crisis that officially surfaced in early 1989. The line of demarcation between bank and building association was beginning to crumble as each began to encroach on the other's traditional preserves.

The major difference between US and UK banking regulations that developed in the 1970s and 1980s was that although quite similar, despite time lags, the American regulations always tended to be very specific while those in the UK tended to be loosely intrepreted. The Garn Act in the US was very specific about the expanded powers of depository institutions with the exception of the type of corporate bonds that they were eligible to purchase. British legislation maintained distinctions, such as that between bank and deposit-taker, that would be abused quickly as in the case of Johnson Matthey. Although there are other instances of American oversights in financial regulations, many coming somewhat late after a crisis had developed, the additional financing possibilities in the American markets remained much wider than those in the UK. As a result, narrowness in interpreting an institution's operating boundaries often led to crisis or abuse. Important for the markets during the 1980s especially was one simple fact: looseness in regulatory language on either side of the Atlantic led to problems. The Banking Act of 1979 and the Garn Act are two prime examples.

THE MARKET COLLAPSE OF 1987

Immediately after the 1929 stock market crash in the United States, the Republicans, then in power in the White House and in Congress, coined the term 'market break' to describe the precipitous price fall in the stock indices. This was used in preference to the term 'crash', to imply that the widespread price drops were thought to be only temporary. History would certainly prove that theory incorrect but when the term was again applied to the market collapse in October 1987, it was more appropriate. But other similarities persisted that had a strange irony.

The market collapse that spread rapidly from the United States to all of the other major stock markets in October 1987 proved to be one of the stranger market phenomena of the twentieth century. On 19 October, Black Monday, the American stock market indices fell about 25 per cent, causing panic selling and numerous margin calls that only added to continued liquidations. Specialists were inundated with orders and many market-makers in the over-the-counter market did not respond to sell orders from their customers, only fuelling some deep-rooted suspicions about that market's overall efficiency and ability to cope with heavy volume. But the sudden change of market direction was not only domestic; within a few hours all of the major markets found themselves in the same position. On the surface, it appeared that the American markets were again exporting a crash in a fashion similar to 1929.

Given the economic circumstances surrounding the market collapse, the speed with which it affected the individual markets was astonishing. No fundamental economic news of a negative nature was present at the time the American stock market indices began to fall. There was an aggregate of economic and political indicators that could have instigated massive selling but many of them never came to fruition. One notable factor was a fear that Congress would somehow eliminate the tax deductibility of interest payments for companies, as it had done for individuals in the Tax Reform Act of 1986. That would have seriously affected junk bond companies which by that time had issued about $250 billion worth of bonds in addition to the bank debt they had also acquired. Exceptions to the general deductibility of corporate interest payments never reached fruition but the fear that it instilled in investors played a part in the massive market selling spree.

Many investors feared the same sort of negative influences experienced earlier in the decade caused by inflation and interest rates, and with the general fear that interest rates would have to be raised to aid the weak dollar, the news began to turn bearish for the markets in the weeks prior to Black Monday. The foreign exchange market also had a role in the collapse, as Destler and Henning (1990) demonstrate. After Alan Greenspan raised the discount rate in August 1987, his first official act as Paul Volcker's successor, the United States appeared to be headed in the same direction as Germany and Japan. But Treasury Secretary James Baker indicated that he was not in favour of further American rate increases despite the fact that the Louvre Agreement required one if that meant keeping the dollar from depreciating.[5]

This official confusion cast a cloud over exchange rate stability at the time and showed divisions within the G5. More importantly, it came at a time when the markets were generally jittery in the wake of the other factors. If the dollar declined, a resurgence of inflation was feared as the American's penchant for foreign-made manufactured goods was well entrenched. Stability in the face of consumerism was preferable to keeping voters happy with relatively low interest rates. The dollar decline of the previous two-and-a-half years was not without its benefits. In 1986, as the dollar fell against the yen and the Deutschmark, Japanese car manufacturers had to raise the price of their cars sold in the US in order to offset lost revenues. The American car manufacturers, beginning to regain some lost ground after years of decline, took the opportunity to raise their prices as well, but not as much as the Japanese. As a result, 1986 was a year of record profits for the car manufacturers after miserable results only a couple of years before.

When the selling began in the stock markets, it was not totally unexpected although the magnitude of the price falls certainly was not anticipated. But the puzzling part of the collapse remained in its transmission mechanism: why did all the markets move together so quickly?

One thing that the markets did share in common was a bevy of increasingly pessimistic economic news that only served to make many market participants nervous in the weeks prior to the market break. Earlier in October, Citicorp announced the largest banking loss in history, caused mainly by the sale of many non-performing sovereign loans. The fall of the dollar since the Louvre Agreement suggested to some that the United States might have to raise its interest rates to bolster the currency. And the Federal Reserve was coming under increasing criticism concerning the amount of easy money available for the merger and acquisition (M&A) trend in general and junk bond financings in particular.

The overall market decline was perhaps the best evidence that the marketplace had become internationalised in the fifteen years since the collapse of Bretton Woods. The drop in New York prices was quickly followed by a drop in London prices by an even greater proportion. Although it is difficult to account for investor sentiment on an international basis, the actual price transmission is somewhat easier to understand in a mechanical sense. The actual internationalisation itself lies at the heart of the matter. Price falls in American shares in New York set off limit orders in other shares, many British, which were traded as American Depository Receipts (ADR) in New York.[6] British ADRs are the most widely traded foreign securities in New York and would be expected to be sold first if a selling trend developed. The fall in UK prices in New York then set off further price falls in London in domestic UK shares as well as foreign shares. The London Stock Exchange has the largest number of foreign shares listed of any major stock market. The same shares' price falls in London then set off selling in other markets in a similar manner. Turnover continued strong in London, however, due to the gilts market, which picked up the slack from equities turnover in a typical 'flight to quality' phenomenon. The worldwide price falls can be seen in Table 6.2.

With the aid of computer-driven programmes, the price falls were in some cases automatic even before a panic of any sort developed. When some herd instinct did develop, regardless of its local origin, it was mostly attributed to domestic investors who sold out of fear or because they were unable to meet margin calls. International investors, although aware of the same factors as domestic investors, appeared to be less of a factor, remaining on the sidelines.[7] Despite the fact that internationalisation lay at the heart of the matter, the panic selling appeared to be mainly among domestic investors, not those who invested cross-border.

Table 6.2 October 1987 changes in world stock prices

Country	Per cent stock price change
Australia	-58.3
Hong Kong	-56.3
Singapore	-40.1
Mexico	-38.7
United Kingdom	-26.1
Belgium	-23.2
West Germany	-22.9
Netherlands	-22.6
France	-22.0
Canada	-21.8
United States	-21.5
Japan	-12.6

Source: Paul Bennet and Jeanette Kelleher, 'The International Transmission of Stock Price Disruption in October 1987'. Federal Reserve Bank of New York *Quarterly Review*, Summer, 1988

What Table 6.2 reveals is that the economies with the closest ties through the foreign exchange markets and the capital markets had the widest swings in their stock prices during October 1987. For about two years after the collapse, the American securities industry retrenched, effectively ending the bull market for Wall Street expansion. Japan had the smallest reaction because the Tokyo stock market had the least linkages with foreign markets of any of the major stock exchanges, i.e., the least number of foreign shares listed or the absence of over-the-counter trading in foreign shares. As a result, the panic that developed affected Tokyo least and other markets were not substantially affected by it in turn. Ironically, Japan's traditional isolation served it well temporarily during the market break.

While no banking panics developed during the break, there were notable victims nevertheless. One of the victims of the market break was the M&A trend that had developed in the post-1982 recession years. In the five years prior to the 1987 market collapse, mergers and leveraged buyouts proceeded at a record pace in the United States. Many of the mergers in turn sparked market speculation since many investors actively sought out companies thought to be targets, hoping to buy before merger plans were announced. Many of those stocks had price/earnings ratios not justified by their financial performances and once the wave of selling hit the market they were among the first to be sold.

The combination of the change in capital gains tax and accelerated depreciation changes in the Economic Recovery Tax Act of 1982 made many companies attractive buys for those seeking assets valued at pre- or early inflation prices. The price of buying existing companies was cheaper than beginning new start-up ventures and the boom in M&A began. A similar phenomenon

139

developed in Britain. Although the gross values were less than those in the US, the number of actual companies acquired by others was actually larger than in the United States. The market break in 1987 did not seriously diminish the UK trend as the actual numer of companies acquired and their gross value actually increased substantially between 1987 and 1989.[8] When the trend did begin to slow, it was because of the effects of the UK recession. Figure 6.1 shows the values of the trend in both Britain and the US.

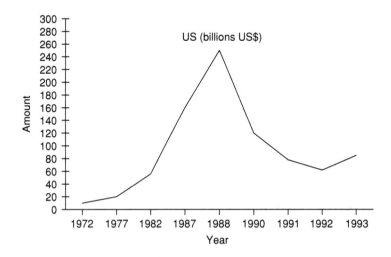

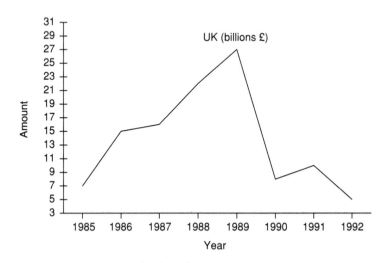

Figure 6.1 Total value of merger activity, US and UK

Source: Securities Data Co. and Central Statistical Office, *Financial Statistics*, various issues

The American trend in mergers was aided in no small part by the ideological stance of the Reagan administration. Tolerating many more horizontal mergers than previous (mostly Democratic) administrations, little resistance was offered to most of the large mergers, operating under the assumption that they would provide more efficiency and economies of scale after the mergers than before. This attitude also spilled over to the banking sector where many interstate mergers were being arranged between banking companies that would have been unheard of a decade before.

Although many of the largest mergers of the period appeared to be horizontal, those in the banking sector were permitted for different reasons than those in the corporate sector.[9] Mergers of banking companies were more difficult because of the restraints imposed by the McFadden Act and the Bank Holding Companies Act. A corporate merger could be blocked by the Justice Department if it was deemed to present a potential for restraining trade rather than fostering it. Banking mergers, on the other hand, were not permitted across state lines. In fact, even within the states themselves, banking was often limited by state legislatures. For instance, in 1980 only twenty-two states permitted statewide branch banking. Eleven allowed only limited branching within their states and seventeen allowed only unit banking (single bank offices only), the latter mostly in the midwest. As a result, there were both federal and state laws to circumvent if a bank was to operate outside its home state.

The banking laws started to crumble after the banking crisis began in the early 1980s. When Continental Illinois effectively failed in the spring of 1984, a consortium of commercial banks had to be assembled in order to protect its depositors. After that time, the Federal Reserve began to adopt a more creative approach to failing banks rather than to simply step in with the aid of the Federal Deposit Insurance Corporation (FDIC) to ensure the failing banks' deposits and orderly reorganisation. If profitable banks could be found to shore up those which were failing then geographical constraints should be effectively removed since it might be too optimistic to assume that a buyer for a failing bank could be found in the same state.

During the early part of the decade, interstate bank mergers began slowly but the trend picked up momentum as the number of insolvent banks increased nationwide. The rate of banking failures was greater than that evidenced during the Depression years and the size of the failures was also larger. Many smaller state banks were being absorbed by larger, healthier state and federally chartered banks, a trend that had been seen several years before in the thrift industry during its first crisis in 1981. Although there were several Federal Reserve rulings on the matter as well as a Supreme Court opinion, it was the state legislatures themselves that eventually decided if and when out-of-state banks should be allowed to acquire banks in their states. By the end of the decade, even those most opposed to out-of-state banks operating within their states would reconsider their positions.

141

THE HAMMERSMITH SWAPS DEBACLE

One of the stranger chapters in recent financial history occurred in 1987 in an unlikely setting for a major crisis in the swaps market. Since swaps had begun to grow exponentially since the earlier part of the decade, fears began to be raised that this new uncontrolled market could pose a serious risk for banks or even the financial system because of its unregulated nature. While that fear proved true to an extent, no one would have foreseen where it eventually would emerge.

Swaps began their history in the Euromarket as structured deals whereby borrowers with existing floating-rate debt and fixed-rate debt would swap their interest payments with each other. The transaction was in turn guaranteed by a commercial bank. As financial engineering became more sophisticated and the number of variations on debt instruments increased, so did the varieties of swaps. Borrowers could swap zero-coupon debt for floating-rate debt or any other of countless combinations with the intent of changing the annual cash outflows on the debt. Swaps thereby provided flexibility for borrowers, providing them with alternatives to being locked into their present coupon payments or calling the debt itself, incurring an expense in the process.

Quickly thereafter, swaps became highly marketable. In place of one of the two borrower counterparties in a transaction, a dealer (investment bank or commercial bank) stood ready to quote prices for swaps and act as counterparty for companies desirous of swapping. In this case, the flexibility was increased for companies could swap as often as they liked. As they did, the market risks also increased at the same time. The dealers assumed two risks in these circumstances: they were exposed to the swap as both a dealer and as a guarantor. As long as the dealer remained the counterparty to a swap it guaranteed the other party's interest payments in case of default. But the dealers were willing to assume these risks in order to participate in the market.

Their incentive for doing so was twofold. First, they were able to carve out market niches for themselves and, second, they were able to speculate on the direction of interest rates or exchange rates at the same time. A dealer who felt that interest rates were going to fall would attempt to receive fixed-rate payments while paying out floating-rate payments. As time progressed and rates did decline, the payments would decline while the receipts would remain steady, presenting the dealer with a profit. If rates went in the opposite direction then the dealer would lose. But this profitable scenario could still prove inefficacious if the payer of the fixed-rate debt defaulted to the dealer and the dealer was required to continue paying the agreed-upon interest. What originally was a profitable situation still had the potential for a loss to the dealer, especially if it did not know its customer particularly well.

In the unregulated market, the potential for client abuse was always present since any company that wanted to swap interest or currency payments technically could do so as much as it wanted, especially in the absence of close managerial controls. The first major swaps problem was a perfect illustration of this but it occurred at the municipal level, not at the corporate level where most of the swapping occurred.

The London Borough of Hammersmith and Fulham was the counterparty that eventually cost a group of international banks over a billion pounds in swaps losses. In 1987, Hammersmith's auditor discovered that the borough had engaged in various types of swaps totalling about £110 million. At the time, the borough's operating budget was about £85 million. Clearly, this was an excessive amount of swaps exposure since attempting to hedge more than the budget was imprudent. But within the next two years the problem burgeoned. By 1989, Hammersmith had engaged in over £6 billion worth of swaps, an amount that no excuse of hedging could even remotely justify.

Hammersmith's auditor sued and the case wound its way through the courts. The eventual decision dismayed many of the banks that had entered into swap arrangements with the borough. The lower courts ruled that Hammersmith had no business engaging in the swaps for speculative purposes although they did acknowledge that hedging was perfectly valid in some instances. But the amounts suggested that Hammersmith was not a hedger *per se* and consequently the swap agreements were invalidated. The House of Lords ruled the same on appeal and, as a result, the banks that had served as Hammersmith's dealers had to unwind the swaps and absorb the losses themselves.

The Hammersmith case was resolved in quite a different fashion than most other financial fiascos. By asserting that the borough had no business speculating with swaps, the British courts effectively told the group of banks involved that the ball was firmly in their court. By not keeping abreast of Hammersmith's activities in the swaps market, they had only themselves to blame for the losses they would incur when Hammersmith's swap book was unwound. The courts were underlining the unregulated nature of the market, telling the banks that it was their problem if they did not know their client well enough to realise that it may have been overextended. Perhaps most unusually, the Lords effectively reversed an old principle that has governed the financial markets in both Britain and the United States for most of this century: under no circumstances would the markets be allowed to lead financial institutions and regulators. In this case, the courts were dictating to the markets after a crisis had occurred. This was something of an unusual occurrence in finance.

Whether the Hammersmith affair had a sobering effect upon banks is doubtful because the swaps market proceeded to develop new products at a rapid pace and the volume of swaps continued to grow geometrically. By the end of the 1980s, the market was estimated at about $3 trillion worth of currency and interest rate swaps outstanding.[10] The growth of the market can be seen in Figure 6.2. In all cases, the swap guarantees booked by the banks were recorded as contingent liabilities, not assets. The banks had discovered a source of revenue that did not require booking an asset and therefore did not involve bank capital calculations, at least prior to 1988 when capital requirements were discussed on a continual basis at the Bank for International Settlements. The swaps market became the natural successor to the problems created by the developing country debt crisis and would soon itself come under closer scrutiny by regulatory authorities. Hammersmith had become an object lesson for both banks and regulators that would not be forgotten.

The swaps market remained perhaps the most nightmarish of all financial markets to understand and regulate because of its complexity and over-the-counter nature. In the interest rate swaps sector alone, dealers were able to create hundreds of variations of swaps by combining the features on corporate bonds that had been developed over the previous ten years. When a dealer or a customer was not comfortable with a swap, it could be swapped again to achieve the desired results. The net result was that one swap generated perhaps dozens more. If a default occurred anywhere in the chain, it had the potential to do serious harm to any or all of the other counterparties. Ultimately, the guarantor bank dealers would be effected, underlining the systemic risk to the entire market.

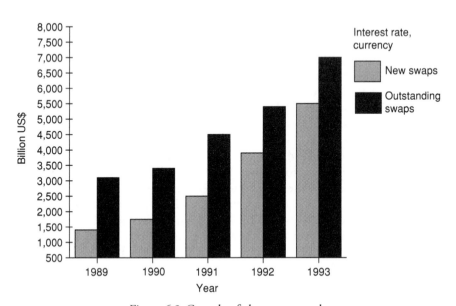

Figure 6.2 Growth of the swaps market

Source: International Swaps & Derivatives Association

Because of the over-the-counter nature of the market, no regularly reported accounts were available in the financial press for the general public. No major English-speaking financial newspaper regularly followed swaps, reported on the size of the market, or wrote about it except to periodically warn about its potential dangers to the financial system. The market developed an ominous reputation, portrayed as a behemoth with the potential to destroy the international financial structure because of its closely inter-related nature that spanned international boundaries and monetary systems. While that characterisation is difficult to qualify, Hammersmith remains the only major swaps debacle since the market began.[11]

The Hammersmith affair coincided with the Bank for International Settlements (BIS) accords that raised primary capital requirements in the industrialised countries by the beginning of 1992. Capital requirements including discussions on how to include swap exposures began almost immediately after the Hammersmith case became publicised. Despite the Hammersmith problem, the BIS discussions represented one of the first times in post-Second World War history that regulators anticipated poten-tial problems in a sector of the marketplace and sought to remedy them before they turned into a full-blown financial crisis. Unfortunately, swaps and derivatives discussions continued well into the next decade without any firm rules to regulate the market. But the discussions themselves served as a warning that regulators were casting a more discerning eye toward the derivatives activities of financial institutions even when they only had powers to recommend rather than regulate legally.[12]

QUIET BEFORE MORE STORMS

By the end of the 1980s, both the British and American banking systems appeared relatively calm after a decade of deregulation and rapid change. The stock markets were still feeling the effect of the collapse of 1987 although the indices began to rebound within six months of the initial price drops. The American agricultural credit crisis of 1985–86 had been resolved by legislation and some of the harshest effects of the debt crisis began to abate. But each country's financial system again would soon be shaken by remnants of the past that had stubbornly refused to die.

Despite the rebound in the British economy in the latter 1980s, nominal and real interest rates remained high when compared to those in the United States or in Britain's major European competitors. Controlling the money supply had proven difficult for most of the decade although the burst in the money aggregates had fuelled a high degree of consumerism and another property price explosion. As a result, consumers tolerated the high mort-gage rates and consumer interest rates because prices and wages were rising, although interest paid took a larger portion of the pay cheque than it did in France or Germany.

High interest rates supported the pound against the dollar and other major European currencies and, by the late 1980s, the pound was near the $2.00 level again for the first time in more than a decade. Its level against the Deutschmark, at around DM2.90–3.00, was also fairly high. This was the background in which Britain decided to finally join the exchange rate mechanism (ERM) of the EC – a decision that had been put off continuously since Britain first joined the EMS in 1979. Lower interest rates in continental Europe proved appealing to the UK, especially if currency stability could be achieved in the process.

When Britain did join the ERM in September 1990, the high interest-rate differentials between itself and Germany persisted. The net effect was that a reduction in German interest rates would spell reductions for the UK. But the negative side was that if German rates rose, UK rates would probably have to follow. If they did not, there would still not be any room for a reduction in British rates. Unfortunately, Britain's joining coincided with the beginning of the prolonged recession in the UK and German reunification, which would alter the normally expected reduction in German interest rates.

After the 1988 presidential election in the United States, another thrift crisis appeared that would eventually dwarf that of 1981–82. Throughout the second half of 1988, the Federal Savings and Loan Insurance Corporation (FSLIC), the thrifts' counterpart of the FDIC, met increasing demands from many thrifts seeking protection for their depositors. However, the incipient crisis in the industry did not find a place in the election contest between George Bush and Michael Dukakis and the Republicans were returned to power. But soon after the inauguration in January 1989, Congress quickly put together a rescue package for the industry with a speed that astonished many observers both for its scope and swiftness. Within a few short months following the election, a problem previously acknowledged as growing but assumed to be under control had emerged to bankrupt the FSLIC and force Congress to construct a new regulator for the thrift industry. When combined with British entry into the ERM, the early 1990s were quickly approaching, promising anything but a halcyon period for the markets.

7

BANKING REFORM AGAIN

Part of the prosperity of the 1980s was due to the absence of a recession for an historically long period after 1982. Not until 1990 did the economies of Britain and the United States begin to register the sort of growth normally associated with an economic slowdown. But the recession would have a different impact in each country. In the United States, it would signal the lowest interest rates since the 1950s. In Britain, it coincided with Britain's entry into the ERM, added to the unemployment queue and lasted almost two years longer than it did in the US. Exchange rates played a prominent role on both counts. The recession would trigger lower exchange rates and interest rates but not without some initial embarrassing costs.

The new volatility in the foreign exchange market and its impact upon government policies gave added credence to the idea that governments could no longer ignore the prosperity to which consumers had grown accustomed over the previous decade. When faced with the dictates of the ERM, Britain decided that lower interest rates were more important than the mechanism itself, which infringed upon its monetary sovereignty. The Americans, on the other hand, recognised that the recession spelled lower interest rates and a weaker dollar. That provided an opportunity to practise benign currency neglect again and to allow the yen to appreciate without intervention, allowing the US merchandise trade deficit to improve. The lessons of the post-Bretton Woods era were entering a new phase: there was now some precedent for allowing exchange rates to take their natural course, especially when interest rates were pointing down. The anti-EC forces in Britain and those Americans favouring harsher treatment for the Japanese would not be the only ones to benefit as a result. Consumers would also gain significantly by the phenomenon.

But the early 1990s was not only a period of exchange rate considerations. Bank regulation and deregulation in the United States was still a current topic of discussion. The thrift crisis and the increased capital requirements imposed by the Bank for International Settlements (BIS), scheduled to begin in 1992, required additional legislation from Congress to prevent even more banks from failing. In the mid-1980s, the Federal

Reserve and the Bank of England had worked together closely with the BIS to strengthen the capital requirements at banks in the developed countries. Prior to 1988, the increasing requirements were domestic matters for each central bank to impose on its own institutions. In 1988, an accord was reached that required all banks in the developed countries to maintain 8 per cent capital on their books by 1992, the year it was anticipated that further European economic integration would occur. When combined with domestic banking and thrift legislation by Congress in 1989 and 1991, those capital requirements became a centrepiece of US banking reform.

Despite the success of the BIS agreement and the example that it provided of international central bank co-operation, more international banking problems were still to come. One of the greatest sources of embarrassment to the Federal Reserve and the Bank of England occurred in 1991 when the Bank of Credit and Commerce International (BCCI) had to be closed in both the US and Britain. Originally established as an international bank with an extensive branch network throughout the developing world, BCCI at first operated in Britain as a licensed deposit taker, placing most of its liabilities in the money market. Later, when the Banking Act was passed in 1987, it fell under the aegis of the Bank of England's supervisory functions. When gross irregularities were reported in its lending policies and treasury operations, both central banks quickly withdrew its licenses to operate in their countries, effectively putting it out of business.

The subsequent closing of BCCI worldwide cost depositors an estimated $20 billion and was something of an anomaly in a world of increasing capital controls and bank regulation mandated by the BIS agreement in 1988. The affair demonstrated the lack of control by domestic monetary authorities when international banks with no effective regulation in their home-based countries operate on a global scale (BCCI's major shareholders were from the United Arab Emirates). Although the Federal Reserve and the Bank of England operated in tandem to close the major operations of BCCI, they were severely criticised for acting too late to protect depositors who had seen their funds disappear through fraud and mismanagement.

The early 1990s also added several cornerstones to the development of consumer democracy. Although the thrift crisis (outlined below) is usually thought of as a masterful cover-up of political and financial ineptitude by the management of many thrifts across the country, both Congress and regulators appeared to discover and acknowledge the problem very late, after the problems had reached crisis proportions. Although quickly acknowledged by the new Bush administration early in 1989, the continuing crisis nevertheless helped defeat George Bush in the 1992 election. When combined with the brief but sharp increase in oil prices at the time of the Gulf War, it provided a reprise of the sort of events that had taken their toll on earlier administrations. Since the collapse of the Bretton Woods system, recessions had a negative impact on incumbent presidents in the United States – the sort of phenomenon not seen in Britain since the 1970s.

Recognising the increasing power of consumers, the political opposition in the United States realised that consumerism was a force that must be acknowledged regardless of the sorts of policies that it eventually wanted to introduce. The presidential election of 1992 and the anti-incumbent campaign that dominated the congressional elections of the early and mid-1990s give testimony to the trend. This was also the greatest challenge to Labour in Britain during the 1980s and early 1990s that went unmet. While the Conservatives expanded credit and exploited a general feeling of prosperity, Labour was still remembered as the last party to deal with the IMF for a standby facility during a period of intense labour–management hostility, electric power blackouts and declining British prosperity. Labour offered little to consumers other than generally time-worn promises that appeared ironically out of date. Similarly, the Republicans lost the 1992 presidential election because of the general notion that budget deficits, government borrowing and easy money in the 1980s led to a recession that threatened livelihoods during a general period of technological change in the United States. Voters were probably more disgruntled with the first recession in eight years and those associated with it, rightly or wrongly, and that contributed to a Republican defeat after twelve years in power.

The 1990s would witness new institutional developments in the banking industries in both the US and Britain. The Americans were still attempting to adapt their banking system to the new, rapidly changing international financial environment while the British were beginning to experience attempts at consolidating building societies into commercial banks. Although the Third World debt crisis had receded and banks were adding fresh capital to their balance sheets, the American banking system was again facing a crisis of major proportions that had the potential to seriously undermine the financial system. Oddly, it came from a sector of the banking community that should have been well on its way to recovery. And when compared with the developments in the financial markets in derivatives trading and new product development, it also appeared strangely out of step with the times. When combined with the BCCI affair, it helped prove that the financial system was still in a precarious position despite years of legislation.

THE THRIFT CRISIS REVISITED

Within weeks of George Bush's election victory in November 1988, the second crisis in the thrift industry within a decade began to surface. The FSLIC had been pushed to the brink by rescuing savings institutions and was technically bankrupt, unable to provide protection for any more thrift depositors. This crisis was much more serious than the one that occurred in 1981, prompting the Garn–St Germain Act to be passed, liberalising thrift institutions in particular. But it had become apparent that access to adjustable rates of interest had not helped the thrifts as originally intended. If anything, adjustable rates of interest were sometimes poorly managed by the thrifts and their operating risks had increased substantially in some cases. Thrifts had proven to be poor lenders and even poorer managers of interest rate risk.

The thrifts' problem was manifold. Many had used the deregulatory legislation to invest in junk bonds although the amounts of corporate securities they could purchase were still limited. Others had loaned heavily to commercial real estate ventures in what had become a saturated market characterised by high vacancy rates by the late 1980s. Still others had engaged in outright fraud: making soft loans to directors and officers and offering doubtful investment products to their depositors. This combination of practices had forced many to the brink of insolvency. The entire thrift industry in Rhode Island had to be temporarily frozen while state regulators there sorted out methods to preserve deposits.

Many of these problems were not headline news items in 1989, but Congress finally passed the first major legislation in decades to correct the structural problems in the thrift industry six months after it was first introduced. The Financial Institutions Reconstruction, Recovery and Enforcement Act of 1989 (FIRREA) provided the most sweeping thrift legislation since the Hoover administration had created the Federal Home Loan Bank Board in 1932, extending far beyond the provisions of the Garn–St Germain Act. The Act effectively merged the functions of the FSLIC into the FDIC (since the thrift insurance corporation was effectively bankrupt) and provided a new regulator to clean up the industry's problems.[1]

Of the myriad provisions of the FIRREA, the best-known institution to emerge was the Resolution Trust Corporation (RTC), the agency charged with the actual clean-up and obtaining the necessary funding. The RTC had the unenviable task of disposing of assets of closed thrifts in order to help settle customer's deposits. Losses on the asset sales plus the deposit cover were originally estimated to cost approximately $50 billion but the number was later increased to around $300 billion when the extent of the industry's problems became better known. The public outrage was oddly muted throughout most of the first two years of the problem, although massive disintermediation of thrifts did occur in early 1989 when the problems first publicly surfaced. Many deposits found their way to the safety of FDIC-protected institutions although, ironically, the FIRREA would make the FDIC responsible for guaranteeing thrift deposits as well as commercial bank deposits.

The thrift crisis prompted much debate over the nature of moral hazard,

a topic embedded in American deposit insurance that had been discussed several times in the 1970s and 1980s. As the thrift crisis deepened, the entire deposit structure in American banks and thrifts came under the worried glance of regulators and commentators. *The Economist* stated that 'the Treasury is rightly alarmed by the contingent liability posed by the $2.9 trillion of insured deposits in America's banks and thrifts plus about a further trillion on uninsured deposits at America's banks'.[2] The old concern of unethical behaviour on the part of bankers, using deposit insurance as a cover for their imprudent lending, was again surfacing, finally with more than ample proof of the weaknesses of providing 100 per cent insurance on deposits of $100,000 or less per account. Bankers not particularly careful in their lending policies could effectively use such deposits as a basis for imprudent lending at little cost to themselves.

But comprehensive deposit insurance was not the only underlying problem behind the thrift crisis. Many thrifts were able to act with relative impunity because of their distance from the banking community. Many were small, state-chartered institutions operating within narrow geographical areas. Because of their relative remoteness from money centres, their actions and policies did not fall under the constant scrutiny of the money markets or securities analysts (many, as building societies, were mutual associations). Their insularity also kept them relatively naive over the years to developments in the financial markets that eventually would be more open to them after the Garn–St Germain Act. Their environment made many of them susceptible to sharp practices practised on them by dishonest operators and aggressive investment bankers.

The bail-out and restructuring of the thrift industry fell under the aegis of the Office of Thrift Supervision (OTS), the Treasury-related agency that encompassed the RTC and its funding arm, the Resolution Funding Corporation, or Refcorp. The functions of the Federal Home Loan Bank Board, founded during the early years of the Depression, were abrogated and replaced by the new agency. The district Home Loan Banks were kept intact although the FIRREA clearly set out to abolish the Board, called by one commentator an 'Act of anger', since the new legislation clearly sought to distance the new institutions it created from those that had preceded it.[3] The clear implication was that the FHLBB had failed in its regulatory duties by allowing the thrift crisis to develop without intervening or raising adequate alarms.

Refcorp was the only part of the new apparatus that would play a visible role in the financial markets. It was given borrowing authority for the long term, borrowing for 30 years' maturity in the bond market. Beyond the first $20 billion, subsequent issues were defeased (backed) by zero coupon US Treasury issues to ensure that principal would be repaid in timely fashion. Refcorp became the one government-related agency with no assets to speak of so the defeasances were necessary to back the bonds and market them effectively. By amortising the borrowings over the long term, it became clear that the thrift problem was not going to disappear as quickly as might have been hoped. Equally, the interest costs of the bail-out would be cosmetically reduced if spread over a long time period.

The thrift crisis prompted many solvent savings institutions technically to change their charters to those of savings banks or, in some cases, commercial banks. Those that remained profitable began to distance themselves from the S&L industry in general so that they would not suffer further disintermediation by savers. That technically made the S&L industry even smaller after the failed institutions were removed from the count. That was the beginning of a trend toward the eventual disintegration of thrift institutions in general. They were too small to compete in the new banking environment and tarnished with a reputation that the few successful ones wanted to eschew in favour of becoming more like full-service banks. The declining number of thrifts can be found in Table 7.1.

Table 7.1 Number of thrifts in the US

Year	Number	Assets (billions US$)
1987	3,147	1,300
1988	2,949	1,400
1989	2,597	1,200
1990	2,342	1,010
1991	2,096	875
1992	1,855	795
1993	1,669	775

Source: Office of Thrift Supervision

True to the competitive nature of banking, the FIRREA also unleashed a small wave of bidding for deposits among some banks and thrifts reminiscent of the interest rate 'wars' of the mid-1980s. The marginal thrifts and banks began to raise their deposit rates in order to attract customers. While there was nothing wrong with the practice, the problem of moral hazard again raised its head. Weak institutions would pay more for deposits than others, suggesting that they would make riskier loans to compensate for the additional cost. Ironically, the deregulation of the 1980s had the potential to quickly overtake the newer strictures of the FIRREA, designed to lessen moral hazard and provide for healthier institutions.

As soon as this problem was recognised, Congress acted to pass the Federal Deposit Insurance Corporation Improvement Act (FDICIA) of 1991. Allowing weak institutions to operate alongside the stronger, called regulatory forbearance, was putting the strong institutions at a disadvantage because it would only increase their insurance premiums paid to the FDIC as more and more of the weaker institutions failed. As a result, the improvement act allowed regulators to close a depository institution if its ratio of capital to risky assets fell below 2 per cent and remained as such for 270 days. That would allow the regulators more latitude; they no longer had to wait for an institution's capital to diminish to zero before acting. That would also help the RTC sell the institution's assets to potential investors.

However, another part of the FDICIA acknowledged indirectly that deposit insurance was inadequate to cover potential deposits at the largest banks and as a result they could not be allowed to fail. The precedent for this sort of thinking was the FDIC's bail-out of all of the depositors of Continental Illinois in 1984 regardless of the size of their deposits. The policy became known as 'too big to fail'. Continental Illinois was bailed out because of the potential damage that its outright failure could have done to the financial system. Much of its funding came from the whole-sale CD market and any failure to honour those obligations might have caused problems at other banks. That sort of knock-on effect, known as systemic risk, was the major concern of the FDIC throughout the years of the banking crisis.

But outright adherence to 'too big to fail' would place the banks and regulators back essentially where they were during the days of Regulation Q by admitting that the FDIC would have to rescue the largest banks regardless of their lending practices. Many alternative suggestions appeared that sought to solve the problem; one of the better-known suggested replacing the traditional deposit/loan relationship with one generally called 'narrow banking'.[4] This would have restricted depository institutions to investing deposits in risk-free Treasury securities only. Although the idea was not adopted, the provisions of the FDICIA nevertheless sought to limit the idea of comprehensive insurance at large banks while admitting that it is still technically impossible for a large bank to fail. The Act mandated limits on interbank risk and interbank credit, and required the access to funds through the payments system to be speeded up by using a net settlement basis.[5]

The thrift crisis coincided with the 1990–92 recession and the slowing of issuing activity in the junk bond market. Many thrifts had purchased junk bonds as high-yielding assets only to see their values diminish. The diminished values hurt the thrifts' asset values and once they were no longer willing buyers of the bonds, the junk market slowed considerably as the recession began. The Garn–St Germain Act served little useful purpose here: by liberalising thrifts' assets in 1982 it had opened the back door to junk bond investments. Once hailed as a great piece of deregulatory legis-lation, the Act only served as further proof that liberalising regulation for its own sake often could have nasty consequences unforeseen at the time that it was passed. The entire thrift crisis had proved that events in the marketplace were again leading regulators and that despite the comprehensiveness of remedial legislation the markets were still several steps ahead of congressional and regulatory attempts to strengthen financial institutions.

MONETARY SOVEREIGNTY AGAIN

While the thrift crisis was causing problems for the American banking system, British attention was turned to the ERM and the pound's role within it. Britain joined the mechanism in September 1990, having waited eleven years since first joining the EMS and finally abandoning exchange controls in 1979. As mentioned in the previous chapter, Britain's entry was cautiously welcomed but the circumstances under which it joined were less ideal. When it joined, it would be pegged to prevailing interest rates and exchange rates in the EC, which would prove less than beneficial to both sterling and the ERM itself.

Despite the success of the British economy in the latter 1980s, interest rates remained stubbornly high for most of the period. When the UK officially joined the ERM, its interest rates became tied inexorably to those in Germany, the ERM leader for setting interest rates and, consequently, for exchange rates as well. For all practical purposes, German monetary policy was sovereign within the ERM and that fact posed problems for those in Britain opposed to further integration. But being tied to the ERM had its potentially positive side as well. While British monetary policy had not always proven successful, being tied to a highly successful policy in Bonn was viewed as favourable for Britain. But that did not take into account the reunification of Germany and the German government's pledge to rebuild the reunified east. In order to attract foreign funds for that endeavour, interest rates on Bundesrepublik bonds would have to be relatively high and remain that way in order to protect the exchange rate at the same time.

Politically, the costs of German reunification collided with the provisions of the Maastricht Treaty passed in early 1992. The high value of the ECU and the pound against the dollar helped keep Britain's interest rates high and began to hurt its trading position. The treaty itself bore the seeds of its own destruction in a sense by allowing for referendums on its terms. The French and the Irish voted in favour in 1992 although the first referendum, in Denmark, received a negative vote, casting a doubt on Maastricht's future. In fact, in the two years immediately following Maastricht, public opinion over the matter of further integration was divided. But one point was clear despite general misgivings in the EC itself: Britain's ambivalence over further economic integration was the greatest among the twelve member states with only about 20 per cent of British voters in favour, the lowest in the EC.[6]

The high value of the pound and high UK interest rates made the UK vulnerable to currency speculation because the currency appeared seriously overvalued given the state of the UK economy. This was the German view, although the Bundesbank made it clear that it was in no hurry to lower German interest rates because capital was still needed from abroad to help finance the rebuilding projects in the east. As a result, currency speculation became rampant in September 1992 and the Italian lira and the pound sterling came under serious selling pressures. In order to maintain sterling's value, the UK raised interest rates by 2 per cent on 16 September and clearly signalled that it would be willing to raise them again if necessary. But it was to no avail because sterling's grid value was broken and the pound was forced temporarily out of the ERM. Within a couple of weeks it became clear that it would not return and that a devaluation had been accomplished *de facto*. The lira suffered the same fate.

Britain's ambivalence about economic and political integration made the post-ERM period crucial for how the devaluation would be received. While the withdrawal was viewed as another symptom of Britain's decline, it was quickly seized upon by Prime Minister Major, who made it clear that it was time to end the recession in the UK. The subsequent interest rate drops that followed helped to revive the economy, moving it closer to the Americans, who were recovering from the economic slowdown, than to the Europeans, who were still in the early stages of recession.

The benefits and costs of leaving the ERM were weighed by Barrell, Britton and Pain (in Cobham 1994). Constructing counterfactual outcomes based upon what may have occurred if Britain had remained committed to the ERM, they calculated that UK output growth would have increased while consumer price inflation would have declined. These conclusions were reached under two scenarios: if Britain had maintained the same parity of the pound in the ERM after September 1992, or if Britain had accepted a devaluation of 6 per cent.[7] In either case, the UK would have benefited. However, the withdrawal raises questions of the political will necessary to achieve any sort of international monetary co-operation. Clearly, the UK authorities took advantage of a bad situation and withdrew, although the results appear to have been an end to recession.

On the other side of the coin, the costs to the UK of the withdrawal were also calculated. The main problem, according to this analysis, was inflation. Based upon the fact that UK long-term gilt rates remained above comparable German rates, the conclusion was that the market was betting upon British inflation over the medium term. Also taken into account was the loss of British credibility at working toward an international monetary standard.[8] However, these purported costs are not particularly compelling. Both points are essentially political and have been seen before in the financial history of the last twenty-five years. First, German interest rates were lower than those in the UK because investors favoured German monetary policy over the British, at least until the effects of UK withdrawal could be determined. Second, in terms of international co-operation, it has been seen that devaluations and depreciations have been used by the UK previously to achieve economic goals, however short-sighted they have been. If international credibility was the only casualty of the withdrawal then the price was worth paying, given the potential political consequences to the Conservatives if lower inflation and economic growth had not been achieved in the long run. It was not the first time that the UK had sacrificed credibility for exchange rates in the post-Bretton Woods period.

Much of the economic success of the UK in the latter 1980s can be attributed to an increase in consumer spending. In the 1980s, consumer spending in the UK rose more than twice the amounts recorded in either of the previous two decades, even when adjusted. Most of that increase came after the inflation and recession that ended in 1982. This was financed by a decrease in the personal savings ratios of UK households that had always been traditionally high. But the trend became more pronounced in the latter 1980s. As Figure 7.1 shows, in 1989 the savings ratio was only half of what it would be in 1992 since the more recession set in, consumers began to save rather than spend. Employment and output also increased in the latter 1980s, only to suffer again during the recession. The political ramifications of this trend were clear. Submitting the UK to high interest rates again would probably continue the trend toward higher

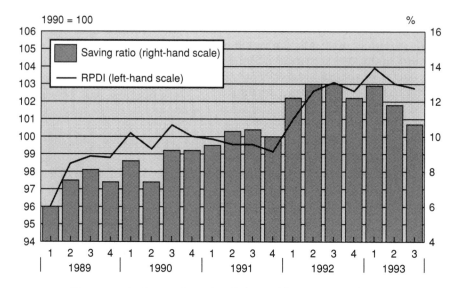

Figure 7.1 Savings ratio and real disposable income in the UK

Source: European Commission

savings, higher unemployment and lower output. Once ERM membership had shown its effects under the interest rate conditions immediately prevailing at the time, there was little incentive for the UK to remain a member.

The collapse of the pound in the ERM can be viewed as another victory for consumer democracy over external monetary forces. By lowering interest rates by almost ten percentage points over the next two years, the UK was able to induce a return to consumer spending after a lengthy recession. When faced with the dictates of the ERM versus the growing demands of consumers and voters, the acceptance of the collapse of the EMS became much easier to tolerate. This is not to ignore the longer-term results that may yet develop, but does illustrate the sort of short-term thinking that has become prevalent in policymaking circles and the markets over the last twenty-five years. Essentially, the British adopted an American stance rather than a European one by making best use of the recession to lower rates and hope for a reaction among consumers.

BENIGN NEGLECT AGAIN

After the Plaza and Louvre agreements, the fortunes of the dollar were as mixed as those of sterling. The decline witnessed after 1987 helped the US merchandise trade deficit decline somewhat as exports increased in many sectors on the back of the cheaper currency. But in 1988–89, the dollar staged a strong rally that eroded some of the gains made by the Deutschmark and the yen after 1986–87. That particular rally had strong political overtones because it came in an election year, when George Bush successfully succeeded Ronald Reagan. On the surface, it appeared that strong dollar politics had come into vogue again.

As Destler and Henning (1989) noted, the strong dollar of 1988 helped quiet the financial markets and certainly did not harm George Bush's chances of election.[9] It came on the back of modest interest rate rises prompted by the Federal Reserve and was supported by the Treasury in the weeks preceding the election itself. While it did spark rumours of an international conspiracy among central bankers to elect George Bush, the financial markets certainly helped by remaining strong throughout the next several months. The dollar did not show weakness again until the recession prompted a lowering of interest rates about a year later. This fall in exchange values also hurt the pound, which remained strong until the ERM crisis in September 1993.

After 1989–90, the Deutschmark became the strong currency supported by high interest rates and a central bank determined to keep the exchange rate high. In order to rebuild eastern Germany, the Federal Republic committed itself to a strong Deutschmark and relatively high interest rates to support it if necessary. That policy was successful between 1988 and 1992 as the growth in real GDP and non-residential fixed investment in Germany was greater than that in the United States or OECD Europe.[10] While that policy hurt the ERM considerably, it helped the United States trade position by reducing demand for the dollar. As the dollar weakened, the new Democratic administration realised in 1993 that some political and trade gains could be made by not intervening to support it on a large scale. The persistent merchandise trade deficit, although improved since the mid-1980s, benefited because foreign manufactured goods were becoming more expensive. Benign neglect was appearing again, this time under totally different conditions than those prevailing during the early Reagan years. The pound and Deutschmark against the dollar can be seen in Figure 7.2.

When the Federal Reserve began to raise interest rates in the winter of 1994, publicly fearing a rise in inflation, signs became clear that the US had emerged from recession and was on the road to a fairly strong economic recovery. But again, the exchange rate became a crucial issue. As the yen rose to the 100 level against the dollar, pressure began to mount on the Clinton administration to intervene and strengthen the dollar to help the Japanese, who were in the throes of recession. However, little was done to strengthen the currency and the yen climbed to new post-war highs, reaching 98 yen/dollar in the spring and summer. The administration apparently was ambivalent about defending the dollar against the yen, especially in the face of intense American–Japanese trade negotiations being conducted at the time. The interest rate increases prompted by the Federal Reserve were publicly said to be aimed at curtailing inflation but several

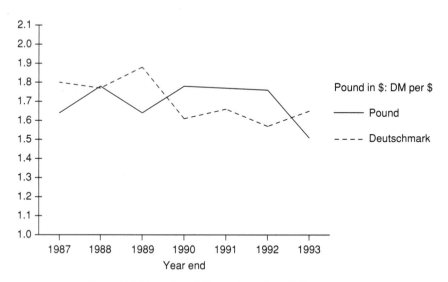

Figure 7.2 Pound and Deutschmark v. dollar, 1987–93

Source: Federal Reserve *Bulletin*, various issues

of the rises, well announced unlike those in the past, did coincide with the negotiations at delicate stages, suggesting that interest rates were being used as a tool in the discussions with the Japanese. Japanese concessions on opening more of their domestic market to the Americans could possibly result in an American interest rate rise, helping ostensibly to strengthen the dollar and improving Japan's export capacities to the US.

On the opposite side of that coin was the size of the export balance itself: some $60 billion per year, two-thirds of which was with the United States. With an imbalance of that size, the Americans would appear to have a small bargaining chip since the consumer was already well enamoured of Japanese goods, as reflected in the merchandise trade deficit. However, when combined with the Japanese banking crisis caused by a massive amount of non-performing loans on the books of Japanese banks and other commercial lenders, it became apparent that the yen/dollar relationship was extremely important to the Japanese because, without a favourable level, manufacturing exports would not be able to sustain the slack caused by losses in the banking sector. The other problem was also more long term: would American consumers continue to buy Japanese goods in the future if a weak dollar had allowed American manufacturers to become more competitive in the domestic marketplace both in terms of increasing quality and price?

BRANCH BANKING AND INVESTMENT BANKING REVISITED

In 1994, after years of piecemeal reforms, Congress finally passed the Interstate Banking Act, which effectively removed all remaining barriers to interstate bank branching. Finally, commercial banks could open branches across state lines without restriction. The McFadden Act had finally been superseded after 67 years. Although interstate banking after a fashion had been practised since the early 1980s, no longer were a variety of excuses needed to practise it.

Originally, both Citicorp and the Bank of America had taken over banking operations in other states in the early 1980s. At the time, the rationale used by compliant regulators was that if the banks had not stepped into the breach, the institutions they had bought would have failed. A takeover by out-of-state banks was better than FDIC assistance and certainly more efficient. But the failing bank doctrine could not be used on a widespread basis because of the intrinsic disincentives for potential buyers. But it was quickly followed by other rationales that helped break down the interstate barriers.

In the mid- to latter 1980s, the regulators began to allow mergers on an interstate basis if all banks were from the same Federal Reserve district. Shortly thereafter, the failing bank doctrine was again applied as the Texas banking system entered a crisis and several large Texas banks were purchased by out-of-state money centre and regional banks. Then, as the banking crisis began to weaken the banking systems of other states, notably in the south-west, many state legislatures removed their local restrictions and many mergers began to occur. But in all cases, the actual provisions of the McFadden Act were still intact: banks acquired others but did not establish *de novo* branches across state lines.

The Interstate Banking Act finally helped banks realise geographically what they had previously been able to accomplish only by loopholes in the banking laws. Credit card services had been offered nationwide for years, as had wholesale banking services. In most cases, they established subsidiaries through their holding companies in order to engage in these practices. Some thrifts had even attempted to open 'nationwide' services by making use of the automated teller machine facilities allowed them by the deregulatory legislation of the early 1980s. While some were successful and others less so, the extraordinary legal manoeuvring of the past would no longer be necessary. The bankers' dream of operating nationwide as Canadian banks had always done had finally become a reality after sixty years of waiting.

But one vestige of the past remained. The commercial banks were still technically prohibited from crossing the lines laid down by the Glass–Steagall Act and performing investment banking services, notably the underwriting of corporate securities. This function was still mainly in the province of the investment banks. But again, during the 1980s the once stringent regulatory atmosphere had been relaxed in the name of greater economies and efficiency as well as because of considerable pressure from some of the commercial banks.

Beginning in the late 1980s, the Federal Reserve began allowing a select group of commercial banks to begin underwriting corporate bonds. Shortly thereafter, the same group was allowed to underwrite equities as well. This foray into previously forbidden areas was justified by the Federal Reserve's liberal interpretation of a provision of the Glass–Steagall Act that allowed commercial bank subsidiaries with trading experience in bonds (primary dealers in government bonds) to begin underwriting on a limited basis.[11] Within a short period of time, several of them had acquired substantial expertise and rose quickly in the league tables of major underwriters in corporate securities.

One of the major factors blocking further integration between the commercial and investment banking sectors has been the blurred lines created by financial innovation. Uses of swaps and derivatives have proliferated to the point that no one, including users and regulators, is certain of the long-term economic effects that these instruments will have on the marketplace. Originally developed by investment banks, much of the trading has been dominated by commercial banks because of their larger capital bases and client bases. More akin to the risks associated with foreign exchange trading than with those normally identified with traditional commercial banking, the sheer size of the markets has slowed down further discussions of allowing either type of banking institutions into the other's territory. Beginning in 1993, corporate losses were being experienced as many companies announced losses attributed to derivatives or swaps trading. The losses recorded by Metallgesellschaft in Germany were the corporate world's version of the Hammersmith debacle, at least until that time. That and losses by companies around the world, caught in the interest rate increases in the United States in 1994, illustrated that many treasurers were not aware of the exposures that they had assumed in swaps and derivatives, or were too naive in assessing the amount of damage that could be done to their positions if interest rates rose after the fact and currency exposures followed suit.

Despite the weakness in the banking sector and the revolution in financial services, the American and British financial systems have changed substantially in the last twenty-five years. They and many other economies have fared much better than would have been thought in the sort of environment that the original Bretton Woods system sought to prevent. This has been accomplished by a tacit acceptance that markets and institutions are two steps ahead of attempts to control them and should remain there unless they pose a greater threat to the financial system as a whole. By attempting to use the currency markets to their own advantage, governments in both countries have come to recognise that consumers prevail over time and that to ignore them would be politically fatal.

CONCLUSION

In the years preceding the fiftieth anniversary of the Bretton Woods Conference in 1994, the idea of returning to a fixed parity system of some sort has resurfaced several times. The intrinsic volatility of the floating exchange rate regime has led to renewed calls for some parity system to replace the riskiness of the present system in order to avoid some of the more serious exchange fluctuations witnessed in the last twenty-five years. However, the recent experience within the ERM and the move away from dollar sovereignty since the 1970s makes the return to some form of parity system less likely.

The history of the financial markets and exchange rates over the past twenty years suggests that the markets effectively have been leading the lawmakers and regulators of both Britain and the United States rather than the other way round. The markets have shown an unwillingness to respond to political pronouncements or to jawboning unless they have experienced serious discipline exercised by governments that goes beyond cosmetic, short-term measures designed to make consumers happy in election years. And, even when discipline apparently has been applied, financial markets and institutions still sometimes go their own way. Despite the Banking Act of 1979, the Johnson Matthey affair still managed to embarrass the Bank of England while the Garn–St Germain Act could not stave off the whole-sale destruction of the thrift industry. In these and other cases, the American record of preventing further financial crisis is worse than the British. It has taken over sixty years for the American banking system to shed the Depression-era legislation that encumbered its ability to grow geographically and diversify its offerings of new products.

Consumerism finally won the day by helping to break down the barriers that hindered banking and cost depositors additional interest under the old interest rate ceilings. The introduction and success of money market funds and adjustable-rate mortgages were both products designed to appeal to consumers previously frustrated by banking regulations designed to protect banks from dangers no longer present in the financial system. In the process, the markets, and especially the foreign exchange market, have opened a new page in the development of consumer democracy in both the US and Britain.

Also militating for the status quo in the present day foreign exchange market are the gains that consumers have made since 1971. Access to imports, easy credit and a wide array of consumer choices has made a return to a parity system difficult since that would necessarily imply a central currency/ies anchoring a system. Others would then become tied to those interest rates and monetary policies. That is plausible when a country has something distinct to gain by applying discipline to its markets (Ireland within the ERM as an example) but is much less beneficial when it erodes consumer confidence or implies a temporary decline in the standard of living.

In the Britain of the 1960s or 1970s, still reminiscent of being a great industrial and manufacturing power, devaluations became a tool by which to adjust the price of exports without having to become more efficient or competitive. Consumption increased steadily in the 1960s while capital formation lagged and that trend began to take its toll. While British capital investment declined for most of the 1970s, consumers' expenditures declined significantly after 1972 and did not show signs of resurgence until 1978, two years after the IMF standby facility. Capital investment declined again until 1982 when the recession ended and the British boom began, following that in the United States. Britain experienced strong consumer spending under the Conservatives due to unusually high interest rates in the second half of the 1980s that kept the pound higher than might otherwise have been the case, helping to satisfy consumers' demand for foreign goods when they were deemed superior to British goods. Consumers were demanding better than British industry could produce and the exchange rate would not always compensate when convenient. A tension appeared that would require careful balancing: a weak exchange benefited industry while a strong rate benefited consumers. When that balance could be achieved, the image of a declining Britain producing shoddy manufactured goods could be overcome.

The Thatcher revolution embodied this trend and made no claims to Britain remaining an industrial and manufacturing power. Consumer democracy also had a political side that helped revolutionise British society in the 1980s, making the Thatcher revolution more radical than the Reagan revolution in the US. As Rubinstein's (1993) historical argument shows, in the contemporary period the Tory government solidified its natural power base in the south-east of Britain, away from the older manufacturing strongholds in the Midlands and the north. The new Conservative party was also free of the fundamental illusion of all recent governments – that Britain could be restored to her former position as an industrial power of the first rank by direct and purposeful intervention in, and on behalf of, manufacturing industry. Recognising that Britain's recent economic strengths were in services and trading rather than manufacturing *per se*, the Conservatives fashioned a consensus around consumerism much as Reagan was concurrently structuring in the US. The result was a long period in power. Withdrawal from the ERM was an acknowledgement that consumerism took precedence over surrendering monetary sovereignty to the EC in 1992 without clear benefits. It was also an acknowledgement that the sterling/dollar relationship was still vital to UK interests; a high pound rate against the dollar was as detrimental to British interests at the time as the high rate against the Deutschmark.

Experience has shown that the foreign exchange market increasingly has made its will felt and governments have had little recourse but to follow. On occasion, governments have tried to make some capital out of embarrassing foreign exchange market conditions. In 1969, Harold Wilson blamed international speculators for the pound's problems as his government officially devalued for what would be the last sterling devaluation of the Bretton Woods era. In 1971, Richard Nixon did the same as the United States abrogated the dollar's theoretical convertibility into gold and devalued against the other major trading currencies. The Bank of England made it clear to the market in 1976 that it preferred dollars to be used in a single case of dealing with another central bank, in a clear attempt to force down sterling. That move had somewhat embarrassing consequences because it touched off a run on the pound. The IMF standby loan followed, leading to the inevitable descriptions of Britain having sunk to the level of a Third World country. Again, in 1992, when sterling left the ERM mechanism, speculators (this time, hedge fund managers) were blamed for sterling's travails although it was almost universally acknowledged that the pound was overvalued both in dollar and Deutschmark terms. The clear evidence in all of these cases was that limited political opportunism could easily be made out of foreign exchange matters. Floating exchange rates make life more simple for governments and cause less public embarrassment.

The development of a high state of consumer democracy in the United States and Britain has been fostered under the floating exchange rate regime. Consumers now have manifold choices of consumer goods and financial services due to clever exploitation of exchange rates and political opportunism by governments dexterous enough to capitalise on currency fluctuations. When the dollar's exchange rates were high, the Reagan administration used the attractive interest rates accompanying them to lure foreign capital to help finance the budget deficit. Consumers used the strong rates to buy a record amount of foreign manufactured goods, helping to transform American industry in the process. In this sense, the exchange rate mechanism served to help modernise many parts of American manufacturing. Large, inefficient motor cars were replaced by more efficient models able to compete with foreign imports. Quality control also was re-examined to determine whether any foreign methods could be employed to make domestic workers more efficient and content in the process. American industry owed many qualitative gains not to the Japanese or the Germans in the first instance but to the exchange rate.

Ironically, Britain's withdrawal from the ERM in 1992 was a devaluation of the same sort that the US adopted in 1971 when the Bretton Woods system collapsed. Within a few years of that devaluation, the US trade deficit narrowed considerably. Again, in the latter 1980s, after the dollar was forced down by the Plaza and Louvre agreements, the US trade balance again improved. These sorts of experiences have proved that governments have learned the embarrassing lessons of official devaluations. In the post-Bretton Woods era, under floating exchange rates the same sort of practices have prevailed but devaluations now have become depreciations (unless they occur within a mechanism such as the ERM) and have been much easier to justify publicly. The markets have traditionally led both the American and British governments in the post-war era and have continued to do so. Under floating exchange rates, governments have been able to recognise this without severe embarrassment, the anguish of the pound in the ERM being the one notable exception.

But the conditions that helped create and sustain contemporary consumer democracies have made life difficult for companies and banks that must make use of foreign exchange in an increasingly volatile world. Financial innovation has helped companies and investors cope in an unstructured environment, making discussions of a new 'system' of foreign exchange much less urgent than it was twenty-five years ago. Swaps and financial derivatives have grown exponentially because the corporate world needs them to help offset risks in the current interest rate and foreign exchange environment. Excesses in the new marketplace will certainly occur, as the Hammersmith and Metallgesellschaft affairs illustrate, but the clear sign is that ingenuity will no longer wait for government intervention but will simply act in its place.

But even though finance is proud of its record since 1971, the larger political issues of institutional intermediation still loom. Volatile market conditions have always been said to be conducive for traders in derivatives markets but they can have just the opposite effect upon smaller traders. The declining numbers of small investors in both the US and Britain since 1970 attest to this despite the popularity of newly privatised industries in the UK under the Conservatives in the 1980s and 1990s. While many of the newly empowered institutional investors have shown that they are willing to tackle difficult social issues such as investment in politically incorrect regimes or excessive executive compensation at companies in which they have a stake, the record is not long enough to prove that the benefits of the trend outweigh its potential pitfalls. More intermediated funds means more aggregate institutional power in the financial markets, as the exponential growth in the foreign exchange market has shown.

Similarly, in this new world of intermediated and institutionalised investment, the off-balance sheet liabilities of Britain and the United States require careful monitoring so that they do not create a moral hazard that would potentially dwarf the thrift crisis in the US. Properly applied, these contingent liabilities can help investment projects in the developing world and elsewhere take shape. If applied poorly, the crisis they are capable of producing could be monumental in scale.

On the weight of the historical evidence since 1971, a return to a Bretton-Woods type system will no longer be appropriate in advanced consumer democracies. The EC and Japan will not cede monetary sovereignty to the United States as they did in 1944 and any system that tried to accommodate all of the major currencies equally would probably be too complicated. The foreign exchange system of the future has already arrived. Following the old adage, it has actually been with us for some time. A return to a Bretton-Woods type system does not have the political will behind it to succeed. Britain and the United States have been using the value of their currencies for politically expedient ends for over three decades. But it is only recently that short-term posturing has proved beneficial because revaluations and (especially) devaluations have become things of the past without structured regimes for exchange rates.

CHRONOLOGY

1968   Prime Minister Wilson devalues the pound.

1969–70   Oil is discovered in the North Sea.

1971   President Nixon severs convertibility of dollar into gold, devaluing the dollar in August.

1972   Sterling allowed to float and exchange controls introduced on transactions of overseas sterling areas in June.

1972   The weekly bank rate replaced by the minimum lending rate, or MLR (one half of 1 per cent above weekly Treasury bill tender rate).

1972   Wage and price controls introduced in Britain for ninety days.

1973   Britain, along with Denmark and Ireland, becomes a full member of the European Community.

1973   The general currency float begins in June.

1973   OPEC imposes total ban on oil exports to the US.

1973   The Bank of England launches the Lifeboat on behalf of the fringe banks.

1973   OPEC raises the price of oil to $11.00 per barrel.

1973   Prime Minister Heath announces three-day working week to begin in January.

1974   The coal miners' strike in the UK begins in February.

1974   Prime Minister Heath resigns after losing general election and is succeeded by Harold Wilson.

1974   Short working week ended after miners accept pay offer. Three-day working week ends.

1974   OPEC ban on oil exports to US is lifted.

1974   President Nixon resigns in August.

1975   Margaret Thatcher assumes leadership of Conservative party.

1975   The American stock exchanges abandon fixed commission rates.

1976   James Callaghan succeeds Harold Wilson as Prime Minister.

1976   Britain negotiates a well-publicised IMF drawdown facility to shore up the pound.

1979   Second OPEC oil price shock sends price toward $35 per barrel.

1979   Parliament passes the Banking Act.

1979   Britain abandons exchange controls.

1979   Conservatives return to power in general election

1979   Federal Reserve announces a change in the direction of monetary policy when Paul Volcker is appointed Chairman by President Carter.

1980   Congress passes the Depository Institutions Deregulation and Monetary Control Act.

1980   Jimmy Carter announces special credit controls in an attempt to control inflation.

1980   Pound reaches $2.45 in November.

1982   Congress passes the Depository Institutions Act (Garn–St Germain Act).

1982   Congress passes the Economic Recovery Tax Act.

1982   The Mexican debt crisis begins

1984   Continental Illinois Bank technically fails and requires assistance from the Federal Reserve and Federal Deposit Insurance Corporation.

1984   Johnson Matthey Bank requires assistance from the Bank of England.

1985   The dollar reaches its historic high against the pound, $1.10 spot. The dollar also reaches post-war highs against many other currencies in March.

1985   The G7 nations, meeting at the Plaza Hotel in New York, agree to intervene in foreign exchange markets to lower the value of the dollar.

1985   Parliament passes the Building Societies Act.

1986   Parliament passes the Financial Services Act, or 'Big Bang'.

1986   The Tax Reform Act is passed in the United States.

1987   Parliament passes the Banking Act, succeeding the 1979 Act.

1987   Louvre Agreement on exchange rates.

1987   The major stock markets fall worldwide, with the New York and London markets losing approximately 20 per cent of their values.

1987   The London Borough of Hammersmith and Fulham is found to have engaged in excessive speculation in the swaps market.

1989   Congress passes the Financial Institutions Reconstruction, Recovery and Enforcement Act (FIRREA).

1990   Britain joins the Exchange Rate Mechanism (ERM) in October.

1991   Congress passes the Federal Deposit Insurance Corporation Improvement Act.

1992   Britain abandons the ERM in September.

1993   ERM bands widened to 15 per cent.

1993   British Parliament ratifies the Maastricht Treaty on European union, the last EC member to do so, in August.

1994   The dollar touches post-war lows against the yen, 100 yen per dollar, in the spring.

1994   Congress passes the Interstate Banking Act.

NOTES

1 THE SYSTEM DISSOLVES

1 *New York Times*, 16 August 1971.
2 Ibid.
3 Alastair Burnet, *America, 1843–1993: 150 Years of Reporting the American Connection* (London: The Economist, 1993), p. 215.
4 The US dollar, Deutschmark, yen, pound and French franc. Other previous entrants were dropped in the early 1980s.
5 See Robert Solomon, *The International Monetary System, 1945–76*. New York: Harper & Row, 1977, pp. 209 ff.
6 Originally Regulation Q was imposed so that no one bank would have an unfair advantage over another by being able to offer higher interest rates on deposits. In theory, all banks were then on a level playing field when competing for business.
7 The alternative is to raise money in the money market by selling certificates of deposit (CDs) and using those funds for lending.
8 Portfolio investment by foreigners occurs when a foreign person or corporation buys financial assets, usually shares or bonds, in another country's market. Foreign direct investment occurs when a foreign owner acquires a controlling interest in a company in another country. The exact definition of controlling interest can vary from country to country.
9 For a history of foreign investment in the United States since 1920 see Charles R. Geisst, *Entrepot Capitalism: Foreign Investment and the American Dream in the Twentieth Century*. New York: Praeger, 1992.

2 EMERGING CRISES

1 See Daniel Yergin, *The Prize: The Epic Quest for Oil, Money and Power*. New York: Simon & Schuster, 1991, especially Chapters 28–30.
2 Oil is priced in US dollars regardless of where it is produced, making the dollar the unofficial currency of many of the smaller oil producing countries. Therefore, when the dollar declines, those countries' ability to import is diminished unless the price of oil is raised commensurately.
3 In the *International Monetary System, 1945–76* (New York: Harper & Row, 1977), Robert Solomon put this point in trade terms. Using Saudi Arabia as an example, he noted that the price rise was unjustified using a trade argument since the population of Saudi Arabia had more money than would ever

be required after the price rise and that Saudi Arabia had a positive balance with the United States and others even before the decision was made to raise prices. See pp. 290 ff.

4 The market was referred to as the parallel market because it did not involve the discount houses, those money market dealers that stood between the clearing banks and the Bank of England. Essentially, these sort of banks could sell short-term notes in the market assuming that the depositor would continue to roll over the instrument each time it became due at a different rate of interest. The note was assumed to be medium-term rather than short-term.

5 As Margaret Reid noted, despite the size of the secondary banking sector, it was dwarfed by the size of the Euromarket operating from London. This was due to the secondary role sterling played in international finance when compared to the dollar. See *The Secondary Banking Crisis* (London: Macmillan, 1982).

6 Ibid. A consortium bank was a Eurobank that was owned by other banks, British and foreign. They usually accepted deposits in the Euromarket, made loans, traded foreign exchange and underwrote and traded Eurobonds.

7 New York Stock Exchange, *Fact Book*, 1988, p. 61.

8 Most commercial banks that participated in the guaranteed student loan programme were more than happy to sell the loan because the default rates of students were among the highest for any sort of loan, a problem that emerged almost as soon as the programme began in 1958.

9 See Charles R. Geisst, *Entrepot Capitalism: Foreign Investment and the American Dream in the Twentieth Century* (New York: Praeger, 1992) for a more thorough history of foreign investment in the United States during this period.

3 RESPONDING TO INFLATION

1 See Brendan Brown and Charles R. Geisst, *Financial Futures Markets* (London: Macmillan, 1983), Chapter 5 for a discussion of those factors that spelled success or disaster for new options and futures instruments.

2 The Ginnie Mae future, being based upon the thirty-year Ginnie Mae mortgage-backed security, had what was known as a 'par cap' attached to it. This meant that the actual futures price could never exceed par regardless of the price of the underlying security. Traders had limited means of making gains on the future when interest rates fell and futures prices should have risen to whatever level the market dictated. Eventually, as interest rates did fall, the future fell into disfavour and eventually ceased trading.

3 Futures on these two instruments eventually were discontinued and replaced in the market by Eurodollar futures, a better hedging instrument for banks because of the central role of Eurodollars in both domestic and international financing.

4 The ERISA had both institutional and personal sides. On the institutional side, it created the Pension Benefit Guaranty Corporation, or Penny Benny. This agency was designed to provide insurance for private (corporate) nonfunded pension funds. On the personal side, it created the individual retirement account, or IRA, an account that the individual could create to help augment his or her retirement funds by setting aside a specific amount of tax deductible funds each year.

5 The American Stock Exchange in New York did develop an options market of its own shortly after the CBOE became established.

6 During the years following the market crash of 1929, many stocks were manipulated by traders who used options in conjunction with other dubious trading practices. These subsequently were prohibited by the Securities Exchange Act passed in 1934.

7 American options differed from what was known as European options in one major respect: American options could be bought or sold in a secondary market while European options had no secondary market in which to trade. On expiration, they simply could be exercised or allowed to expire.

8 OECD, *Economic Survey*, March 1975.

9 Robert Bacon and Walter Eltis, *Britain's Economic Problem: Too Few Producers*. 2nd edn (London: Macmillan, 1978), pp. 119 ff.

10 Henry Kissinger, *White House Years* (Boston, MA: Little, Brown, 1979), p. 959 ff.

11 Bacon and Eltis, *Britain's Economic Problem*, p. 5.

12 Daniel Yergin, *The Prize: The Epic Quest for Oil, Money and Power*. (New York: Simon & Schuster, 1991), p. 670.

13 Central Statistical Office, *United Kingdom Balance of Payments, 1967–1977*.

14 Malcom Crawford, 'High-Conditionality Lending: the United Kingdom', in John Williamson, ed., *IMF Conditionality* (Washington, DC: Institute for International Economics, 1983), p. 421.

15 See Brendan Brown, *Money Hard and Soft on the International Currency Markets* (London: Macmillan, 1978), especially Chapters 1 and 3.

4 RISING INSTITUTIONALISM

1 New York Stock Exchange, *Fact Book, 1992*, p. 70.

2 Ibid., p. 71.

3 In Britain, gilts traded on the London Stock Exchange and their turnover figures were reported along with those for ordinary and preference shares. In the United States, US Treasury obligations trade over the counter among recognised dealers and are not listed or traded on stock exchanges.

4 Central Statistical Office, *Share Register Survey Report, End 1992* (London: CSO, 1994).

5 New York Stock Exchange, *Fact Book*, 1976.

6 The exception was that thrifts were able to offer one quarter of 1 per cent more interest on deposits than commercial banks.

7 See Charles R. Geisst, *Visionary Capitalism: Financial Markets and the American Dream in the Twentieth Century* (New York: Praeger, 1990) and Thomas Stanton, *A State of Risk: Will Government-Sponsored Enterprises be the Next Financial Crisis?* (New York: Harper Business, 1991) for the historical and legal background to the presumption of government guarantees for public but non-governmental agency debt.

8 The total face value of federal credit and insurance programmes in fiscal year 1992, including the obligations of the mortgage assistance agencies, deposit insurance programmes and other GSEs amounted to approximately $6.6 trillion. See Thomas Stanton, 'Federal Credit Programs: the Economic Consequences of Institutional Choices,' *The Financier*, February 1994, I, (1), p. 22.

9 The Garn–St Germain Act, or Depository Institutions Act, allowed savings and loan institutions additional latitude in expanding their offerings to customers while also allowing them to purchase assets previously prohibited.

10 Stanton, *A State of Risk*, pp. 154–55.

5 BANKING REFORMS ON BOTH SIDES

1 See Edward P.M. Gardener (ed.), *UK Banking Supervision: Evolution, Practice and Issues* (London: Allen & Unwin, 1986), p. 75.

2 Ibid., p. 93.

3 The prime rate is determined by adding a spread of about 1 per cent to 1.50 per cent on top of the commercial paper rate. Eurodollar rates are more closely aligned to the commercial paper rates and the spread added to them is usually smaller.

4 The McFadden Act, passed in 1927, prohibited banks from opening *de novo* branches in other states. Although effectively circumvented in the 1980s, the law is still on the books although in the 1970s it was considered more inviolate than it was in the 1980s and 1990s.

5 It is often forgotten that the Glass–Steagall Act of 1933 applied only to banks that were federally chartered. Prior to 1933, these institutions were referred to as 'national banks'. Banks that were chartered only by the state in which they operated did not fall within the regulatory ambit of the Federal Reserve but were subject to their own state banking laws, which often were more lenient than those of the central bank.

6 A reverse repurchase agreement, or reverse repo, is an arrangement where the Federal Reserve sells Treasury bills to its primary dealers with an agreement to buy them back within a short period of time. Its other side, the repurchase agreement, or repo, is just the opposite: a buy with a sell-back to the dealers.

7 See William Greider, *Secrets of the Temple: How the Federal Reserve Runs the Country* (New York: Simon & Schuster, 1987), pp. 185 ff.

8 Margaret Thatcher, *The Downing Street Years* (New York: HarperCollins, 1993), p. 54.

9 Ibid., p. 53.

10 Quoted in I.M. Destler and C. Randall Henning, *Dollar Politics: Exchange Rate Policymaking in the United States* (Washington, DC: Institute for International Economics, 1989), p. 27.

11 Ibid.

12 Prior to 1980, 20 per cent was the figure used for determining foreign control.

13 Edward M. Graham and Paul Krugman, *Foreign Direct Investment in the United States* (Washington, DC: Institute for International Economics, 1989), pp. 34–35.

14 Securities Industry Association, *The International Market: Growth in Primary and Secondary Activity* (New York: Securities Industry Association, 1987), pp. 12–13.

15 Graham and Krugman, *Foreign Direct Investment*, pp. 10–11.

16 In 1981–82 the total assets of the thrift industry in the US, both federally chartered and state chartered, were about $700 billion, so a market of potentially $140 billion existed at the thrifts alone for junk bonds.

17 An adjustment was made in the swap pricing to reflect any differences in credit risk between the two parties involved in the swap.

6 BIG BANG AND BEYOND

1 Charles R. Geisst, *Entrepot Capitalism: Foreign Investment and the American Dream in the Twentieth Century* (New York: Praeger, 1992), p. 131.

2 The percentage of bank capital is calculated by dividing the amount of shareholders' equity on its books by the amount of total loans. In generating revenue

by not booking a loan (derivatives are not loans), banks avoided having these new instruments included in their capital requirements. Later in the 1980s and early 1990s, exposure from derivatives was included in banks' capital requirements.

3 Central Statistical Office, *Share Reigister Survey Report, End 1992*. (London: CSO, 1994), p. 18.

4 See Charles R. Geisst, *A Guide to Financial Institutions*, 2nd edn (London: Macmillan, 1993), Chapter 7.

5 I.M. Destler and C. Randall Henning, *Dollar Politics: Exchange Rate Policymaking in the United States* (Washington, DC: Institute for International Economics, 1989), pp. 62–63.

6 An ADR is a receipt for foreign stocks trading in the New York market. The holder of the ADR is the beneficial owner of a specific number of shares of a foreign equity. The benefit of ADRs to investors is that they are valued in dollars rather than the foreign currency.

7 Robert Aderhold, Christine Cumming and Alison Harwood, 'International Linkages Among Equities Markets and the October 1987 Market Break,' Federal Reserve Bank of New York *Quarterly Review*, Summer 1988, p. 45.

8 In addition to the increasing values noted in Figure 6.1 in the UK, the number of companies acquired by others was 696 in 1986, 1,125 in 1987, 1,499 in 1988 and 1,337 in 1989, the year in which the gross values were the highest. See Central Statistical Office, *Financial Statistics*.

9 In addition to the RJR/Nabisco merger, valued at $24 billion, the other large mergers of the 1980s included Chevron/Gulf (both oil companies), Philip Morris/Kraft (tobacco and food), Bristol Myers/Squibb (pharmaceuticals), and Time Inc./Warner Communications (communications and publishing).

10 Counting outstanding swaps is something of an imprecise science. If two parties agree to swap either interest rates or currencies, the amount calculated is determined by adding the total principal amounts involved and dividing by two. Critics contend that may be valid for currency swaps where principal amounts of currency are actually exchanged but interest rate swaps do not involve principal amounts, only interest payments.

11 The closing of Drexel Burnham Lambert in 1990 also required an estimated $25 billion of swap arrangements to be terminated, with many of the firm's counterparties having to settle for a discount on their swaps.

12 In the early 1990s, swaps activities at commercial banks in the United States came under close scrutiny by shareholders as well as regulators and many institutions heavily involved in the markets realised that poor performance in the derivatives markets could lead to severe share price falls. Also, the activities of several mortgage assistance agencies were examined by a federal oversight board to determine whether or not the agencies were overextended in the swaps market; that is, had too much exposure given their congressionally mandated purposes.

7 BANKING REFORM AGAIN

1 The new legislation created two separate funds within the FDIC, one for banks and the other for savings institutions.

2 *America 1843–1993: One Hundred Fifty Years of Reporting the American Connection* (London: The Economist, 1993), p. 261.

3 Lawrence J. White, *The S & L Debacle: Public Policy Lessons for Bank and Thrift Regulation* (New York: Oxford University Press, 1991), p. 180.

4 For example, the narrow banking alternative offered by James R. Barth and R. Dan Brumbaugh in *The Changing World of Banking: Setting the Regulatory Agenda* (Annandale-on-Hudson, NY: Jerome Levy Economics Institute, 1993.) Under this plan, deposits are invested in risk-free Treasury securities only, offering a lower rate of interest. The bank's profit is confined to the small interest rate spread between them.

5 See Larry D. Wall, 'Too Big to Fail After FDICIA', Federal Reserve Bank of Atlanta *Economic Review*, 78(1) January/February 1993.

6 Public opinion poll, Autumn 1993, cited in *The Economist*, 19 September 1994.

7 Ray Barrell, Andrew Britton and Nigel Pain, 'When the Time was Right? The UK Experience of the ERM,' in David Cobham, (ed.), *European Monetary Upheavals* (Manchester: Manchester University Press, 1994), p. 129ff.

8 Ibid., p p. 133 ff.

9 I.M. Destler and C. Randall Henning, *Dollar Politics: Exchange Rate Policymaking in the United States* (Washington, DC: Institute for International Economics, 1989), pp. 69 ff.

10 William Branson, 'German Reunification, the Breakdown of the EMS, and the Path to Stage Three', in David Cobham, (ed.) *European Monetary Upheavals* pp.17 ff.

11 Specifically, Section 20 of the Glass–Steagall Act, the 'engaged principally' clause, prohibited a commercial bank from being engaged principally in securities underwriting or trading. However, subsidiaries that primarily traded Treasury securities could do so because their primary business lay elsewhere. As a result, many commercial banks entered the securities business through the back door. Some Canadian commercial banks also entered the business through their American branches because of the provisions of the Free Trade Agreement signed by the US and Canada. Originally, the commercial banking subsidiaries that entered the underwriting ranks had to do so by forming their own syndicates, not participating in those of the traditional investment banking underwriters.

BIBLIOGRAPHY

Bacon, Robert and Walter Eltis (1978). *Britain's Economic Problem: Too Few Producers.* 2nd edn. London: Macmillan.

Barth, James R. and R. Dan Brumbaugh (1993). *The Changing World of Banking: Setting the Regulatory Agenda.* Annandale-on-Hudson, NY: Jerome Levy Economics Institute.

——(1992). *The Future of American Banking.* Armonk, NY: M.E. Sharpe.

Brown, Brendan (1979). *The Dollar Mark Axis on Currency Power.* London: Macmillan.

——(1978). *Money Hard and Soft.* London: Macmillan.

Brown, Brendan and Charles R. Geisst (1983). *Financial Futures Markets.* London: Macmillan.

Burnet, Alastair (1993). *America, 1843–93: 150 Years of Reporting the American Connection.* London: The Economist.

Cairncross, A. and B. Eichengreen (1983). *Sterling in Decline.* Oxford: Blackwell.

Callaghan, James (1987). *Time and Chance.* London: Collins.

Central Statistical Office. *Financial Statistics,* various issues.

——(1994). *The Pink Book 1993: United Kingdom Balance of Payments.* London: HMSO.

——(1994). *Share Register Survey Report.* London: Central Statistical Office.

Cobham, David (ed.) (1994). *European Monetary Upheavals.* Manchester: Manchester University Press.

De Grauwe, Paul (1989). *International Money: Post-War Trends and Theories.* Oxford: Clarendon Press.

Destler, I.M. and C. Randall Henning (1989). *Dollar Politics: Exchange Rate Policymaking in the United States.* Washington, DC: Institute for International Economics.

Dornbusch, Rudiger (1988). *Exchange Rates and Inflation.* Cambridge, MA: MIT Press.

Einzig, Paul (1973). *Roll-Over Credits: The System of Adaptable Interest Rates.* London: Macmillan.

Federal Reserve System. *Bulletin,* various issues.

Gardener, Edward P.M. (ed.) (1986). *UK Banking Supervision: Evolution, Practice and Issues.* London: Allen & Unwin.

Geisst, Charles R. (1990). *Visionary Capitalism: Financial Markets and the American Dream in the Twentieth Century.* New York: Praeger.

——(1992) *Entrepot Capitalism: Foreign Investment and the American Dream in the Twentieth Century.* New York: Praeger.

Graham, Edward M. and Paul Krugman (1989). *Foreign Direct Investment in the*

United States. Washington, DC: Institute for International Economics.

Greider, William (1987). *Secrets of the Temple: How the Federal Reserve Runs the Country*. New York: Simon & Schuster.

Group of Thirty (1993). *Derivatives: Practices and Principles*. Washington, DC: Group of Thirty.

International Monetary Fund. *Financial Statistics*. Washington, DC: International Monetary Fund, various issues.

Kaldor, Lord (1982). *The Scourge of Monetarism*. Oxford: Oxford University Press.

Kissinger, Henry (1979). *White House Years*. Boston, MA: Little, Brown.

Krugman, Paul (1992). *Currencies and Crises*. Cambridge, MA: MIT Press.

Organisation for Economic Cooperation and Development. *Country Reports*, various issues.

Reid, Margaret (1982). *The Secondary Banking Crisis*. London: Macmillan.

Revell, Jack (1973). *The British Financial System*. London: Macmillan.

Rubinstein, W.D. (1993). *Capitalism, Culture and Decline in Britain, 1750–1990*. London: Routledge.

Shaw, E.R. (1978). *The London Money Market*. 2nd edn. London: Heinemann.

Solomon, Robert (1977). *The International Monetary System, 1945–76*. New York: Harper & Row.

Stanton, Thomas (1991). *A State of Risk: Will Government-Sponsored Enterprises Be the Next Financial Crisis?* New York: Harper Business.

Thatcher, Margaret (1993). *The Downing Street Years*. New York: HarperCollins.

United States Department of Commerce. *Survey of Current Business*. Washington, DC: US Department of Commerce, various issues.

Wall, Larry D. 'Too Big to Fail After FDICIA', Federal Reserve Bank of Atlanta *Economic Review*, 78(1). January/February 1993.

White, Lawrence J. (1991). *The S & L Debacle: Public Policy Lessons for Bank and Thrift Regulation*. New York: Oxford University Press.

Williamson, John (ed.) (1983). *IMF Conditionality*. Washington, DC: Institute for International Economics.

Yergin, Daniel (1991). *The Prize: The Epic Quest for Oil, Money and Power*. New York: Simon & Schuster.

INDEX